LIVING IN THE SHADOW OF THE SECOND COMING

LIVING IN THE SHADOW OF THE SECOND COMING

ENLARGED EDITION

TIMOTHY P. WEBER

Academie Books

1415 Lake Drive, S.E., Grand Rapids, Michigan 49506

from Zondervan Publishing House

LIVING IN THE SHADOW OF THE SECOND COMING: AMERICAN PREMILLENNIALISM
1875–1982
Copyright © 1983 by The Zondervan Corporation
Grand Rapids, Michigan

Library of Congress Cataloging in Publication Data

Weber, Timothy P.

Living in the shadow of the Second Coming.
Revision of the author's thesis, University of Chicago.

Bibliography: p   Includes index.

1.   Millennialism—United States—History.
2.   United States—Church history.   I.   Title.
BR525.W36   1979   236'.3'0973   78-14201
ISBN 0-310-44091-2

This is an enlarged edition of a book published in 1979 by Oxford University Press, Inc.

From Edmund Grosse: *Father and Son*, edited with an introduction and notes by William Irvine. Riverside Editions No. B 88; reprinted by permission of Houghton Mifflin Company; copyright © 1965 by William Irvine.

Henry W. Frost, "The Dying Heathen," and J. J. Robinson "Is Social Service Part of the Apostasy?" Used by permission, Moody Bible Institute of Chicago.

From *Our Hope*, XXI (Jan. 1915). Reprinted by permission

From Shirley Jackson Case: *The Millennial Hope*. Reprinted by permission of The University of Chicago Press; copyright © 1918 by The University of Chicago.

From Lelia N. Morris: *What If It Were Today?* Copyright 1912. Renewal 1940 extended by Hope Publishing Co., Carol Stream, IL 60187. All Rights Reserved. Used by permission.

Printed in the United States of America

83   84   85   86   87   88 / 10   9   8   7   6   5   4   3   2   1

Preface

No one writes a book by himself. The author's name on the title page actually represents a host of helpers who can not possibly be enumerated or adequately thanked. Authors, however, should try anyway.

This study began as a doctoral dissertation at the Divinity School of the University of Chicago, so most of my appreciation goes to librarians and former teachers. The staffs of the libraries of the University of Chicago and the Moody Bible Institute of Chicago deserve high marks for patience and expertise. The idea for this book originated in Jerald C. Brauer's course on American revivalism. During his class on the history of social reform movements in nineteenth- and twentieth-century America, Arthur Mann helped me see the social consequences of premillennialism in a completely new light. Not only did these two men stimulate my thinking, they read and evaluated my finished work.

Chief thanks, however, belongs to Martin E. Marty, my dissertation adviser and *Doktor Vater*. His constant interest, enthusiasm, and suggestions made graduate studies a rare pleasure.

Though the dissertation was written at the University of Chicago, it was revised for publication during my first two years on the faculty of the Conservative Baptist Theological Seminary, Denver, Colorado. Colleagues on the faculty and able students helped me sharpen my thinking more than they knew. Special thanks in this regard goes to the students who took my course on Evangelicalism and Social Action in the winter of 1978. They prodded me to rethink some of my ideas on premillennialism's impact on evangelicalism's social involvement.

Finally, and most significantly, I want to thank my wife, Linda, to whom this book is dedicated. Only male graduate students and their wives fully understand and appreciate the sacrifices of those fearless women who are married to would-be Ph.D.s. Linda loved, supported, and encouraged me through years of labor. She saw to it that research and writing schedules were set and kept. Though she was involved each step along the way, she will never fully know how important she was in the writing of this book. In a pitifully small way, this study is partial payment of the enormous debt of love I owe.

                                                            T. P. W.

Denver Conservative Baptist Seminary
Denver, Colorado
September 1978

NOTE ON THE NEW EDITION

This book updates and expands one that was published in 1979 by Oxford University Press. The original work covered the half-century between 1875 and 1925; this edition continues the story into the early 1980s. Chapters 8 and 9 are completely new, as is most of the conclusion. The subtitle has been changed to reflect more accurately the updated book's content.

                                                            T. P. W.

Denver, Colorado
May 1983

Contents

To Linda Lee Weber

LIVING IN THE SHADOW OF THE SECOND COMING

Introduction

One of the least expected developments in American religion since World War II has been the evangelical renaissance. Though many observers assumed that conservative Protestantism could never fully recover from the fundamentalist debacles of the 1920s, by the 1970s evangelicalism had emerged as a powerful and highly visible force on the American religious scene.

Signs of evangelical renewal are everywhere. At a time when most "mainline" denominations are struggling to reverse declining memberships and contributions, many evangelical groups are experiencing impressive growth. In fact, evangelical enterprises in general are doing better than ever. Missionary agencies, colleges and seminaries, and evangelistic organizations are in obvious ascendancy, to say nothing of the unprecedented profits of evangelical book publishers.

None of this has escaped the notice of the media. In addition to the constant reporting about evangelical institutional gains, the conversions of men like Charles Colson (Watergate conspirator and Nixon "hatchet man"), Eldridge Cleaver (exiled Black Panther Party leader), and Larry Flynt (publisher of the pornographic *Hustler* magazine) have received wide coverage in the

3

press. Even more significant was the election in 1976 of evangelical Jimmy Carter to the presidency of the United States. Such national reporting suddenly focused public attention on the "born-again" movement, which some experts say may include fifty million people in America.

At the same time, however, this public scrutiny has uncovered deep divisions within the movement. Despite its current power and prestige, evangelicalism cannot present a united front to the rest of the world. Now acceptable and generally respected throughout the culture, evangelicals apparently are left with no one to fight except each other. They are seriously at odds over the doctrine of biblical inerrancy, the role of women in the church, the practice and meaning of charismatic gifts, strategies and methods in mass evangelism, the relationship between evangelism and social action, and the use of wealth and natural resources in a needy world. Evangelicals are beginning to realize that such division may cause their movement to self-destruct precisely at the time of its greatest potential for real impact in this century.[1]

Whatever the future holds for American evangelical religion, one of its most noticeable elements is the interest in, even obsession with, biblical prophecy. Once considered the preoccupation of relatively few fanatics, eschatology (the doctrine of "final things") has come close to reaching cult status in American society, or at least in a significant part of it. Biblical prophecy has always been an important topic for fundamentalists and large numbers of evangelicals. They have been preaching sermons, writing books, holding conferences, and splitting churches over it for decades. But it has not made much of an impact beyond those circles until fairly recently.

The bursting of these former bounds is due in large part to Hal Lindsey's *The Late Great Planet Earth,* a popularly written attempt to show that ancient biblical prophecies about events leading up to the personal second coming of Jesus Christ are being fulfilled in our own time.[2] The significance of Lindsey's book is not so much its thesis. As we shall see, his interpretive approach has been around for a long time. Rather, the book is noteworthy because it has been able to reach many people who are outside of those groups traditionally receptive to its message. Previously, books on prophecy could be found only in Christian (i.e. evangelical) or Bible bookstores. But *The Late Great Planet Earth* began showing up in drugstores, supermarkets, and "secular" bookstores, right alongside gothic romances, cheap westerns, and books on the latest fads: dieting, organic gardening, the personal lives and loves of Hollywood celebrities, and UFOs. As a result, over twelve million copies of Lindsey's book have been sold since 1970. To ensure an even wider audience, the book was made into a documentary-style feature film which appeared in commercial theaters throughout the United States in early 1978.

About the same time the evangelical interest in eschatology started seeping into the wider culture, the academic community began taking notice as well. In the same year *The Late Great Planet Earth* was published, the University of Chicago Press issued a study entitled *The Roots of Fundamentalism*, by Ernest R. Sandeen.[3] In his ground-breaking work, Professor Sandeen argued that the fundamentalist controversy in the 1920s was actually the product of a much older fundamentalist movement, which consisted of an alliance between the advocates of the conservative Princeton theology and the "premilliennialists," so called because they believed that Jesus Christ will personally return to earth before establishing his millennial kingdom. Sandeen showed how this new premillennial movement came to the United States via Great Britain, captured the allegiance of prominent evangelicals, spread through various Bible and prophetic conferences, Bible institutes, and popular literature, and eventually joined forces with other conservative evangelicals, mainly of the Princeton variety, to do battle with theological liberalism in the American churches.

Regardless of the merits of Sandeen's thesis, *The Roots of Fundamentalism* did for the scholarly world what *The Late Great Planet Earth* did for non-evangelical popular culture: it focused attention on a vital and persistent strain in American religion, the interest in biblical prophecy. The premillennialists in Sandeen's study are the forerunners and spiritual ancestors of those who currently read and believe Lindsey's book.

Since premillennialism is well anchored in nineteenth-century American evangelicalism, others besides Sandeen have noticed it. The standard histories of American religion deal with the movement, concentrating mainly on its rise and spread after the Civil War, its basic tenets, and its rather negligible effects on the majority of those in the churches. Invariably, these accounts present premillennialism as a reactionary movement of the socially disinherited, psychologically disturbed, and theologically naïve.[4]

Not surprisingly, premillennialists have viewed their own movement in a more favorable light. Their work, however, tends to deal more with biblical and theological issues than with historical ones. In fact, most of their scholarly energies are devoted to trying to settle the many disagreements which they still have over the details of their prophetic interpretations.

Yet neither the studies of insiders nor those of outsiders have provided an altogether clear picture of the historical rise of this prophetic movement, which still claims millions of adherents. Needless to say, it is impossible to know everything about the past. Despite their efforts, historians can examine only the traces which the dead have left behind. Furthermore, once these traces have been collected and analyzed, historians can rarely agree on what they mean. Yet, even if it is only to justify their monthly paychecks, professional historians keep trying.

One way to get a different perspective on the past is to ask different questions. As everyone knows, the kind of answer one gets is closely tied to the kind of question that is asked. Consequently, historians often poke around in well-worked piles of historical data with new sets of questions, hoping to uncover something previously hidden from view.

Sometimes the search for new analytical angles develops into a distinct historical approach. For example, some historians who are impressed with the techniques of psychotherapy treat the people of the past in the same way a modern psychiatrist might a patient on his couch. These practitioners of "psychohistory" probe into long-dead psyches, trying to discover hidden motives, suppressed drives, and elusive neuroses that might help explain why things happened the way they did. Other historians, equally impressed with the adaptability of computers, try to program the past, confident that the high-speed analysis of historical data ("quanto-history") will reveal what other methods have not.[5]

Another relatively new perspective that can help historians is what Robert F. Berkhofer, Jr., calls *A Behavioral Approach to Historical Analysis*.[6] This behavioral method endeavors to supplement more traditional approaches, not exclude them. By concentrating on what people actually did in the past the historian can better evaluate what the same people said they were doing or even thought they were doing. He can discover the true beliefs and values of individuals or groups. What people *do* frequently speaks louder and is more revealing than anything they *say*, or *claim to believe*.

This behavioral approach can be extremely helpful for the student of the history of Christianity. The Christian faith has always been a curious blend of belief and behavior, doctrine and duty, profession and practice. The New Testament abounds with behavioral directives. Christians in the apostolic age were often told to "be doers of the word and not hearers only" (James 1:22). The Apostle Paul repeatedly urged his readers to let their conduct conform to their convictions about Jesus Christ and the new life they had found in him.

Christians, therefore, have always been expected to live out the implications of their faith. Naturally, Christians have not always done so, and sometimes they have not even been certain of what was expected of them. But few would deny that daily or personal behavior was supposed to be a direct reflection of theological beliefs. Too often historians of Christianity have studied the cognitive or theological aspects of the church's history to the neglect of how beliefs were translated into daily life.

This behavioral approach has already been applied to the study of American religion, with some interesting results. Dr. Martin E. Marty, church historian at the University of Chicago, demonstrated in his *A Nation of Behavers* that it makes more sense to classify religious people in contemporary America by their religious behavior than by the more traditional denominational or even theological labels.[7]

It seems certain, therefore, that the Christian past may reveal some interesting new insights if it is approached in a behavioral way. Consequently, this book seeks in a modest way to ask behavioral questions about the history of American premillennialism between 1875 and 1925. For example, what difference did believing in the imminent second coming of Christ make in the way people actually lived? How do modern, educated people behave in a growingly complex industrial society, when they are firmly convinced that this age might suddenly be turned into the age to come by the personal return of Jesus Christ? How do they conduct their personal and corporate lives, and how do they interact with the major social, political, and international events of their time when this conviction becomes a part of them?

After briefly setting the new premillennialism in its historical context, we shall explore what premillennialists believed the Bible taught about the coming of Christ. More specifically, we shall examine their methods of biblical interpretation, their conclusions, and their novel chronology of the end times. Special attention will be given to the unavoidable tension built into their system: since they refused to set dates for the return of Christ, they had to live as though Christ might return at any moment—*and*, at the same time, as though he might not come for years.

After establishing the eschatological beliefs of these evangelical premillennialists, we will determine their practical consequences in behavior. First we will explore how premillennialists adjusted their personal lives in light of a possible any-moment second coming, and how revivalists found in premillennialism a valuable aid for winning souls.

Then we shall see what belief in the imminent second coming did to the inherited evangelical commitment to social reform and world evangelization. Other chapters will include an analysis of premillennialists' response to World War I, their distinctive behavior toward Jews and the new Zionist movement, and, finally, their adjustments to the turbulent times after that war.

Since the intricacies of biblical prophecies are still mysterious to most people, it is necessary to say a brief word about Christian millennial thought in general.[8]

Broadly speaking, Christian millennialism is the belief that there will be a long period of unprecedented peace and righteousness, closely associated with the second coming of Christ. Christians can be divided into three groups, depending on whether they take the millennial reign of Christ literally and where they place Christ's return in relation to it.

Amillennialists (literally, "no-millennialists") interpret biblical references to the millennium figuratively and contend that the millennial reign of Christ occurs in the hearts of his followers. Postmillennialists, on the other hand, believe that Christ will return *after* the church has established the millennium through its faithful and Spirit-empowered preaching of the gospel; while premillennialists expect Christ to return *before* the millennium in order to establish it by his might.

Premillennialists are further divided into two subgroups on the basis of their fundamental approach to prophetic texts. Historicist

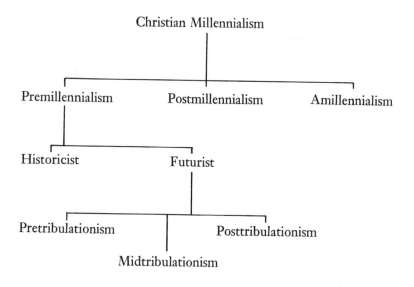

CHART I
Varieties of Christian Millennialism

premillennialists believe that the prophetic Scriptures, especially those in Daniel and Revelation, give the entire history of the church in symbolic form. Thus they look into the church's past and present to find prophetic fulfillments and to see where they are in God's prophetic timetable.

Futurist premillennialists argue that none of the prophecies of the "last days" have been fulfilled in the history of the church, and they expect them all to come to pass within a short period just before the return of Christ. For them, all the great events prophesied in the Bible still await fulfillment. All futurist premillennialists agree on the basic outline of future events. At the end of the present age, human society will grow worse and worse until the Antichrist will gain control, throwing the world into a reign of terror (the "tribulation") mainly directed against all those who will not recognize his divine pretensions. At the end of the tribulation, the reign of Antichrist will be destroyed at the Battle of Armageddon by the triumphant return of Christ. Having disposed of Antichrist and his forces and having bound the power of Satan, Christ will establish his millennial kingdom, which will end after a thousand years with an easily subdued revolt by Satan, the resurrection of the dead, the judgment, and the creation of a new heaven and a new earth.

While futurist premillennialists agree on this script for the future, they disagree on the exact timing of the church's "rapture." The rapture is the "catching away" of the church to meet Christ in the air (I Thess. 4:15-17). Pretribulationists believe that the church will be raptured before the rise of Antichrist and the beginning of the tribulation. Midtribulationists, on the other hand, contend that the church will be raptured during the tribulation, after Antichrist's rise to power, but before God begins to pour out a series of preliminary judgments on the earth in anticipation of Christ's return. Posttribulationists say that the church will live through the entire period and be rescued at the end of the tribulation by the rapture at the time of the second coming.

The premillennialism that gained a wide following among American evangelicals in the last quarter of the nineteenth century was called "dispensationalism" (for reasons which shall become apparent) and is classified as futurist and pretribulational. When first introduced it quickly overcame and nearly supplanted its older posttribulational rival. For that reason this book is primarily about the religious behavior of dispensationalists, although there does not appear to be any substantial difference between their behavior and that of their other brethren in the premillennialist movement. Even though "dispensationalist" and "premillennialist" are used almost interchangeably in this study, it must not be forgotten that there are other kinds of premillennialists as well. Though all agree on the basic tenets of premillennialism, there is often disagreement on many of the details. Since this study concentrates on religious behavior and not on biblical interpretation, the subtle, and not so subtle, hermeneutical differences between them are usually passed over as non-essential to the story.

Though dispensationalists are the primary focus of the book, non-dispensational premillennialists can consider this study part of their history too. Despite the fact that premillennialists did not always agree on every detail of prophetic interpretation, their actions were pretty much the same.

I

Rightly Dividing the Word of Truth

Study to shew thyself approved unto God, a workman that
needeth not to be ashamed, rightly dividing the word of truth.

II Timothy 2:15 (KJV)[1]

After the Civil War the last thing most American evangelicals
expected was a resurgence of premillennialism. Belief in Christ's
personal return to set up his earthly kingdom had always had its
faithful witnesses in the churches, but few people imagined that
it would ever again be able to attract a significant number of adherents scattered throughout the evangelical denominations or
isolated in premillenial denominations. Premillennialists will always be with us, many thought, but premillennialism is gone forever as a force in American Protestantism.

To be sure, premillennialism had seen better days. The Puri-
tans, for example, had been overwhelmingly premillennial, but
since the middle of the eighteenth century their original eschatological vision had been steadily giving way to postmillennialism,
which contended that the world will have its millennium before
Christ's triumphant second coming.[2] Most of the credit for this
shift usually goes to Jonathan Edwards, America's leading theologian before the Revolutionary War. In a 1739 series of lectures
later published as the *History of the Work of Redemption*,[3] he
borrowed the earlier views of Daniel Whitby and Moses Low-
man to argue that instead of coming after the mighty return of

Jesus Christ, the millennium will arrive through "the preaching of the gospel and the use of the ordinary means of grace."[4] Contemporary revivals of religion pointed to "the dawning, or at least a prelude of the glorious work of God . . . and there are many things that make it probable that this work will begin in America."[5]

As strange as that theory sounded in 1739, by the early nineteenth century increasing numbers of evangelicals enthusiastically supported it. In the years since Edwards's predictions, two massive religious awakenings had swept America clean of its infidelity and irreligion. Suddenly the millennium seemed easily within reach through the dual agencies of revival and social reform. Evangelists prodded sinners to be born again, and evangelical do-gooders founded societies for the abolition of slavery, for temperance, for alleviation of the miseries of the poor, and the like, in order to make the country as Christian as possible. So successful were their efforts that by the mid-1830s evangelical leaders were declaring that "the millennium is at the door" and "if the church will do her duty, the millennium may come in this country in three years."[6]

Despite the fact that most American evangelicals were preparing for the millennium, Christians elsewhere in the world were running for cover. America might have been on the verge of the millennial kingdom, but all hell was breaking loose in other places. Events surrounding the French Revolution, for example, made the unblinking optimism of the postmillennialists seem naïve. Consequently, premillennialism had a modest revival.

For anyone to gain a respectful hearing for his millennial views, he had to demonstrate their correspondence with current events. This was especially true of historicist premillennialists, who believed that biblical prophecies of the "last days" provided an overview of the entire church age. Accordingly, those premillennialists were eager to show that the Pope's exile from Rome in 1798 at the hands of French troops was an exact fulfillment of the prophecies in Daniel 7 and Revelation 13. Those passages predicted that after 1260 "days" the reign of the Beast or Antichrist would end and they would be followed shortly by the coming of the Son of Man. In typical Protestant fashion, the Beast was identified as the Roman papacy, and in typical historicist fashion, the "days" of the prophecy were converted into years. By dating the rise of the papacy at A.D. 538, premillennialists could claim by simple arithmetic that the events in 1798 were dramatic fulfillments of the prophecy.[7]

Encouraged by such success, premillennialists turned their attention to the next major event on God's prophetic calendar—the second coming of Christ. The exile of the Pope proved its imminence, and the prophecy in Daniel 8:14 provided the year. Daniel had predicted that 2300 "days" after the "desolation of the sanctuary," Messiah would come. Using Bishop Ussher's chronology to date the profanation of the Jerusalem Temple by Nebuchadnezzar (457 B.C.), premillennialists converted days to years and calculated Christ's coming in about 1843.

Once provided with the basics of "millennial arithmetic," anyone could play the date-setting game; and historicist premillennialists on both sides of the Atlantic did so, with predictable success. America's most famous premillennialist before the Civil War was William Miller, a rather unassuming Baptist preacher from Vermont. Using such methods, Miller began to publicize his views and by 1839 had acquired a considerable following.

What started as one more diversion in the "burned-over district" of western New York soon exploded into a full-blown religious phenomenon. Under considerable pressure from his followers, who may have numbered a million in the Northeast, Miller calculated a foolproof arrival date for Jesus—October 22, 1844. Although the "Millerites" probably did not gather on roofs and hill tops in white "ascension" robes to await the Lord's appearing, as their enemies alleged, they became the laughing stocks of American evangelicalism when Christ failed to appear. Excluded from most of the churches after the "Great Disappointment," many of the Millerites formed their own denomination (Seventh-Day Adventist) and wrote off all the rest of Protestantism and Roman Catholicism as the great whore of biblical prophecy (Rev. 17). Thus the modest premillennial revival of the early nineteenth century was brought to what most assumed was a total and permanent end. To say the least, by 1845 premillennialism had fallen on hard times, as far as American evangelicalism was concerned.[8]

Yet by 1875 a new kind of premillennialism, called "dispensationalism," began gaining wide acceptance among the same evangelicals who had considered the earlier Adventists fools and heretics. Given the rather embarrassing recent history of premillennialism in the United States, its sudden rise and prosperity were nothing less than amazing. In order to succeed where their predecessors had failed, the new premillennialists fought to establish two related truths: that they had nothing essentially in common with the discredited Millerites and that they were just as evangelical and orthodox as the rest of the Protestant mainstream.

The new premillennialists had little difficulty proving their first claim because, as anyone who took the time could discover, they had a substantially different approach to biblical prophecy than their historicist brethren had had. Dispensationalists used a "futurist" interpretation of prophecy which held that no "last days" prophecy will be fulfilled until just before Christ's return. They likewise rejected the historicists' "year-day theory" for dating prophetic events and the idea that the papacy was the biblical Antichrist. Since they denied that prophecies were intended for the church age as a whole, they were for the most part relieved of the dangerous and often embarrassing task of matching biblical predictions with current events, and the task of setting dates for the second coming.[9]

Before coming to the United States in force after the Civil

War, the new premillennialism had flourished in Great Britain earlier in the century, thanks in large part to the influence of the Plymouth Brethren. Founded around 1830 by evangelicals who were dissatisfied with the spiritual condition of the established church, the Brethren were a loosely organized group of believers who met informally for the Lord's Supper, prayer, and Bible study.

One of their most gifted teachers, John Nelson Darby (1800–1882), developed a new variety of futurist premillennialism, called "dispensationalism," after his division of biblical and subsequent history into eras, or dispensations. C. I. Scofield, one of Darby's later American followers who provided American premillennialists with a *Reference Bible* containing his views, defined a dispensation as "a period of time during which man is tested in respect of obedience to some specific revelation of the will of God."[10] Furthermore, "these periods are marked off in Scripture by some change in God's method of dealing with mankind, in respect to two questions: of sin, and of man's responsibility. Each of the dispensations may be regarded as a new test of the natural man, and each ends in judgment—making his utter failure in every dispensation."[11]

As dispensationalists have been contending from that time to this, there is nothing especially radical about dividing history into periods. But the charges of novelty which fellow premillennialists (including futurists) leveled against them did not concern historical periodization. What separated dispensationalists from their fellow futurists was their strict literalism when interpreting biblical prophecy, their absolute separation of Israel and the church as the two distinct peoples of God, and some conclusions which grew out of these two presuppositions.[12]

Everything in the dispensationalist system seemed to rest on the conviction that God has two completely different plans operating in history, one for an earthly people (Israel) and one for a heavenly people (the church).[13] Thus, "rightly dividing the word of truth" meant more than keeping one's dispensations straight. At all costs, the dispensationalists insisted, one must maintain the distinction between the two peoples of God.

God's plan for his earthly people had been revealed through a series of covenants between Israel and her Lord. In the Abrahamic Covenant (Gen. 12:2–3), God had pledged to make Abraham the father of a great nation through which the rest of the world will be blessed. Because that covenant was unconditional, it was a covenant of grace, dependent only on God's faithfulness. In the Mosaic Covenant (Exod. 19–20), the Jews, foolishly, Darby thought, had agreed to keep God's law. Instead of begging God to release them from the law's demands, the Jews had agreed to live by it, thus making their earthly fortunes conditional on their obedience.

Fortunately for the Jews, the Abrahamic Covenant was still in effect, and the sacrificial system permitted the people to remain in God's good graces. In the Davidic Covenant (II Sam. 7:4–17), God promised to preserve David's royal line forever, and though he might occasionally have to punish David's descendants for their disobedience, God pledged never to cancel his commitment to David's house.

Even as the Jews were being carried off into captivity, the prophets of Israel reaffirmed the covenant to David by promising a future restoration of the throne by Messiah, David's true and ultimate son. Messiah would reign in God's place, under a new covenant in which the external laws of Moses will be replaced by a new, inward law capable of producing true righteousness (Jer. 31:31–34, 33:15–16).[14]

In the meantime, however, God's earthly people had to suffer through Gentile domination. In a series of prophetic visions (Dan. 7–9), the prophet Daniel saw these "times of the Gentiles" in terms of the rise of four successive Gentile world powers. After a specified period, which the prophet described as seventy weeks after one of the Gentile rulers issues a decree allowing the rebuilding of the city of Jerusalem, Messiah would come to re-store David's throne (Dan. 9:24–27).

The prophet was even more specific about the seventy weeks than that. During the first seven weeks, the city would be rebuilt. Sixty-two weeks later Messiah would appear, but he would be rejected ("cut off"). During the final week an evil ruler would attempt to destroy the Jews, but he would be prevented from do-ing so by the returning Messiah, who would vindicate God's peo-ple and restore his father's line.

Confusing as the prophet's visions might seem to some, dispen-sationalists believed they told them as much as they needed to know about the first and second comings of Christ. Because the Hebrew word translated as "week" actually means "a seven," dis-pensationalists claimed that the prophet originally meant seventy "sevens" of years (490) between the royal decree and the estab-lishment of Messiah's kingdom.[15] Thus, if one could accurately determine the date of the decree to rebuild Jerusalem, he should be able to count ahead to the "cutting off" of Messiah and the es-tablishment of his kingdom. After considerable effort, dispensa-tionalists were able to show that Jesus was put to death 483 years (sixty-nine weeks) after Artaxerxes' decree that allowed some Jews under Nehemiah to return to work on Jerusalem's fallen walls (Neh. 2:1–8).[16] By that reckoning, Jesus should have re-turned seven years later (after Daniel's seventieth week) to estab-lish the kingdom. What happened?

To resolve this obvious difficulty, dispensationalists devised a "postponement theory," to the effect that when the Jews rejected Jesus as their Messiah, Christ postponed his scheduled return and unexpectedly turned his attention to the Gentiles. As a result, God suspended his prophetic timetable at the end of Daniel's sixty-ninth week and set to work building up a new people, a heavenly people—the church.[17]

C. H. Mackintosh, whose popularizations of Darby's theology sold well in the United States, explained the theory clearly.

The Messiah, instead of being received, is cut off. In place of
ascending the throne of David, He goes to the cross. . . .
God signified His sense of this act by suspending for a time
His dispensational dealings with Israel. The course of time is
interrupted. There is a great gap. Four hundred and eighty-
three years are fulfilled; seven yet remain—a cancelled week,
and all the time since the death of Messiah has been an un-
noticed interval—a break or parenthesis, during which Christ
has been hidden in the heavens, and the Holy Ghost has been
working on earth in forming the body of Christ, the church,
the heavenly bride.[18]

In essence this meant that the Christian church had no prophecies of its own. It occupied a mysterious, prophetic time warp, a
"great parenthesis," which had no place in God's original plans.
As Mackintosh explained, "It is vain to look into the prophetic
page in order to find the church's position, her calling, her hope.
They are not there. It is entirely out of place for the church to be
occupied with dates and historic events. . . . The Christian must
never lose sight of the fact that he belongs to heaven."[19]

This perspective left dispensationalists, to say nothing of the
church, in a difficult position. According to their reasoning, the
church is in the world but can lay claim to none of the prophecies of future earthly events. As we have already seen, dispensationalists blushed at the thought of assigning earthly prophecies
to God's heavenly people. Furthermore, as every dispensationalist
knew, the Bible bulged with predictions of future events. Daniel's
seventieth week, postponed for the time being, must occur sometime. This time of trouble, called the great tribulation by all premillennialists, was described in great detail in Revelation and
other places (e.g. Matt. 24 and II Thess. 2). To complicate matters even further, dispensationalists believed that God was un-
willing or unable to deal with his two peoples or operate his two
plans at the same time. Consequently, it seemed necessary to re-
move the church before God could proceed with his final plans
for Israel.

This rather difficult problem was easily solved by dispensationalism's most controversial and distinctive doctrine—the secret, pretribulational rapture of the church.

In premillennialist jargon, the rapture was the "catching away" of the church at the second coming of Christ. The Apostle Paul provided the biblical evidence:

> For the Lord himself shall descend from heaven with a shout, with the voice of the archangel, and the trump of God; and the dead in Christ shall rise first, then we which are alive and remain shall be caught up together with them in the clouds, to meet the Lord in the air: and so shall we ever be with the Lord (I Thess. 4:16–17).

Up to the early 1830s, it seems that all futurist premillennialists had seen the rapture in conjunction with the second coming of Christ at the end of the tribulation. But dispensationalists, taking their cues from the creative teaching of John Darby, separated them. At the rapture, they said, Christ will come *for* his saints, and at the second coming, he will come *with* his saints. Between these two events will occur the tribulation, which dispensationalists equated with Daniel's seventieth week and the reign of Antichrist. In this way the church will be removed from the scene so that God can resume his prophetic countdown and his dealings with Israel.[20]

The pretribulation rapture was a neat solution to a thorny problem, and historians are still trying to determine how or where Darby got it. Samuel Tregelles, prominent biblical scholar of his day and one of the Plymouth Brethren, charged that the idea originated in about 1832 during an ecstatic utterance in the congregation of Edward Irving, where the charismatic gifts of the Spirit were alleged to have been poured out.[21]

A newer though still not totally convincing view contends that the doctrine initially appeared in a prophetic vision of Margaret Macdonald, who was a teenager from Glasgow, Scotland, in the early part of 1830. According to some recently discovered (and confusing) manuscripts, Miss Macdonald claimed special insight into the second coming and may have even advocated a pretribulation rapture of the church. Shortly after her vision of the end, Margaret began speaking in tongues and became, along with other members of her family, one of the main attractions of a charismatic type of revival in western Scotland. Deeply disturbed by the reports of a new Pentecost, the Plymouth Brethren commissioned Darby to investigate. He arrived in the middle of 1830 and, according to his own testimony twenty-three years later, actually met and heard Miss Macdonald. According to recent theory, Darby returned home totally against the so-called outpouring of the Spirit, but borrowed Margaret Macdonald's view of the rapture, modifying it at a number of points and fitting it into his system, without ever acknowledging his debt to her.[22]

Possibly, we may have to settle for Darby's own explanation. He claimed that the doctrine virtually jumped out of the pages of Scripture once he accepted and consistently maintained the distinction between Israel and the church.

> It is this conviction, that the Church is properly heavenly in its calling and relationship with Christ, forming no part of the course of events of the earth, which makes its rapture so simple and clear; and on the other hand, it shows how the denial of its rapture brings down the Church to an earthly position, and destroys its whole spiritual character and position. Prophecy does not relate to heaven. The Christian's hope is not a prophetic subject at all.[23]

Now that the heavenly people of God have been removed, Darby and his followers went on, the divine script can be played out to the end. Shortly after the church's rapture, the Antichrist will be revealed. Promising peace in a time of world chaos, the Antichrist will make a covenant with the newly restored state of Israel, pledging to protect it from hostile neighbors. Treacherously, he will suddenly suspend all religious practices of the Jews and then brazenly demand to be worshipped as God. In order to solidify his political and religious power, the Beast will begin a reign of terror against all who refuse to accept his pretensions, in this case, Jews who have turned to Christ since the church's rapture. In retaliation for the attacks against his people, God will pour out terrible plagues on the earth, which will throw most of mankind into agony and despair.

Finally, things mount to a crescendo. Forces from north, south, east, and west will converge on Israel in a last attempt to destroy God's people and God's influence in the world. As the world's armies gather in Armageddon, a valley in northern Israel, Christ and his previously raptured saints will break through the clouds and destroy them.

After this awesome display of power, the Antichrist and his followers will be cast alive into the lake of fire, the nations of the world will be judged according to how they treated God's earthly people, and Satan will be bound and thrown into the bottomless pit.

Then, when Daniel's seventieth week is over, the victorious Messiah will restore the throne of David and the millennial kingdom will begin. Since all ancient prophecies concerning Israel must be fulfilled literally, the millennium will be a Jewish kingdom, complete with a restored temple, daily blood sacrifices, and a powerful King Jesus reigning from Jerusalem and exercising Jewish hegemony over the rest of the world. Thus all the prophecies originally intended for Christ's first advent (before the Jewish rejection had forced their postponement) will be fulfilled at the second.

After a thousand years of Christ's kingly rule, Satan will be freed to foment one last rebellion. After it is quickly squelched, the resurrection of the dead and the last judgment will occur. Once everyone who has ever lived is assigned to his proper place in heaven or hell, God will create a new heaven and earth as an eternal dwelling place for his people.

That, in barest outline, is the dispensational premillennialism which began gaining acceptance in the evangelical denominations after 1875. Dispensationalists had little trouble proving that their brand of premillennialism differed from that of the Millerites. The Millerites were historicists; they were futurists. The Millerites set dates for the second coming; they theoretically could not because there were no temporal bearings to take in the "great parenthesis" of prophetic time. God's countdown was suspended until the church would be taken out of the way. The second coming would take place soon after the rapture; but the rapture, not part of God's "earthly" prophetic plans, could occur at any time. It was imminent.

Dispensationalists had only slightly more difficulty in establishing their orthodox and evangelical credentials. Their task might have been more formidable had it not been for the fact that the rise of theological liberalism forced all conservative evangelicals into a close, defensive alliance. Conservatives needed each other in the battle against liberalism in the churches, and, under those circumstances, dispensationalists received a hearty welcome in more conservative evangelical circles.

Historians of American religion have characterized the five or six decades after the Civil War in terms of conflict and creativity, realignment and reorganization, activity and aimlessness. They speak of "ordeals of transition," the dissolution of the "evangelical empire," the "spiritual crisis of the Gilded Age," and the "ordeal of faith" in churchgoing America.[24]

Once appearing invincible and immovable, American evangelicalism was thrown into chaos by immense and unprecedented social and intellectual crises which beset the nation after the Civil War. The rise of the city, the almost overwhelming influx of immigrants and the unsettling problems arising from rapid industrialization called into question some of the more traditional evangelical approaches to society and economics and forced the churches onto new and unfamiliar terrain in their attempts to meet them.[25]

Similarly, the churches were threatened by new, revolutionary ways of thinking. The rise of the theory of evolution called into question traditional ways of looking at the universe and the nature of man. Biblical higher criticism, comparative religion, and the new social sciences caused many evangelicals to doubt the traditional views of biblical inspiration and authority and the finality of the Christian faith.[26]

As might be expected, evangelicals dealt with these theological challenges in various ways. As early as 1872, Henry Ward Beecher, for forty years the pastor of the Plymouth Congregational Church in Brooklyn and one of the most influential preachers of the nineteenth century, told divinity students at Yale that unless ministers re-evaluated the traditional faith in light of modern thought, they would be left behind by "the intelligent part of society."

> If ministers do not make their theological systems conform to the facts as they are; if they do not recognize what men are studying, the time will not be far distant when the pulpit will be like a voice crying in the wilderness. And it will not be "Prepare the way of the Lord," either.[27]

Consequently, many evangelicals tried to redefine the traditional evangelical faith in terms compatible with modern thought. Evangelical liberals kept close ties with the tradition by affirming the finality of the Christian religion, the uniqueness of Jesus, the special nature of the Bible as divine revelation, and the centrality of personal religious experience. Modernists, on the other hand, showed less concern about retaining historic Christian categories. Their approach, though not that different from evangelical liberals initially, led them to far more radical conclusions. Whereas evangelical liberals affirmed the outlines of the tradition and tried to bring them in line with modern thought, modernists seemed to affirm the methods of modern science and then examined the tradition to see what could stand up to scientific scrutiny.[28]

Without question, liberals did manage to retain the allegiance of many modern people by their adaptations to modern thought; but more conservative evangelicals thought they had accommodated themselves too far. While redefining the old gospel in terms that modern people could understand, they had robbed them of their ancient meanings. While making the story and message of Christ palatable for modern people, they had stripped them of their spiritual power. Some conservatives openly wondered whether liberalism was even Christianity at all.

As with the liberals, conservative evangelicals responded to the challenges of the time in divers ways.[29] But in the long-standing evangelical tradition, they could forget their sectarian differences in order to do battle against a common enemy—in this case, liberalism and the growing denial of the old gospel. Conservatives banded together, and dispensationalists were included. Though their premillennialism placed them outside the main nineteenth-century evangelical tradition, conservatives considered them well within the tradition on other, more essential points, and thus welcomed their assistance in the battle to save the churches.

No better example of conservative cooperation can be found than the Bible conference movement that got started in 1875 with the organization of the Believers' Meeting for Bible Study, which soon changed its name to the Niagara Bible Conference. Meeting for two weeks each summer, the Niagara conferences provided a gathering place for conservative evangelicals to hear the older evangelical doctrines confirmed and preached. Though they could have made much of their differences, evangelicals from a variety of denominations "gathered by one Spirit unto the name of the Lord, to worship in perfect sympathy and fellowship, and in utter forgetfulness of all differences, before one Father."[30]

The new premillennialists were at the Niagara Conferences from the beginning and eventually became the dominant force in their leadership. When the summer conference of 1878 decided that it needed statement of faith, premillennialists helped frame one. The result was a theological statement that the vast majority of conservatives in the revivalist-evangelical tradition could support. In addition to the plank on premillennialism, the "creed" affirmed the inspiration and authority of the Bible, the Trinity, the fall and sinfulness of man, the absolute necessity of personal conversion to Christ, justification by faith alone, the centering of the whole Bible in Christ, the importance of the work of the Holy Spirit in the life of the church and the individual believer, the inclusion of all true believers in the true church of Christ, and the final separation of all people for eternal life or damnation.[31]

Though such a statement obviously ignored vast areas which had been important to Christians in the past, such as the sacraments and church government, it did express what many believed were essentials in light of the liberal restatement of traditional beliefs. It would be easy to show that the Christian gospel has at times meant much more than the contents of the Niagara Creed, but it would be difficult to show that it had ever meant much less—as far as American evangelicals were concerned.

Premillennialists worked hard at keeping their ties with other conservative evangelicals strong. They consciously portrayed themselves as evangelicals who believed the same things—with the exception of eschatology—that their brethren did. William Pettingill, for example, denied the charge that premillennialists were totally consumed with doctrines concerning the last day. A premillennialist, he said, is not one who "thinks, sings, prays, and dreams about nothing else but the second coming of Christ." Premillennialists' beliefs about the Lord's return were completely compatible with other evangelical beliefs about Christ's divinity, virgin birth, substitutionary atonement, physical resurrection, and current intercession for believers.[32] Another premillennialist claimed that "if you accept the second coming you are under bonds logically to accept the doctrines with which it is so indissolubly bound up. The second coming is so woven into these basic doctrines of the Christian faith . . . that you cannot deny the one without denying the other."[33]

Premillennialists and other evangelicals could get along, but occasionally the premillennialists felt the need to go their own way. Within three years of the founding of the Niagara Bible Conference, some of its premillennialist leaders and their followers desired more explicit exposition of the new premillennialism than other evangelicals were willing to bear. Consequently, a call was issued for the First American Bible and Prophetic Conference, which was held in New York City at the Holy Trinity Episcopal Church in late October of 1878.[34] Those convening the conference noted that "when from any cause some vital doctrine of God's Word has fallen into neglect or suffered contradiction and reproach, it becomes the serious duty of those who hold it . . . to bring back the Lord's people to its apprehension and acceptance."[35]

This first conference went so well that in time six more were held: Chicago in 1886; Allegheny, Pennsylvania, in 1895; Boston in 1901; Chicago again in 1914; and Philadelphia and New York in 1918.[36] As the years passed, the new premillennialism (i.e. dispensationalism) came to dominate more and more of the proceedings, clearly edging out other kinds of futurist premillennialism. By stressing this from of eschatology, the new premillennialists were broadening their own movement while at the same time they were accentuating the differences which separated them from the rest of the evangelical community in the United States.

Possibly more daring because of their growing influence and respectability in evangelical circles, premillennialists frequently made rather extraordinary claims for their distinctive doctrines. Not only was dispensationalism compatible with other evangelical doctrine, it helped establish it. Reuben A. Torrey claimed a premillennial doctrine of the second coming was the ultimate antidote for all infidelity and the impregnable bulwark against liberalism and false cults.

> In the truth concerning our Lord's return is the safeguard
> against all current heresies, errors, and falsehoods. . . . One
> who knows the truth concerning the Second Coming of
> Christ has proof against them all. For example, no one who
> knows the truth concerning the Second Coming of Christ
> could possibly be misled by Christian Science, Millennial
> Dawnism [Jehovah's Witnesses], Occultism, Theosophy, or
> Bahaism. It is remarkable how all forms of error touch the
> doctrine of Christ's Second Coming, and are shattered by the
> truth revealed about it in the Scriptures.[37]

William Bell Riley called premillennialism "the sufficient if not
solitary antidote to the present apostasy."[38] To arrive at a premillennialist position, one had to correctly and literally interpret the
Bible, thus ensuring that one grasped the other essential doctrines
of the faith as well.

Naturally, when premillennialists began to make such claims
for the virtue and power of their distinctive doctrine they an-
noyed their conservative allies, who thought they could stand firm
without it. Under such circumstances, the differences which separated premillennialists and other conservatives became obvious.

Despite the cooperation in a common cause, premillennialists
were still a small minority within conservative evangelicalism.
From time to time, leaders in the mainstream spoke out against
their allies, especially when they implied that the rest of their
brethren were wrong about eschatology. In the 1880s A. A.
Hodge, the Princeton Seminary professor whose doctrine of biblical inerrancy was espoused by most premillennialists, called the
pretribulational rapture of the church "an unscriptural and un-
profitable theory." Francis Patton, conservative Presbyterian and
president of Princeton University, often associated with premillennialists, but he said, confidentially, "I am not foolish enough to
be one of them."[39]

Much later, J. Gresham Machen, fundamentalism's greatest theologian, demonstrated the ambivalent attitude that many conservatives had toward their premillennial allies:

> The recrudescence of "Chiliasm" or "premillennialism" in the modern church causes us serious concern; it is coupled, we think, with a false method in interpreting Scripture which in the long run will be productive of harm. Yet how great is our agreement with those who hold the premillennial view: They share to the full our reverence for the authority of the Bible, and differ from us only in the interpretation of the Bible; they share our ascription of deity to the Lord Jesus, and our supernaturalistic conception both of the entrance of Jesus into the world and of the consummation when He shall come again. Certainly, then, from our point of view, their error, serious though it may be, is not deadly error; and Christian fellowship, with loyalty not only to the Bible but to the great creeds of the church, can still unite us with them.[40]

For people who prided themselves on a literal interpretation of the Bible, Machen's kind words were little consolation. Though they participated fully in the conservative evangelical alliance, at times premillennialists felt lonely and isolated. In the 1880s James H. Brookes, a leading dispensationalist who was, for the most part, highly regarded within the Presbyterian Church, frequently felt on the outside. On one occasion he tried unsuccessfully to get the General Assembly to take a stand on the status of premillennialism within the church: either declare premillennialists heretics or give them the open hearing they deserve. Speaking from his own experience, Brookes warned other premillennialists to be ready "to be gored and tossed on their way to meet Him in the air."[41]

Clearly, premillennialists did not like to be reminded of their minority status within the evangelical movement, especially when they claimed to be preservers of the evangelical tradition. C. H. Mackintosh, a British subject, nonetheless spoke for his American brethren when he described the burden that all premillennialists shared.

> There is something peculiarly painful in the thought of having so frequently to come in collision with generally received

opinions of the professing church. It looks presumptuous to contradict, on so many subjects, all the great standards and creeds of Christendom. But what is one to do? . . . But we would impress upon our readers the fact that it is not at all a question of human opinion or of a difference of judgment amongst even the best of men. It is entirely a question as to the teaching of Scripture. There have been, and there are, and there will be, schools of doctrine, varieties of opinion, and shades of thought; but it is the obvious duty of every child of God and every student of Christ to bow down in holy reverence, and hearken to the voice of God in Scripture. If it is merely a matter of human authority, it must simply go for what it is worth; but on the other hand, if it be a matter of divine authority, then all discussion is closed, and our place—the place of all—is to bow and believe.[42]

In an age when a doctrine's validity was often judged by who believed it, premillennialists set out to show that what they lacked in quantity they made up for in quality. As a result, they became master list-makers, as though compiling long lists of premillennialists would convince others of the validity of their biblical interpretations.

In 1891 James Brookes published a list of premillennialists from the United States, Great Britain, and Germany.[43] Twenty-two years later the editors of the *Christian Workers Magazine*, which was published by Moody Bible Institute, printed a list of 245 "eminent exponents of premillennialism."[44] The list was mainly composed of contemporary premillennialist leaders, but what raised a few eyebrows and protests was the inclusion of such "premillennialists" as Martin Luther, John Calvin, Philip Melanchthon, John Knox, Richard Baxter, and John and Charles Wesley.

When the editors published an even longer list two years later, the resulting protest brought a retraction of sorts.[45] The editors admitted that some people on the list were not premillennialists in any sense whatever, but they had felt justified in including them because they were not *post*millennialists. The only real criteria for making the list, the editors confessed, were believing that Jesus was coming back and that there would be no millennium *before* his coming. In fact, as it turned out, one did not even have to believe in a literal millennium:

> This is all we are contending for. In other words, it is not a millennium for which we are looking, but for Him. If our brethren differ with us as to the first, but agree as to the second, we are still happy. It is only when they admit a millennium and postpone His coming until the close of it, that we are unhappy. We had rather they were anti-millennialists than postmillennialists.

With these criteria, the editors assured, the list should stand as is, with only one exception—Cornelius Woelfkin, a former premillennialist who had denied his earlier convictions to become a leader of the liberals in the Northern Baptist Convention.[46]

All such lists were obviously intended to encourage identity-conscious premillennialists and to demonstrate to skeptical evangelicals that premillennialism was an honorable tradition with respectable supporters.[47]

There was only one thing wrong with list-making: anyone could make one. In 1919 James Snowden, a postmillennialist theology professor from Western Theological Seminary (Presbyterian) in Pittsburgh, surveyed 236 theological professors from twenty-eight seminaries in eight denominations. Among these he could locate only seven premillennialists. "This fact may be allowed to speak for itself. . . . It is hard to kick against the pricks of such scholarship, and in the long run it has its way."[48]

Premillennialists may not have had a majority of seminary professors on their side, but they could point to a number of respected and prominent evangelicals in their movement who were known neither for their eccentricities nor for their tendencies to follow after foolishness. D. L. Moody, "Mr. Evangelical" to nearly everyone at the end of the century, was an early premillennial convert, and nearly every major evangelist after him adopted his eschatology: George Needham, W. J. Erdman, Major D. W. Whittle, J. Wilbur Chapman, Leander Munhall, Reuben A. Torrey, and Billy Sunday.

A number of leaders in the evangelical world missions movement accepted the doctrine: among them Robert Speer, long-term secretary of the Presbyterian Board of Foreign Missions, A. T. Pierson, editor of the authoritative *Missionary Review of the World,* and A. B. Simpson, Presbyterian minister and founder of the Christian and Missionary Alliance.

But probably more important were the prominent pastors who gave their large congregations steady doses of the new premillennialism. James H. Brookes, probably the most influential of them all, served as pastor of the Walnut Street Presbyterian Church in St. Louis from 1858 to 1897. Adoniram Judson Gordon was pastor of the Clarendon Street (Baptist) Church in Boston from 1869 to 1906, while George Bishop served with equal distinction at the First Reformed Church of Orange, New Jersey, from 1875 to 1906. In addition to his evangelistic work, W. J. Erdman filled Presbyterian pulpits in Chicago, in Jamestown, New York, in Boston, and in Asheville, North Carolina, between 1875 and 1895. Before giving up the pastorate for writing and conference work, Arthur Tappan Pierson was the minister of churches in Detroit, Indianapolis, and the prestigious Wannamaker's Bethany Tabernacle in Philadelphia. Cyrus I. Scofield served at the First Congregational Church of Dallas from 1882 to 1895. Those men, and scores like them, initiated thousands into the premillennial understanding of the Bible.

The new premillennialists not only had their share of respectable evangelical leaders; they produced their own through a number of Bible institutes, which they helped to establish at the end of the nineteenth century. Starting with Moody Bible Institute in 1886, conservatives founded those specialized schools as a hedge against the New Theology and higher criticism. The Bible institutes were not theological seminaries; they were training schools for Christian lay workers. Seeing no need to burden his students with the laborious study of Greek and Hebrew, D. L. Moody declared that his school's main intent was to produce "gapmen"— "men who know the Word" and could "go into the shops and meet these bareheaded infidels and skeptics" in order to appeal to them "in the name of Jesus Christ."[49] Moody wanted his gapmen to know their Bibles, but he desired evangelists, not exegetes.

Almost without exception, the institutes taught the new premillennialism. Yearly they produced an enthusiastic corps of men and women for church agencies, home and foreign missionary societies, and the pastoral ministry. For example, in 1900 Moody Bible Institute sent out 137 graduates into various positions:

22 preachers and teachers in evangelistic work
19 pastors (mostly in frontier and rural churches)
13 missionaries under the American Sunday School Union
16 home missionaries
8 foreign missionaries (plus 1 under appointment)
11 workers in city and rescue missions
9 "pastor's assistants" and church visitors
6 educational workers (Bible teachers, etc.)
5 YMCA secretaries
4 YWCA secretaries
1 deaconess
1 hospital chaplain
1 nurse in training for foreign missionary service
1 church chorister
19 continuing college studies.[50]

That number, however, represented only those who actually finished the two-year training course. In the early years, especially, the percentage of students who earned a diploma was small. Most students stayed only a short time in order to gain specialized training in some area of interest. Possibly as significant as those who finally earned their MBI diplomas were those who came only for a few days, weeks, or months of study. Multiply that kind of influence by the fifty or so Bible institutes in existence by 1900 and one can see how premillennialism spread throughout the churches.

It is difficult to overestimate the influence of the premillennialist leadership in the spread of the movement and its growing respectability in wider evangelical circles. In fact, many who looked back to their becoming premillennialists noted the influence of the great leaders of the movement.

Many of the most prominent leaders of the new premillennialism were known as "doers." They were successful pastors, evangelists, missions executives, and gifted Bible teachers, who attributed their success to their belief in the imminent second coming. Henry Ostrom was an evangelist who claimed that his turning to premillennialism was partly due to the successful image of premillennialist leaders.

> I do not mean to say that the apparent outstanding success of these godly men became conclusive. . . . But it did do this for me—it started me again to [study] my Bible . . . and I have been led almost to the conclusion that where men do not accept this teaching of the truth of God, they are usually possessed of such an element of uncertainty about the reliability of the whole Bible that their approach to Christian work is not quite as sure-footed as it would be if they accepted this truth.[51]

Even though most evangelicals after the Civil War had no premillennial background, many were willing to reconsider the issue after hearing a premillennialist with impeccable conservative credentials expound it. James M. Gray, dean and president of Moody Bible Institute for thirty years (1904–34), told how he became a premillennialist after attending the first prophetic conference in New York in 1878. Though he had already completed his theological education, he was highly impressed by such an array of Bible teachers who were convinced that Jesus might be coming soon. Arno C. Gaebelein, an early pioneer in Jewish missions and editor of the premillennial *Our Hope*, resisted the teaching until he met the likes of Brookes, Erdman, Gordon, and Pierson at the Niagara Bible Conference. William Pettingill, dean of the Philadelphia School of the Bible, was first drawn to premillennialism through a Bible study group of devout believers in the Rochester, New York, YMCA. Robert McQuilkin, president of Columbia Bible College in South Carolina, had been taught by William J. Erdman in the Philadelphia YMCA. Others recorded that they had been first reached by the writings of these men.[52]

Such influential teachers exuded more than personality and enthusiasm, however. In their teaching of the new premillennialism they demonstrated a clear continuity between their position and traditional evangelicalism on a number of significant points.

First and probably foremost was the commitment to biblicism. At a time when conservatives were honestly concerned about the impact of higher criticism on the status of the Bible in the churches, premillennialists stood firmly for full biblical authority and inerrancy.

Premillennialists opposed higher criticism on a number of grounds. Moody believed that it was "ruining revival work and emptying the churches."[53] No one expended time and energy in practical Christian work unless he was certain of his message. Higher criticism robbed the Christian of religious certainty.

Higher criticism also took away the individual believer's ability to interpret the Bible for himself. The perspicuity of the Bible was one of evangelicalism's most cherished ideas. Most American Protestants believed that the layman could understand the Bible completely on his own. But the findings of higher criticism forced many lay people to doubt their ability to understand anything. Suddenly, nothing could be taken for granted. Questions of authenticity, dating, literary genre, and the influence of other Semitic cultures weighed heavily on anyone trying to read the Bible and come to his own conclusions. A. T. Pierson expressed the frustration of many evangelicals when he stated that "like Romanism, [higher criticism] practically removes the Word of

God from the common people by assuming that only scholars can interpret it; while Rome puts a priest between a man and the Word, criticism puts an educated expositor between the believer and his Bible."[54]

Premillennialists, on the other hand, not only affirmed the inspiration and authority of the Bible, they still maintained that anyone with an open mind and basic intelligence could understand it for himself. One premillennialist, probably saying more than he intended, claimed that "the Scriptures were not for the erudite, but for the simpleminded. . . . All the material needed for our understanding of the matter are contained in the Bible itself." Another claimed that all one needed to understand the Bible was "a bit of spare time daily, some simple, comprehensive plan of reading, a reverent spirit and daily practice with the Book's spirit and teaching."[55]

Not only did the premillennialists preach the principle of every-man-his-own-interpreter, they practiced it. Their most characteristic "proof" was the Bible Reading, popularized in Bible and prophetic conferences. The Bible Reading was nothing more than the public reading of Bible passages which had been selected to illustrate a particular point or doctrine. James Brookes explained how it was done:

> Have your leader select some word, as faith, repentence, love, hope, justification, santification, and with the aide of a good Concordance, mark down before the time of meeting the references to the subject under discussion. These can be read as called for, thus presenting all the Holy Ghost has been pleased to reveal on the topic.[56]

In this way, premillennialists assured their audiences, only God could be heard. One Bible Reader was grateful that "little that is human is introduced save the expository" comments of the speaker before each new subject, which "form the connecting links whereby the harmony and fulness of the Word . . . will be more readily appreciated."[57]

Though one might question such a method, the Bible readings seemed to have a convincing impact on many who heard them. Conservatives who wanted their beliefs based on the Bible alone were naturally impressed when passage was piled on passage. Not only was the Bible Reading tailor-made for those insisting on biblical authority, it was easily adopted by laymen for their own study. Anyone could buy a Concordance and develop his own readings. Premillennialists were great believers in personal Bible study and encouraged other evangelicals to see for themselves if the Bible taught the premillennial second coming.

A second feature of the evangelical tradition which carried over into premillennialism was historical primitivism. When formulating doctrine, the vast majority of American evangelicals took their cues from the first century. The discipline of church history was just starting to come of age after the Civil War, with many church historians beginning to recognize the development of doctrine over the centuries.[58] But for the rank and file, the faith was "once for all delivered to the saints" during the times of the Apostles. The church's task, therefore, in every age is simply to restate what the Apostles taught—and, of course, their words were found in the Bible alone.

But evangelical liberals were calling all of these time-honored assumptions into question. They spoke of development, change, and transformation. Building their views on an evolutionary model, they were willing to admit that the church of the first century had believed in the personal and premillennial return of Christ, but they felt no obligation to retain its perspective.

George Eckman, a strong opponent of premillennialism, admitted its popularity in the early church, then added that

the lapse of centuries, the record of history, the development of Christianity, and the deepening of Christian experience have put the Christian student of the Bible in a position to place a sounder evaluation upon the doctrine of Christ's second coming than was possible in a previous era. Ancient prophecy is clearer, the words of Jesus are plainer, the writings of the apostles are more intelligible than ever. If we are deceived to-day by false teachers respecting the second coming of Christ, our fault will be greater than that of any who have gone before.[59]

Harris Franklin Rall, a systematic theologian from Garrett Biblical Institute, nearly wrote off the apocalypticism of the Book of Revelation as "something taken over from the Jewish church of which Christianity was ridding itself. More and more the church saw that the world was to be changed and the kingdom was to come by gradual moral and spiritual development."[60]

To conservative evangelicals, such reasoning was the height of folly and arrogance. How could the nineteenth or twentieth century pass judgment on the beliefs of the Apostles? How could modern historians or biblical scholars cast aside something clearly found in the inspired text of Holy Scripture simply because they believed they had a better vantage point from which to judge?

At an 1886 prophetic conference one participant expressed total shock at such a mentality:

> I well remember the shock of surprise . . . with which I read in one of the prominent so-called religious papers of New York City that . . . the doctrine of our Lord's premillennial advent which writer admitted was undoubted held by the early church, did well enough in times of persecution, and sustained the faith of God's people when the church was yet weak and struggling against mighty foes; but now, when the church has become strong and is on its world-conquering way, such a doctrine is no longer of any use, being unadapted to a triumphant church, and therefore, whatever in the Scriptures seems to inculcate this doctrine must be interpreted in the light of modern history: With such a principle of interpretation, the devil could drive a coach and four through any biblical doctrine whatsoever.[61]

Premillennialists, on the other hand, held on to the first century with a passion. The Bible clearly contained passages on the apocalyptic return of Jesus Christ at the end of the age. If premillennialism was good enough for Peter, Paul, and the Lord Jesus Christ, then it should be good enough for Christians in modern times. Thus, the propensity of evangelicals for historical primitivism was maintained and exploited by premillennialists.

Premillennialism also maintained the overt supernaturalism of the earlier evangelical tradition. American evangelicals historically had believed in an active, intervening God who had not only worked in the history of Israel and revealed himself in Jesus of Nazareth, but who continued to intervene in the lives of people in more modern times. The frontiersman who writhed in spiritual agony at the camp meeting, the more sedate student who found Christ in one of the innumerable college revivals, the urbanite who came to Jesus in one of the massive evangelistic campaigns knew firsthand that God was still able to visit people in supernatural ways. It was comforting to know that God was in control of the universe and occasionally personally intervened in it for the sake of the elect. In short, evangelicalism's God was personal, powerful, and active—supernatural.

Because of its evolutionary framework, theological liberalism blurred the distinction between nature and super-nature. It stressed continuity, process, gradual change. Liberalism did not deny the existence of a personal God (though some forms of it did), but it did tend to downplay the supernaturalism of the earlier tradition. Its God was committed to historical development and had decided not to intervene.

Possibly more than any others on the current scene, premillennialists maintained the supernaturalism of the past. Their world view still had room for angels, demons, lakes of fire which burned forever, and a personal Son of Man who was coming soon on the clouds of heaven to put an end to evil and establish the perfect order. While more liberal evangelicals were becoming increasingly embarrassed by the world view expressed in the Bible, premillennialists felt very much at home there and maintained it in an age of telephones, telegraphs, motor cars, and flying machines.

Their supernaturalism was just the kind of affirmation many Protestants were looking for. Instead of placing God within some historical or evolutionary process, instead of playing down his transcendence for the sake of his immanence, premillennialists still believed in a God who stood outside and above history and human life and would shortly intervene in it through the return of Jesus Christ.[62]

Furthermore, premillennialism provided a way for many evangelicals to maintain their traditional millennialism under changing conditions. Postmillennialism was quickly losing credibility after the Civil War because, in the eyes of most people, things were getting worse, not better. As the evangelical empire began to crumble, the promises of postmillennialism seemed empty and highly improbable.

The disillusionment with postmillennialism was a recurring theme in the testimonials of premillennial "converts." In 1914, for example, Howard Pope, the superintendent of men at Moody Bible Institute, admitted that although he had been trained as a postmillennialist at Yale, his study of missions and world population growth convinced him that the world could not be converted to Christ, as his former teachers had predicted. After realizing his older views did not account for things as they actually were, Pope "was converted to the premillennial view as quickly as Saul was converted to Christ."[63]

Other former postmillennialists said much the same thing. It was becoming harder and harder to read the morning newspaper and remain a firm believer in the imminence of the millennium. According to many people, times were bad, possibly worse than any time in living memory. Premillennialism was far more believable under the circumstances.

Many analysts believe that the changing times was the most important factor in the rise of premillennialism after the Civil War. During difficult times people need an escape and promise of better times ahead. Shirley Jackson Case, for example, called premillennialism a "phase of wartime thinking," while others have attributed it to uneasiness over the rise of industrialism or the apparent disintegration of American society.[64]

There is much truth in this "deprivation theory." Premillennialists made much of the current state of society and interpreted it as "signs of the times." Political corruption, pornography, intemperance, the rise of monopolies, the desecration of the Lord's Day by immigrants worldliness in the church, liberal theology (which was equated with apostasy), international conflicts, forest fires, earthquakes, revivals, the rise of cults like Christian Science and Millennial Dawnism, the invention of the airplane, polio and influenza epidemics, changing weather patterns, the rise of Zionism, the sinking of the Titanic, the partitioning of Europe after World War I, radio, and countless other events or trends were seen as proof that premillennialism was correct and the end of the age might be approaching.

Even its detractors realized that premillennialism seemed realistic and plausible. But premillennialism's rise cannot be explained on environmental or even psychological grounds. Though the rest of this study will document how premillennialism led its advocates to interact with their times, there can be no adequate social or environmental explanation that does not take into account the current state of Protestantism and the significant ways that premillennialism reflected important elements in the historical American evangelical tradition.

In the last analysis, premillennialism must be seen as an authentic part of the conservative evangelical movement at the end of the nineteenth century that gained popularity among those conservatives who favored a rather literalistic interpretation of Scripture, and who recognized in premillennialism a way to remain both biblical and evangelical under difficult circumstances.

2

Occupy Till I Come

Behold, now are we the sons of God, and it doth not yet appear what we shall be: but we know that when he shall appear, we shall be like him, for we shall see him as he is. And every man that hath this hope in him purifieth himself, even as he is pure.

I John 3:2–3

Occupy till I come.

Luke 19:13

Utterly convinced that Jesus Christ would appear on October 22, 1844, many Millerites took decisive action. Some left their jobs, boarded up their businesses, confessed to unsolved crimes, sold their farms and everything they owned, and let their crops go unharvested so that they could spread the word of Christ's coming and meet him with clean consciences and free of debt.[1] As the expected day approached, thousands of people found it difficult if not impossible to live normal lives.

While the new premillennialists were just as serious about their beliefs, they never acted in similar ways. In fact, their dispensational interpretation of biblical prophecy made it impossible for them to do so. They were convinced that the rapture might occur at any moment; but then they also had to recognize that it might not occur for years or even in their lifetimes. Since the church was living in suspended prophetic time, there was no way to tell. Unlike the Millerites, they could not calculate Christ's coming.

To other evangelicals who were used to equating premillennialism and the Millerites, the behavior of the dispensationalists looked tame and even insincere. They claimed to believe in the imminent second coming, but their lives did not seem to reflect their convictions. James Snowden charged that despite all their talk about waiting and watching for the return of the Lord, dispensationalists acted no differently than anybody else.

> What do they do that is different from what other Christians . . . do on this subject? If their theory is true, it must lead them to do something that is distinctive of them, that corresponds with and grows out of and fulfills their doctrine, something that other Christians, such as postmillennialists, do not do. As far as we can make out, they do not differ in their practice from other Christians, unless it be that they hold "prophetic conferences" and carry on a propaganda to convert other Christians to their view. They do not engage in any distinctive or special kind of Christian service that fulfills their doctrine. . . . On pragmatic principles, if this doctrine is true, it should "make a difference."[2]

To the outsider at least, it looked as though dispensationalists did not take their own doctrines very seriously.

Were they as inconsistent as Snowden implied? There seemed to be ample evidence. Dwight L. Moody was a confirmed premillennialist who believed in the imminent coming of Christ. During one of his revivals in the late 1870s, he claimed that "the moment a man takes hold of the truth that Jesus Christ is coming back again . . . this world loses its hold upon him; gas-stocks and water-stocks, and stocks in banks and in horse-railroads, are of very much less consequence to him then. His heart is free and he looks for the blessed appearing of his Lord, who at His coming will take him into His blessed kingdom."[3]

Yet at the same time Moody was expecting the return of Christ at any moment, he was also busy making long-range plans for two educational institutions, Northfield Seminary for girls and the Mount Hermon School for boys. In the middle of the 1880s, he also helped to found the Bible institute in Chicago which eventually took his name.[4]

Moody was not the only premillennialist practicing such apparently inconsistent behavior. As we have already seen, dispensationalists were avid educators in the Bible institutes. James M. Gray, a leading dispensationalist and president of Moody Bible Institute after the turn of the century, faithfully preached the imminent coming of Jesus and capably oversaw a massive building program at the Institute. Between 1904 and 1931 Gray helped MBI increase its gross operating expenses from $376,000 to $5,807,059.81; its buildings from 8 to 37; its staff from 42 to 280; and its total student body (including day, evening, and correspondence students) from 1100 to 17,200.[5] While the students were being taught that Christ might return at any moment, the Institute's administrators were building for the future in case he did not.

While some premillennialists wondered if buying life insurance or cemetery plots indicated uncertainty about the imminent return, most dispensationalists never gave it a second thought.[6] Readers of Moody Bible Institute's *The Christian Workers Magazine* might find an article on the imminent coming of Christ for his saints alongside an advertisement plugging Moody Bible Institute Annuities to ensure a safe and secure retirement.[7] Everywhere one looked, it seemed, dispensationalists were saying one thing and doing another.

Realistically, one cannot expect everyone in a movement to live in complete harmony with his stated beliefs. People often fail to think about the practical consequences of their theological positions. But the apparent inconsistent behavior of the premillennialists cannot be explained in such a manner. They were actually living as consistently as their interpretation of Scripture allowed.

Dispensationalists were in an irresolvable bind: they had to live as though Christ might return at any time, but also as though he might delay his coming for years. The Millerites had the luxury of "millennial arithmetic." The dispensationalists, on the other hand, were forced to live with "maybes" and theoretical possibilities. Under such circumstances the new premillennialists did not dare sell their homes, quit their jobs, or break off all earthly ties. Their eschatology demanded that they live both in the present and the future, and most premillennialists recognized the danger of putting too much emphasis on either extreme. When they erred, most dispensationalists seemed to stress the "not-yet" side of their eschatology. They knew that Jesus could theoretically return at any moment, but in the meantime they had to pay their bills, meet their mortgage obligations, and raise their families. Even the success of their movement among evangelicals in America demanded careful, long-range planning: schools had to be founded, books had to be written, and conferences had to be organized and promoted. It seemed that they had to be forward-looking even to spread the news of Christ's possible imminent return.

The critics of premillennialism were not the only ones to recognize these inconsistencies. Premillennialists themselves knew that the normal demands of life in the world threatened to rob them of their enthusiasm and certainty about the possibility of the Lord's imminent appearance. Consequently, dispensationalists were constantly reminding each other to be in a perpetual state of expectation and anticipation. Their literature was filled with exhortations to watchfulness and joyful waiting.

They likened themselves to the soldier on picket duty who knows that his present peace might be shattered by the call to action. Unlike his comrades back in camp who could afford to lie around the camp fires and relax, the sentry must be constantly alert and on his guard. But despite the call to be ready, dispensationalists were hard put to be specific about how they should be waiting for the Lord's return. Without exception, they rejected any extreme or bizarre behavior as counterproductive. In the end, they were forced to suggest run-of-the-mill forms of Christian piety and service. R. A. Torrey stated that premillennialists should prepare themselves through a "separation from the world's indulgence of the flesh, from the world's immersion in the affairs of this life and intense daily earnestness in prayer."[8] Another premillennialist called on his brethren to be ready by "teaching, testifying, giving, sacrificing, suffering, using mind, hands, feet, whatever we have and whatever we can for His honor and for making Him and His will known among men for their welfare."[9] Of course, neither suggestion was distinctly premillennialist. Nearly every other earnest evangelical in America could have made one or the other comment, regardless of his eschatological views.

One way to spur more dedication and expectant activity was to get the faithful to speculate about what they would do if they could know with certainty that Christ's coming was actually imminent. In 1915 Arno C. Gaebelein asked his readers a hypothetical question: What would you do if you *knew* that Christ would return within the year?

There would be the greatest awakening. As it was with the wise virgins [Matt. 25:1–13], there would be an arising and trimming of lamps as never before. The worldliness into which so many of God's children have drifted . . . would at once be ended. There would come a great repentance, a great self-judgment, self-surrender, and turning to the Lord. Furthermore, we would witness a revival of activity, in service for God in every direction. The Gospel would be preached . . . the truth would be circulated . . . there would be prayer meetings such as the church has never known before. But should these results not be with us without such a supernatural revelation [of Christ's coming within the year]? Is it not enough that the Lord has told us in His word that He will come and that He will come suddenly? Are our solemn, significant days not evidence enough that His coming for His saints must be at hand? . . . We do not know when He comes. We do not know if this new year will be the time. But if we really believe that He is coming and that He

may come at any time, we shall witness amongst ourselves as
His people the things stated above.[10]

But knowing that it may happen is not the same thing as knowing
it definitely will happen at a specific time. Try as they might,
dispensationalists could not share—did not want to share—the pre-
cision of the Millerites. Their hermeneutic forced them to live
in the tension of now/not-yet.

In the last resort, there were no guarantees that Jesus would
return in 1915. He would come in his own time. Whenever it
would be, premillennialists knew that they must be ready.

> The Lord Jesus Christ is coming back! He may be here at
> any moment! He may come today! . . . Now this is not a
> foolish assertion that He will come today. Nor is it the set-
> ting of a specific time for Him to come, which would be
> equally foolish and wrong. . . . It is the sober statement of a
> fact, to arouse souls from their carelessness and indifference,
> and point them to the clear testimony of God's only Word
> that the Lord Jesus *is* coming again, and *may* be here today.[11]

In the midst of daily pressures and responsibilities, premillennialists had to keep reminding themselves that "today might be
the day." Gaebelein voiced the prevailing view when he said that
"every night when we retire our last thought should be of Him
and that before another morning comes we *may* meet Him.
Every morning's first thought should be of Christ and that before
another evening appears He *may* come."[12]

Despite the honest sentiment, there was always the danger that
premillennialists might take their doctrine too much to heart and
stress the importance of the "now" to the detriment of the "not-
yet." If one became too enthralled with the possibilities of the
imminent return, he might fail to make proper provisions for the
future and the equally possible "tarrying of the Lord." The premillennialists were after balance, but sometimes it was hard to
come by.

That point is difficult to document because people who overemphasize the present and end up looking foolish do not generally write about their own failures. Other premillennialists would certainly shy away from discussing them for fear they would reflect on the whole movement. However, if one notes the frequency and intensity of the reminders to work and "occupy" until the Lord's return, one gets the impression that the leaders of the movement knew that the doctrine of imminency could just as easily put a stop to work as promote it.

Most likely, then, experiences like that of Edmund Gosse, the famous British literary critic who lived around the turn of the century, were more common than reported. Gosse's father, the equally renowned naturalist Philip Gosse, was a member of the Plymouth Brethren who taught his son to expect the imminent return of Christ. Edmund shared his father's convictions, but tried to turn them to his own advantage on occasion.

> I proposed at the end of the summer holidays that I should stay home [from boarding school]. "What is the use of my going to school? Let me be with you when we rise to meet the Lord in the air!" To this my father sharply and firmly replied that it was our duty to carry on our usual avocations to the last, for we knew not the moment of His coming, and we should be together in an instant on that day, how far soever we might be parted upon earth. I was ashamed, but his argument was logical, and, as it proved, judicious. My father lived for nearly a quarter of a century more, never losing the hope of "not tasting death," and as the last moments of mortality approached, he was bitterly disappointed at what he held to be a scanty reward of his long faith and patience. But if my own life's work had been, as I proposed, shelved in expectation of the Lord's imminent advent, I should have cumbered the ground until this day.[13]

No one knows how many premillennialists, without the "judicious" advice of a wise parent or friend in the faith, despaired of seeking an education or making the most of their possibilities because of the nearness of the Lord's coming.

Clearly then, intense expectancy of the Lord's return could—and did—backfire if it were not tempered with practicality. Some premillennialists must have grown tired of waiting. In 1919 J. C. Massee told the story of a small boy who returned home after Sunday School and announced that "Jesus is coming back to this earth." When his mother asked him when Jesus might be expected, he said, "Oh, I don't know, but soon." The next day the boy rushed home from school and inquired if Jesus had arrived. When his mother said that he had not, the boy concluded that Jesus might have stopped off first at his Sunday School teacher's house and would be along shortly. In the meantime, he informed his mother, he would be outside playing.

Massee concluded that many in the church were like the foolish boy. "We have thought of it, and dreamed of it, and been discouraged. . . . The church has gone out to play."[14] For those who longed for the Lord's return, nothing could satisfy but his appearance. When the years passed without Christ's advent, some were bound to fall away.

Once again Edmund Gosse can illustrate. After returning to boarding school at his father's insistence, he became more certain of Christ's imminence than ever before. His expectancy finally took the form of "unwholesome excitement":

> It was a summer afternoon . . . I was alone, and I lay on a sofa, drawn across a large open window at the top of the schoolhouse. . . . I gazed down on a labyrinth of gardens sloping to the sea, which twinkled faintly beyond the towers of the town. . . . A wonderful warm light of approaching sunset modelled the shadows and set the broad summits of the trees in a rich glow. There was an absolute silence below and around me, a magic of suspense seemed to keep every topmost twig from waving.
>
> Over my soul there swept an immense wave of emotion. Now, surely, now the great final change must be approaching. I gazed up into the faintly coloured sky, and I broke irresistibly into speech. "Come now, Lord Jesus," I cried,

"come now and take me to be for ever with Thee in Thy Paradise. I am ready to come. My heart is purged from sin, there is nothing that keeps me rooted to this wicked world. . . ." And I raised myself on the soft, and leaned up on the window-sill, and waited.

This was the highest moment of my religious life, the apex of my striving after holiness. I waited awhile, watching; and then I had a little shame at the theatrical attitude I had adopted, although I was alone. Still I gazed and still I hoped. Then a little breeze sprang up, and the branches danced. Sounds began to rise from the road beneath me. . . . "The Lord has not come, the Lord will never come," I muttered, and in my heart the artificial edifice of extravagant faith began to totter and crumble. From that moment forth my Father and I, though the fact was long successfully concealed from him and even from myself, walked in opposite hemispheres of the soul. . . .[15]

As any dispensationalist could have observed, Master Gosse had allowed himself to be carried away by his imagination and his flair for the dramatic. But that did not alter the devastating impact of his experience. No one can even speculate on how many other premillennialists were shaken from their beliefs by the weariness of waiting.

Unless dispensationalists drifted into such extremes, their personal behavior was hardly distinguishable from that of other evangelicals. When they successfully maintained the balance between the now and not-yet tensions in their system, they were hard to detect; but when they erred on the side of the not-yet, they were almost totally undetectable from others. But one must not thereby conclude that premillennialism made no difference at all in their personal lives. While the outward actions of premillennialists were not distinctive, many of the reasons they gave for their behavior were. Premillennialists may not have developed a new Christian life style, but they used their beliefs about the second coming to fortify some of the slipping behavioral standards they shared with other evangelicals.

Probably no behavior was more typically evangelical than saving souls. Although different churches and traditions spoke of it differently (being justified by faith, getting saved, owning the covenant), nearly all evangelicals acknowledged the need for a personal encounter with Christ. Pastors and enthusiastic lay people participated in personal evangelism, but the most visible and spectacular form of reaching people with the gospel was revivalism. And, although it was never fully accepted as the only way to bring people to Christ, by the last quarter of the nineteenth century revivalism had won the allegiance of the vast majority of American evangelicals.

Urban revivalism and the new premillennialism developed side by side. As historians of American religion have noted, every major American revivalist since Dwight L. Moody has been a premillennialist. Belief in the imminent second coming of Jesus Christ gave revivalists a valuable and effective weapon in the war for souls.

Revivalists did not make premillennialism a major part of their preaching until after World War I, when the schism within Protestantism made it less necessary to appeal to wide segments in the churches. By 1920 premillennialist revivalists could afford to press their doctrine, while before then they had been careful to remember premillennialism's distinct minority status within the evangelical mainstream.[16] Without always stressing the point in front of audiences that might take offense, revivalists and other premillennialists nevertheless saw their belief about the second coming as an immensely useful device to encourage people to make their decisions for Christ.

On the most basic level, dispensationalism injected a new note of urgency into evangelism. If Christ might come for his church at any moment, then there was simply no time to lose. The time for evangelism was, at least theoretically, very short, and no one knew how much time was left. Moody claimed that "I have felt like working three times as hard ever since I came to understand that my Lord was coming back again."[17] J. Wilbur Chapman, another leading revivalist of the period, testified that premillennialism had been "one of the never-failing inspirations in my ministry. It has constantly stirred me on to increased activity in connection with my evangelistic work, and but for this blessed hope, I think that many times I would have grown discouraged and felt like giving everything up."[18]

Premillennialists viewed the world as a sinking vessel whose doomed passengers could be saved only by coming one at a time into the lifeboats of personal conversion. Since the course of the world was downward, only souls, not societies, could be saved from certain destruction. As Moody put it,

> I look on this world as a wrecked vessel. God has given me a life-boat, and said to me, "Moody, save all you can." God will come in judgment and burn up this world, but the children of God don't belong to this world; they are in it, but not of it, like a ship in the water. This world is getting darker and darker; its ruin is coming nearer and nearer. If you have any friends on this wreck unsaved, you had better lose no time in getting them off.[19]

Premillennialism not only gave its advocates a new incentive for converting sinners; it gave them a new, powerful way to shake them from their spiritual lethargy. In the past revivalists had told their audiences about the uncertainty of life and the dangers of postponing one's decision for Christ. Any person, they warned, might suddenly and unexpectedly die and be rushed into the presence of God. Understandably, hell-fire preachers got good results when they thundered "Prepare to meet thy God" at unrepentant sinners. No one in his right mind wanted to meet God face to face without adequate preparation.

Premillennialists were able to add to this already effective approach. No longer did the sinner only have to worry about dying unexpectedly; now he had to live with the possibility of being

left behind when Jesus returned to rapture the church. Dispensationalists figured that people would like to experience the wrath
of the Antichrist and the horrors of the great tribulation about as
much as they would enjoy dying and going to hell.

The imminent second coming put new pressure on the unconverted, and premillennialist speakers rarely missed the opportunity to remind their hearers that "He is coming! Perhaps this
year; perhaps this month; perhaps tomorrow; perhaps today. Are
you ready?"[20] In his frequently delivered sermon on "The Lord's
Return," D. L. Moody would tell his electrified audience that "the
trump of God may be sounded, for anything we know, before I
finish this sermon—at any rate, we are told that He will come as
a thief in the night, and at an hour when many look not for
Him."[21]

To this possibility the sinner had no response. Theretofore, by
ruling out the remote chance of accidental death, the healthy
sinner could easily convince himself that he still had adequate
time to put off the pleadings of the evangelist. But no one could
do anything to protect himself from the surprise return of Jesus
Christ.

Aware of their advantage, revivalists painted frightening pictures of the horrors awaiting those who missed the rapture of the
church and were left behind. In 1918 one dispensationalist described the horrible scene:

> Multitudes of men and women will, for the first time in their
> lives, call upon the name of the Lord and cry unto Him for
> Mercy. But their cry will not be heard. . . . Often had these
> left-behind ones been warned, but in vain. Servants of God
> had faithfully set before them their imperative need of fleeing
> from the wrath to come . . . only to be laughed at for their
> pains. And now the tables will be turned. God will laugh at
> them, laugh at their calamity and mock at their fear.[22]

In the same year revivalist Reuben A. Torrey put it as well as
anyone when he said,

> Ah, but for you who are out of Christ, unbelievers—When the Lord comes, it means you are to be left behind, left behind when God takes away the restraining power that holds back the manifestation of the Antichrist. Do you want to live in this world when the salt of the earth is gone? . . . I don't. And then darker and darker and darker and darker until it is the midnight of eternal despair. The common argument today for immediate repentance and acceptance of Jesus Christ is that you may die at any moment. That is not the Bible argument. The Bible argument is, "Be ye ready, for in such an hour as you think not the Son of Man cometh." Are you ready?[23]

To make the prospects of being left behind even more graphic, premillennialists reminded hesitant sinners that they would be separated from raptured loved ones and friends. Typical of that kind of appeal was the supposedly true story told by William Evans, a premillennialist who served Moody Bible Institute and the Bible Institute of Los Angeles from 1900 to 1918. After reading the Apostle Paul's passage on the rapture (I Thess. 4), a man retired and dreamed that the next morning he awoke to find his wife and daughter nowhere in the house. A thorough search revealed that all the doors and windows were securely bolted and that their clothes were just where they had left them the night before. Greatly puzzled, the man went to his sister-in-law's, where he discovered that her black maid was also missing. After breakfasting on coffee without cream—the milkman had not made his delivery that morning—the man walked to work, discovering along the way similar stories of missing relatives and friends. When he arrived at work, he found that a number of his employees had not shown up. Needless to say, the churches were open and packed with angry inquirers that evening, once people realized what had happened. Those pastors who remained were severely criticized for not preparing their people for the rapture, but they defended themselves by saying that they had given the people exactly what they had received in seminary.

At that point in the dream, the man awoke screaming. Startled by the sudden outcry, his wife, still by his side, thankfully, asked what was the matter. The man related his dream. He concluded:

> Oh, how glad I was to see her, and to realize that the terrible experience was only a dream! But the more I thought of it, the more solemn seemed the Scripture truths which it contained, and the more I was impressed with the importance of being ready for the coming of the Lord.[24]

A. J. Gordon told a similar story, about two sisters who had heard a sermon on the text, "one shall be taken and the other left" (Matt. 24:40). Upon returning home, the Christian sister begged her unconverted sister to accept Christ, but to no avail. During the night, the Christian left the room they both shared to pray for her sister's soul. When the non-Christian awoke and found herself alone, she immediately wondered, "Has the Lord really come, and has she been taken and I left?" Filled with instant fear, she began to weep loudly, which brought her "raptured" sister on the run. Greatly relieved that the rapture had not taken place, the sister decided that she no longer wanted to take any chances. "Together they wept and knelt and prayed, and before they closed their eyes again they knew that if He should come, they would part no more."[25]

Clearly, then, revivalists and personal evangelists had in the imminent second coming a valuable tool for encouraging commitments to Christ. Though the opponents of premillennialism often tried to downplay its significance, the coming of the Lord to rapture his converted followers at any moment was a boon to all those who wanted to impress on others the importance of an immediate decision for Christ. Tomorrow might be too late.

But premillennialism not only was an effective incentive for the unconverted; it also helped to keep those already saved on the straight and narrow.

American evangelicalism has always been a blend of doctrine

and duty. Although evangelicals disagreed on church government, modes of baptism, and certain particulars of doctrine,
nearly all agreed that true believers in Christ must both believe
correctly and behave properly. Profession and practice went
hand in hand. As a result, evangelicals developed almost the same
ideas about what constituted the ideal Christian life. Though their
lists of "do's and don'ts" differed slightly from group to group,
the standard taboos included breaking the Sabbath, attending the
dance or the theater, use of alcohol and tobacco, and gambling.
Naturally, not all evangelicals could agree on any one particular
list, but most did agree that Christians should avoid "worldly
amusements," however defined, and that they would be immeas-
urably better off if they maintained a close watch on their personal habits and deportment in the world.

Not surprisingly, at times such an approach became superficially legalistic and self-defeating; but it appears that most evangelicals did not find such lists overly oppressive or restrictive.
After all, the guidelines were for the believer's own good, a hedge
against moral ruin and a prod to personal purity.

Such assumptions about the Christian life suffered almost irrep-
arable damage in the late nineteenth and early twentieth centuries.
New temptations in the cities, materialism which resulted from
industrialization, the "new woman" and the resulting pressures
on family life, the unprecedented effects of mass advertising and
merchandising, changing dress styles, new amusements, and such
new ideas as "behaviorism" and Freud's findings on the power of
human sexuality made the earlier evangelical values seem archaic
and irrelevant. The revolution in morals became a serious threat
to traditional life styles and behavior patterns.

Premillennialists claimed that nothing inspired people to holiness of life more than belief in the imminent coming of Christ.
Those who expected Jesus to come soon practiced a strict "separation from the world." In 1888 Samuel H. Kellogg, a premillennialist who had served as a missionary to India and as a seminary

professor, observed that "the modern easy-living, card-playing, theater-going, dancing type of Christian is very rarely found to be one who has learned to look for his Lord's premillennial advent."[26] In fact, dispensationalists frequently hinted that only those with a firm grip on the Lord's imminence could live devout lives. James Gray, for example, claimed that when he had been the pastor of churches in Massachusetts before the turn of the century, his best parishioners had always been premillennialists.

> The members of my church on whose hearts the coming of Christ had made any sensible impression were separated from that whole system of worldliness. They were the working force of my church along spiritual lines, and the most intelligent Bible students. They manifested the greatest power in prayer. They were the most self-denying givers. They lived the most even and consistent lives.[27]

Although they acknowledged that God always observes every act and ascertains every thought, there was something about the possibility of being instantly interrupted by the returning Lord which put extra restraints on would-be deviants. In order to use their doctrine as a deterrent to questionable behavior and as a means of social control, premillennialists only had to ask a single question: Would you want to be doing *that* when Jesus comes?

This theme is scattered throughout premillennialist literature. Robert Speer, the Presbyterian missionary administrator, wanted it to be understood that people should be motivated to be good by more than the imminent return of Christ; but he also found in the doctrine a helpful restraining force during times of temptation:

> I want to speak this word to the man who would be free from unclean personal sin: the next time the temptation comes, fix your mind on the hope of His coming. No man can easily do an unclean and unholy thing expecting at that moment that Jesus Christ might come. Can I cross the threshold of the questionable place? Can I read the questionable

book? Can I be found with that questionable story on my
lips? Can I be caught on the verge of that sin, if I am expecting that at that very moment Jesus Christ may come?[28]

Reuben A. Torrey fashioned a simple rule of thumb from the
doctrine of the imminent rapture, and he used it in every situation: "Do not do anything that you would not be glad to have
your Lord find you doing if He should come. . . . Never go
anywhere that you would not like to have the Lord find you if
He should come." Torrey testified that "it is simply wonderful
how that clears things up."[29]

That method evidently worked for others, too. Premillennialists circulated stories about how their fellow believers had been
saved from sinning by applying similar ethical rules. Evangelist
Leander Munhall told of two members of the same church who
had been walking down the streets of New York City one evening. As they had passed through the theater district, one had
remarked that a certain play had received rave reviews and asked
if the other would like to attend.

"No," he replied, "I don't want to." When asked why not, he
explained that "the Lord might come while I was in such a
place."[30]

In an attempt to maintain even greater conformity, some premillennialists hinted that Jesus might leave behind real believers
who were not living as they should at his coming. In this "partial
rapture" theory, unspiritual and worldly believers who needed to
be purified would have to go through the terrors of the tribulation. Most premillennialists were not willing to go that far; but
one warned that "the bare possibility of being left in the tribulation should stir every Christian heart to double diligence, to
burning zeal, to holy consecration, to high living, and to utter
abandonment of self . . . to the will of Christ in all things."[31]

To enforce the ethical demands of living in the shadow of the
second coming, premillennialists composed hymns and "gospel
songs" to remind the faithful to be ready.

Jesus is coming to earth again,
What if it were today?
Coming in power and love to reign,
What if it were today?
Coming to claim His chosen Bride,
All the redeemed and purified,
Over this whole earth scattered wide,
What if it were today?

Faithful and true would He find us here
If he should come today?
Watching in gladness and not in fear,
If He should come today?
Signs of His coming multiply,
Morning light breaks in eastern sky,
Watch, for the time is drawing nigh,
What if it were today?

Glory, glory! Joy to my heart t'will bring;
Glory, glory, when we shall crown Him king.
Glory, glory, haste to prepare the way,
Glory, glory, Jesus will come some day.[32]

In a hymn entitled "Will Jesus Find Us Watching?" Fanny
Crosby, a blind hymn writer who composed thousands of songs
and poems, asked,

When Jesus comes to reward His servants,
Whether it be noon or night,
Faithful to Him will He find us watching
With our lamps all trimmed and bright?

Blessed are those whom the Lord finds watching,
In His glory they shall share;
If He shall come at dawn or midnight,
Will He find us watching there?

Oh, can we say we are ready, brother?
Ready for the soul's bright home?
Say, will He find you and me still watching,
Waiting, waiting when the Lord shall come?[33]

Premillennialists, then, discovered in their own particular doctrine a way of reinforcing slipping evangelical mores. Apart from their distinctive approach, dispensationalists opposed "worldliness" on the same basis as other evangelicals. For example, they deplored the changing styles in women's fashions, generally considering any rise of the hemline or reduction in the number of petticoats as a disgusting affrontery to modesty and an invitation to masculine lust. In 1916 the editors of the *Christian Workers Magazine* complained that women went to their shops, factories, stores, and offices "arrayed in clothes short at both ends and skimpy in the middle." No wonder, they observed, the women attract "the unworthy attention of ungodly men and . . . inflame their passion to direful results."[34] If pious premillennialists were scandalized in 1916, when skirts rarely if ever rose to more than six inches above the shoe tops, they were close to apoplexy when the "flappers" of the 1920s bobbed their hair, bound their breasts to hide their feminine curves, wore dresses up to their knees, and even rolled their stockings below their kneecaps.

In the resultant controversy over dress styles, the critics of high fashion seemed more concerned about its adverse effects on men than anything else. As one observer noted, all men carried around with them a quantity of "dynamite" which only needed to come in contact with a lighted match to explode. How could Christian mothers allow their daughters to go out with other mothers' sons, dressed in "garb that harlots have ever used as an instrument to lure men to destruction?" Some premillennialists even wanted to hold scantily clad girls responsible for the delinquency of young men.[35]

Dancing had been considered sinful by many evangelicals before the turn of the century, and the development of new and even more daring dance steps did little to mitigate their convictions. The main objection to dancing was that such close proximity between the sexes could result in nothing but a lessening of sexual morality. In 1907 R. A. Torrey admitted that dancing was not a sin—as long as men and women did not do it together.[36] Dispensationalists, like all the more conservative evangelicals, considered the Turkey Trot, Grizzly Bear, Fox Trot, One-Step, Toddle, Shimmy, and Charleston as nothing short of obscene. As a former dancing master confessed, "many of the couples performing these dances should have a marriage license before stepping out on the ballroom floor, and if they had a marriage license, there would be no excuse for committing such acts in public."[37] Every one knew that praying knees and dancing feet never seemed to go together, and that dancing aroused its participants. T. C. Horton of the Bible Institute of Los Angeles once asked his men's Bible class how many had ever danced. Nearly every one of the 300 present raised his hand. When he asked to see the hands of those who had had only "pure thoughts" while dancing, not one was able to respond.[38] Under such circumstances, Christians should avoid dancing. Certainly, one who expected the imminent return of the Lord would not want to be locked in the Grizzly Bear when the Son of Man came on the clouds of heaven.

The theater, and later on the moving picture, received strong denunciation from premillennialists. In 1919 *The Institute Tie* noted the new movie industry's potential for good, but by the next year its editors were claiming that movies contaminated the minds of young people. Movies portrayed immoral or unsuitable stories about robbers, gamblers, drunkards, fighting husbands and wives, and various forms of crime; and they invariably put unwholesome ideas into the heads of all who saw them. After spending Saturday afternoon in the neighborhood movie house, people would find church dull on Sunday morning. One critic claimed that churchgoers who attended the cinema would soon demand ragtime music during worship services and try to bring motion pictures right into the house of God. In 1915 A. C. Gaebelein observed that full movie houses on Sunday evening meant a substantial drop in church attendance. Movies corrupted the young, undercut the convictions of the old, and diverted attention away from the church. Christians, therefore, must have nothing to do with them.[39]

Examples of such sentiments could be multiplied, but the point has already been made: premillennialists maintained the traditional cultural taboos of the evangelical movement, altering their lists of "don'ts" when changing mores made it necessary. What disturbed most Protestants about the revolution of morals in America disturbed premillennialists. They in turn did everything in their power to resist the popular trends, using their doctrine of the imminent second coming of Jesus as added incentive to flee from temptation.

The new premillennialists had in their possession a powerful and effective tool for guiding and regulating personal life. The doctrine of the imminent return of Christ gave evangelists a new weapon in the battle for human souls: the impending rapture of the church gave apathetic sinners a boost to make their decisions for Christ. And the possible arrival of the Son of Man provided all would-be disciples of Jesus with a new motivation to live holy lives, separated from every appearance of evil. For surely "every man that hath this hope in him purifieth himself" (I John 3:3).

But premillennialism gave its advocates much more than mere support for slipping evangelical social taboos. It gave them a new perspective by which to live the Christian life. Despite the criticism that premillennialists cared only for the "great by and by," the belief in the imminent second coming gave added significance to life in the present. Current actions and decisions had ultimate significance because they might be suddenly interrupted by the apocalyptic arrival of Jesus. Life in the here and now, therefore, was crucial. Premillennialists did not see themselves as caught up in some long, indeterminate, evolutionary or progressive stream. They lived on the edge of eternity, only one second from a divine in-breaking. Spiritual commitments, therefore, and even petty ethical decisions took on new meaning.

Though the now/not-yet tensions of their dispensationalism made it hard for premillennialists to live consistently, they certainly provided them with excitement. For believers in the second coming, Jesus' command to "occupy till I come" (Luke 19:13) was no call to stand pat; it was a call to personal commitment and discipleship. The nearness of the Lord's coming gave added meaning to their lives in the present.

3

This Gospel Shall Be Preached

And this gospel of the kingdom shall be preached in all the
world for a witness unto all nations; and then shall the end
come.

Matthew 24:14

One of the most persistent charges against the new premillennialism was that it completely repudiated the earlier evangelical
commitment to win the world to Christ and build a truly Christian America. Optimistic evangelicals and social gospelers who
envisioned a more Christian world through the spread of the
gospel and a more consistent application of Christian principles
to all of life were generally appalled by the apparent pessimism
and defeatism of the premillennial outlook.

In 1918 Shirley Jackson Case of the University of Chicago
summarized the prevailing view of many liberals and socially involved Protestants when he condemned the "inherent pessimism"
of the premillennial world view:

> The story of man's career upon earth is viewed as one long
> process of deterioration from the days of Adam until the day
> of final doom. Life's ills seem altogether too gigantic to be
> overcome by mere human endeavor, and even with such di-
> vine aid as mankind has experienced no gradual process of
> reform can issue successfully. . . . [The premillennialist]
> scorns all efforts made in the name of religion to correct the
> ills of society. Society must not be redeemed; it must be
> damned. . . . To inaugurate any program of social better-

ment or to set the church as a whole upon an upward course would be to thwart the divine purpose and to delay the advent of Christ. Both the world and the church must grow constantly worse in order to meet premillennial ideals. Viewed from this standpoint, the essential function of religion is to insure for a few select individuals a way of escape from the ultimate wrack and ruin to which the world is destined.[1]

Walter Rauschenbusch, America's leading advocate of the social gospel, censured premillennialism's "historical pessimism" and called it a "dead weight against any effort to mobilize the moral forces of Christianity to share in the modern social movement."[2] In his unfavorable study of premillennial eschatology, Presbyterian theologian James Snowden quoted, with obvious approval, a minister from St. Louis who condemned it as "the rankest type of pessimism" and concluded that "it discredits the church, belittles the power of the gospel, and dishonors the Holy Spirit. It makes his work a failure and confesses him to be unequal to the task for which he was sent into the world."[3]

Anyone even slightly familiar with the premillennialist view of things will see some truth in these assertions. But as was often the case, such generalizations about the premillennial outlook were simplistic and misleading. Despite the apparent pessimism and the conviction that the world's spiritual and social course would inevitably be downward until the personal intervention of Christ, premillennialists often did not act as their opponents said they must. World views notwithstanding, premillennialists insisted that they were the world's greatest optimists and frequently did not act as though they believed the world was beyond saving. As one critic was forced to admit, sometimes the actions of the premillennialists were "better than their principles."[4]

Nowhere was that incongruity more apparent than in the area of foreign missions. Despite their views on the dismal future of the world, premillennialists were enthusiastic supporters of evangelical foreign missions. Just as D. L. Moody "felt like working three times as hard" after becoming a premillennialist, others experienced a new desire to bring the gospel to a dying world in its final slide toward inevitable doom.

Robert Speer, secretary of the Presbyterian Board of Foreign Missions from 1891 to 1937, became a premillennialist during his college days at one of Moody's Northfield Conferences, and he noted some years later how "life seemed altogether changed for me in that hour." Part of that change was an increased desire to reach the lost with the gospel before it was too late. According to Speer, premillennialism not only kept Christians morally upright, made them more tolerant of others, and increased their zeal for evangelism, it also prompted them to maximum effort in anticipation of the Lord's return.[5]

Nearly all dispensationalists claimed their belief was an enormous catalyst to the missions movement. Though they sincerely believed that the world could not be converted to Christ in this dispensation, they insisted that their doctrine made them devoted supporters of the missionary cause.

Why did they become so actively involved in an enterprise which was doomed to failure? How could they believe as they did about the future of the present dispensation and still become eager participants and even aggressive leaders in the attempt to evangelize the world?

On the most basic level, premillennialists, like other conversion-minded evangelicals, were totally convinced that all who died without faith in Christ were eternally lost. The same convictions that motivated premillennial revivalists to greater activity made missionaries out of other premillennialists. When this concern for the lost was joined with the belief that Christ's imminent return might cut short opportunity to save them, premillennialists were given a strong drive toward missionary activity.

Premillennialist Henry W. Frost emphasized this dual concern in his poem on the "Dying Heathen":

Hark, there comes the sound of crying
Borne across the restless sea!
Countless heathen millions, dying,
Moan in hopeless agony;
Moan on moan, with none to pity—
So they die eternally.

Lo, the priests are chanting, chanting,
Endless prayers in monotone,
While, like demon-spirits haunting,
Hired mourners shriek and moan;
Incense burns, while souls are dying—
These can ne'er for sins atone!

See the shrines are dimly lighted!
Hear the mourner's measured tread!
Past the chant for souls affrighted,
Now the worship of the dead.
Vain is all that man can offer
For the souls for which Christ bled.

So the countless millions, passing,
Go beyond this earthly light;
So the countless millions, massing,
Enter death's eternal night;
So the days go by, and going,
End our time of doing right!

Christ is coming: judgment awful
Waits the souls who die in sin;
Christ is coming: judgment lawful.
Will the church of Christ begin?
Rouse ye saints, arise, deliver;
They will shine who souls shall win.[6]

With such motivation and urgency, premillennialists had no trouble joining with other evangelicals in the huge missions movement at the end of the nineteenth century.[7] Both groups shared a common concern for the lost and a desire to spread the gospel into all the world. Neither had illusions about the difficulty of the task or the mixed results of missionary effort. John R. Mott, leader in the Student Volunteer Movement for foreign missions, popularized the slogan "the evangelization of the world in this generation," but he warned that evangelism did not always have the desired effects:

> To consider negatively the meaning of the evangelization of the world in this generation may serve to prevent some misconceptions. It does not mean the conversion of the world within the generation. Our part consists in bringing the Gospel to bear on unsaved men. The results are with the men whom we would reach and with the Spirit of God. We have no warrant for believing that all who have the Gospel preached to them will accept it. On the other hand, however, we have a right to expect that the faithful preaching of the Gospel will be attended with conversions. We should not present Christ in an aimless and unexpectant manner, but with the definite purpose of influencing those who hear us to believe on Him and become His disciples. Like St. Paul at Thessalonica, we should preach the Gospel "in much assurance." We are not responsible for the results of our work, however, but for our fidelity and thoroughness.[8]

Most evangelicals could agree with Mott's balanced optimism. They realized that not everyone responded favorably to the gospel, but they expected to reap a huge harvest of souls if they were faithful in their efforts. Postmillennialists were not the only ones who assumed that, given enough time, money, and volunteers, the gospel would spread until "at the name of Jesus every knee would bow . . . and every tongue confess that Jesus is Lord, to the glory of the Father" (Phil. 2:10–11). One of the basic beliefs of many evangelicals in the missions movement was that God intended through such means eventually to bring the whole world under the lordship of Christ.

Some evangelicals, however, began to doubt that the world could ever be converted to Christ through such normal means. Population charts and reports of missionary societies told the story: despite massive efforts and occasional success, on the

whole foreign missions were not keeping pace with world population growth. Never-say-die postmillennialists counseled even
greater efforts, but others began to question postmillennialism's
fundamental assumptions about the course of this age. When
their postmillennial heritage could not be squared with the
events around them, many evangelicals began looking elsewhere
for a more suitable explanation of things. As might be expected,
many turned to premillennialism.

Premillennialism not only offered a different view of the future, it provided a different explanation of what God aimed to do
in this age. To put it simply, God had absolutely no intention of
saving the world before the second coming of Christ. His chief
purpose in this dispensation was to "visit the Gentiles, to take out
of them a people for his name" (Acts 15:14), not to convert the
world.[9] Before Christ's return, God's saving work was limited
to a comparatively small part of the human race, and, therefore,
the church must not think that it was commissioned to win the
world for Christ and turn it into the kingdom of God. The
church's task was evangelization, by which premillennialists
meant the dispensing of the gospel to non-Christian people.
Though there would be conversions, premillennialists quoted the
Bible to show that the response would be nothing like the postmillennialists envisioned. Christians, therefore, must be content
with their minority status and with the apparent failure of their
cause. The lack of overwhelming success was not due to the
church's lack of faith or discipline; it was ultimately the preor-
dained will of God for this age.[10]

William J. Erdman advised a Bible conference audience in
1908 that the church had better try to see things from God's
perspective for a change and live within the boundaries set for it
by God himself.

> Let us be very clear about that. There is a mystery here, we
> do not deny. We would like to see everyone converted. . . .

It is not the purpose now between the first and second comings of His Son to convert all the nations. That conversion
lies beyond the Second Coming. . . . Therefore, let us not
be discouraged, but adapt ourselves to the purpose of God.
Let us not in the least think Christianity or the Holy Spirit
to be a failure.[11]

As every premillennialist was quick to add, accepting God's
plan for this age did not mean abandoning missionary work. On
the contrary, it demanded even more strenuous effort. To borrow
a common premillennialist metaphor, the world was a sinking
ship, and while the church could not keep the ship afloat, it could
at least rescue a few of the passengers.

C. I. Scofield found an ideal setting for the sinking ship/lifeboat
metaphor in 1912, when he addressed a memorial service in Bel-
fast, Ireland, for the victims of the *Titanic* disaster. Obviously
aiming close to home, Scofield warned that "the ship upon which
humanity is crossing the sea of time is doomed," but he added
that God had provided a lifeboat that was large enough to hold
all those who wanted to climb aboard.[12]

Premillennialists were committed to world evangelization even
if very few would actually respond to the gospel. In addition to
caring for the lost, premillennialists saw the second coming directly tied to world evangelization. The key biblical clue was
found in Matthew 24:14: "And this gospel of the kingdom shall
be preached in all the world for a witness unto all nations; and
then shall the end come."

Dispensationalists who taught that no predicted event stood between the present and the rapture of the church naturally felt uneasy when fellow premillennialists made the second coming con-
tingent on the evangelization of the world. To deal with the
unsettling implications of the passage, some dispensationalists
argued that the gospel had already been preached throughout
the world in apostolic times or suggested that while the Lord

could come *for* his saints at any time, he would not return *with* them until evangelization was complete, thus leaving the final responsibility with the Jews, who were expected to be converted during the great tribulation.[13]

Other premillennialists, including some dispensationalists, had no such reservations. To them Matthew 24:14 was the church's rallying cry. The Lord Christ was poised on the battlements of heaven, waiting for the saints to complete their assigned task. Once the evangelization of the world was completed, the second advent would occur.

From that point of view, the church was not a passive participant in the unfolding of God's plan, swept along with no real share in its development. Though the events of the future were fixed, their exact time was dependent on the faithfulness and obedience of God's people. There, at least, premillennialists maintained a firm hold on the importance of the present and their activity in it. Postmillennialists believed that the coming of the millennium was in their own hands. Premillennialists held that the millennium could come only after the personal intervention of Christ. But to this extent they maintained for themselves some determination of when that intervention would occur. While the church could not convert the world, it could determine when Christ would.

William Bell Riley, a consistent dispensationalist most of the time, nevertheless sided with those who believed that the Lord was waiting for the church to finish its task:

> We strive together for the bringing back of the King. . . . We have something to do with His return! We have something to do with His ascension to the throne. We have more to do than John did when he cried, "Come, Lord Jesus, and come quickly." In one sense His crown is in our hands, and it will never bedeck His brow until by our loyalty and love, and unselfish service, and maybe unthinkable sacrifice, we have placed it there. . . . It is ours to hasten the day! Lord help us.[14]

Needless to say, premillennialists with that outlook threw themselves body and soul into foreign missions. Their journals kept readers constantly supplied with news from the foreign fields and reminded them regularly that all believers in the premillennial coming of Christ had a large stake in the evangelization of the world. Brookes's *The Truth*, Gordon's *Watchword*, Moody Bible Institute's *The Institute Tie*, *Christian Workers Magazine*, and *Moody Bible Institute Monthly* all carried regular features on missions, often with pictures of exotic peoples and places and statistics on the work overseas. Though the *Missionary Review of the World* was not a premillennialist journal, its editor, A. T. Pierson, was a leader in the movement and demonstrated his premillennialist concern for the work.

Premillennialists did more than read about missions; they supported them with their treasure and, on occasion, with their lives.

For example, premillennialists played a significant role in the founding and spread of the Student Volunteer Movement (SVM). In 1886 Moody's four-week Northfield Conference was geared to reach and motivate college students for Christian service. One of the Conference's organizers, Luther Wishard, had been pushing for a foreign missions emphasis and had gone out of his way to invite college students who were already somewhat committed to foreign service. A few days after the meetings got under way, those students joined together with the half-dozen foreign students at the conference and organized unofficial meetings dedicated exclusively to missionary concerns.

Two weeks later their enthusiasm caught on among the other participants, and over a hundred young people dedicated themselves to missions after graduation. Many in the "Mount Hermon Hundred" toured other college campuses the following year, urging students to join them. By the next summer conference, over 2000 collegians had pledged themselves for missionary careers.

Though premillennialists never really gained control of the

student movement, they were there at the beginning and contributed much to its outlook and enthusiasm. At the 1886 conference which gave birth to the SVM, the principal speakers were confirmed premillennialists—A. T. Pierson, James Brookes, D. W. Whittle, William G. Moorehead, and A. J. Gordon. When some of the students objected to the extreme biblical literalism of Brookes, Moody made it a point to invite men with other perspectives, including William Rainey Harper and Henry Drummond to later conferences.[15]

Premillennialists were also important in the founding of the "faith missions." Voluntaristic, independent of any formal ecclesiastical support or control, ecumenical, nondenominational, and often geared more to evangelism than church planting, faith missions were ideally suited to premillennialist concerns and strategy.

The biggest and in some ways the best faith mission was J. Hudson Taylor's China Inland Mission (CIM). Born in Yorkshire, England, of pious Methodist parents, Taylor (1832–1905) felt the call to foreign fields early and left for China in 1853 under the China Evangelization Society at the age of twenty-one. Although ill health forced him to return to England after only seven years, he made good use of his time in China. He learned Chinese, took long journeys into the interior, married, adopted Chinese dress to identify more closely with the people, and resigned from his mission board, deciding to rely on God alone for his financial and material needs.

When he returned to England in 1860 there seemed little chance that he would ever return to China, but his deep love for the Chinese and his concern for the unevangelized millions in China grew. In 1865 he undertook the founding of a new mission dedicated to the evangelization of the Chinese interior. Taylor began lecturing around Great Britain, calling for financial support and volunteers. His task was formidable, since he had no denominational support or assistance whatever.

He started by calling for twenty-four volunteers, two for each of China's unevangelized provinces. In 1875 Taylor called for eighteen, seventy more in 1881, and one hundred in 1886. By 1895, the China Inland Mission numbered 641 missionaries and 462 Chinese helpers who served in 260 stations and out-stations, making it the largest missionary agency of its time.

Early in his work, Taylor set down the mission's principles:

1. It was to be interdenominational. Standing in the best evangelical tradition, the mission accepted any committed evangelical Christian who could sign its simple (though conservative) doctrinal declaration.

2. It was open to people with little formal education. In a day when missions were becoming more and more "professional," Taylor recruited people with little formal training and often saw them develop into highly respectable Chinese experts in their own right.

3. It would be directed from China. Taylor believed that to best serve the Chinese the mission should be in constant touch with them. Consequently, he kept as much power for himself as possible and directed operations from China, not from Great Britain.

4. It would encourage its missionaries to adopt Chinese dress and identify as much as possible with the people.

5. It would maintain evangelization as its primary aim. Although establishing churches and education were not ignored, the dissemination of the gospel into unevangelized fields was the unquestioned priority of Taylor and his co-laborers.

Taylor was a premillennialist, and his methods were consistent with his beliefs. Kenneth Scott Latourette's description of CIM's purpose and techniques demonstrates how much Taylor's approach was a reflection of his eschatology:

> The main purpose of China Inland Mission was not to win converts or build Chinese churches, but to spread a knowledge of the Christian gospel throughout the empire as quickly

as might be. To this end, when a province was entered, stations were opened in the prefectural cities and, later, in subordinate ones. Preliminary exploration would, as a rule, precede these steps. The purpose was to cover the entire empire, so far as that was untouched by other Protestant agencies. Once the Christian message had been proclaimed, the fruits in conversions might be gathered by others. The aim was the presentation of the Christian message throughout the empire in the shortest possible time, not the immediate winning of the largest possible number of converts.[16]

It is not surprising, therefore, that the American branch of the mission sent many premillennialists to the Chinese interior. Henry W. Frost, a premillennialist who was in charge of American recruitment for CIM, after the turn of the century frequently filled his quotas with new premillennialists. One of the most famous American volunteers became an evangelical and premillennialist hero—William Whiting Borden, heir of the Borden dairy product fortune.

Born in Chicago to wealthy parents, Borden was reared within the evangelical and premillennial influences of Moody Memorial Church. After finishing prep school he accompanied the Reverend Walter C. Erdman, the son of W. J. Erdman, on a round-the-world tour of foreign mission fields. Two months into the trip, which eventually included Japan, China, India, Egypt, Syria, and Turkey, Borden decided that God was calling him into missionary service.

Borden entered Yale as a committed missionary candidate, but he did not while away his undergraduate years dreaming of exotic evangelistic encounters. In addition to competing in boxing, tennis, yachting, and football, he was twice elected to Phi Beta Kappa. Such activities did not preclude spiritual matters, however. During his four years at Yale he became involved in the SVM, serving two years as president of the Connecticut Valley Student Volunteer Union, was elected "class deacon," and helped found the Yale Hope Mission for Men in New Haven. He was also active in personal evangelism through Bible studies and prayer groups on the Yale campus.

By the time he entered Princeton Theological Seminary in 1909 he was already well known in evangelical circles. During his seminary days he was elected to the boards of Moody Bible Institute and the National Bible Institute in New York and served as a delegate to the Student Volunteer Convention in Edinburgh, representing the American branch of the China Inland Mission. In December of 1911 Borden formally applied as a missionary candidate with CIM, volunteering to go to China's ten million Moslems, who had never had a missionary.

Between his graduation and the end of the year, Borden dabbled in urban evangelism in New York, toured for the Student Volunteer Movement, and was ordained to the ministry in Moody Church. Finally, in December 1912, he set sail for Cairo to study Islamic language and literature under the Reverend Samuel Zwemer, pioneer missionary to the Moslems. In March 1913, barely into his studies, Borden contracted spinal meningitis. He died on April 9, not yet twenty-six years old.

His will demonstrates his commitment to evangelical and premillennial causes: he bequeathed $250,000 to the China Inland Mission; $100,000 each to the National Bible Institute and the Moody Bible Institute; $50,000 each to Princeton Theological Seminary, the foreign mission boards of the Presbyterian Church, USA, the Presbyterian Church, US (South), and the United Presbyterian Church, and the Chicago Hebrew Mission; and $25,000 each to Nile Mission Press and the Africa Inland Mission. To many people, Borden represented the best that American evangelicalism and premillennialism had to offer: he had been a rich man's son who had sacrificed everything for the cause of Christ and the evangelization of the world. Like other premillennialists, Borden had seen no inconsistency in believing the world could not be converted and yet dedicating himself to missionary service.[17]

Another example of premillennialist commitment to world missions is the Christian and Missionary Alliance, founded in 1887 at the merger of the Christian Alliance and the Evangelical Missionary Alliance. The real force behind the merger was A. B. Simpson, a Presbyterian premillennialist who had left his affluent church to work among the poor and unchurched of New York City.[18]

Though the Alliance today approximates a denomination, at the beginning it was merely an association for the advancement of home and foreign missions that drew support from throughout American evangelicalism. Simpson wanted it clearly understood that

> the Christian Alliance is not an ecclesiastical body in any sense, but simply a fraternal union of consecrated believers in connection with various evangelical churches. It does not organize distinct churches or require its members to leave their present church connections. There is no antagonism whatever in the Alliance to any of the evangelical churches, but a desire to help them in every proper way and to promote the interests of Christ's kingdom in connection with every proper organization and work. . . . Let us never forget the special calling of our Alliance work. . . . It is first to hold up Jesus in His fullness . . . to lead God's hungry children to know their full inheritance of privilege and blessing for spirit, soul, and body . . . to witness to the imminent coming of the Lord Jesus Christ as our millennial king.[19]

What held the Alliance together was a zeal for foreign missions, a concern for the needs of the poor and disinherited, and an adherence to what Simpson called the "four-fold gospel": conversion, entire sanctification, divine healing, and the premillennial second coming.

The Christian and Missionary Alliance, along with other groups within the "holiness movement," maintained an unusual balance between old-fashioned evangelism and active social concern. During the 1880s, for example, the Alliance established a rescue mission for women, a home "for rest and healing," a training college for foreign missionaries and urban workers (later called Nyack Missionary College), an orphanage, and various ministries among foreign immigrants. After 1892 the Alliance was sending out between seventy and one hundred missionaries a year.[20]

The Alliance was well known for its generous financial support of foreign missionary causes. In *The Truth*, James Brookes told his readers that the members of the Alliance had raised over $100,000 in a single day at its annual convention in 1896. Not long afterward the Alliance held another rally in Carnegie Hall and donated another $122,000. In 1896 alone, Brookes observed, the Alliance had contributed over $350,000 to foreign missions. In contrast, Brookes wrote that his own Presbyterian Church had held a similar rally for missions in Carnegie Hall and had raised only $5500. True to form, Brookes suggested that the real reason behind the huge difference was the Alliance's commitment to premillennialism.[21]

Whether that was the reason or not, the Christian and Missionary Alliance combined a firm conviction in the premillennial coming of Christ and an aggressive social and missionary program. For them belief in the imminent return of Christ and missionary effort went hand in hand.

In discussing premillennialism's relation to foreign missions, one must not overlook the role of the Bible institutes in supplying a steady stream of eager missionary candidates.

The Bible institutes were founded as practical training schools, not as rigorous academic centers. Their chief aim was to produce a well-trained, biblically literate, and spiritually mature corps of lay people to meet the changing conditions in the nation and the world. Along with training urban workers and evangelists, the Bible institutes were committed to preparing young men and women for foreign service.

A. B. Simpson's missionary training school, founded in 1882, was primarily dedicated to this task, as was A. J. Gordon's Boston

Missionary Training School (1889), which was originally established to provide missionaries for the Congo. Those institutions that were not chiefly founded for missionary training nevertheless provided encouragement and some course work in that direction. From the beginning, Moody Bible Institute maintained a strong missions emphasis, and virtually all other Bible institutes followed Moody's example. The Northwestern Bible Training School was set up in Minneapolis after the turn of the century under premillennialists A. J. Frost and William Bell Riley. In 1907 the Bible Institute of Los Angeles was founded, and shortly thereafter it was joined by the Toronto Bible Training School and the Philadelphia Bible Institute. Those schools were premillennial and missions-minded.

Over the years, Moody Bible Institute maintained a good record of missionary recruitment. Between 1889 and 1923, 1143 Moody students became foreign missionaries. Of that number 818 were still on the field in 1923, serving under 55 denominational and independent mission boards. The largest percentage were in China (227), but others were in Africa (194), India (87), Japan (55), Korea (31), five countries of the Near East (27), the islands of the Pacific (25), Europe (20), Alaska (9), and Southeast Asia (5). Those students who did not travel overseas had a deep concern for those who did. In 1922, for example, the student body at MBI donated $6950 for foreign missions.[22]

The early issues of *The Institute Tie*, published for friends, students, and alumni of the Institute, carried regular reports and prayer requests from alumni on the field. On occasion the editors sadly recorded the deaths of those who had given their lives in missionary service. The Institute lost three alumni in the Boxer Rebellion in 1900 and another in Africa during an uprising over British taxes in 1898.[23]

Such a steady flow of premillennialists into missionary agencies was bound to have an impact on the entire missionary movement. Though it is impossible to determine exactly how many premil-

THIS GOSPEL SHALL BE PREACHED

lennialists were serving overseas at any time, by the 1920s pre-millennialists were claiming that they made up "an overwhelming majority" of the movement. Others estimated that believers in the imminent second coming made up from 75 to 85 per cent of the missionary force worldwide.[24] Those figures were probably in-flated, but there seems to be enough evidence to indicate that American premillennialists were better represented on the mission fields than in the home churches.[25]

With such overwhelming evidence to the contrary, why did non-premillennialists insist that belief in the imminent second coming "cut the nerve of foreign missions?" They failed to rec-ognize that the premillennialists were working with a new philos-ophy of missions which enabled them to deny that the world could ever be converted to Christ, yet work hard to evangelize it. Instead of cutting missionary involvement, premillennialism in-creased it, even when it denied that it could succeed. As one pre-millennialist told the prophetic conference of 1918,

> at such an hour it is not for us to fold our arms and look up, to sigh over conditions around us, to pray to be caught away out of the wreck of this sin-cursed world. . . . I would not cross the street to talk to a crowd of premillennialists about the coming of the Lord unless they were looking for and hastening His coming by sending forth the gospel.[26]

4

The Perfect Solution

This know also, that in the last days perilous times shall come.

II Timothy 3:1

Fear not, little flock; for it is your Father's good pleasure to give you the kingdom.

Luke 12:32

If premillennialism did not "cut the nerve of foreign missions," its opponents were certain that it at least paralyzed the earlier evangelical commitment to social action and reform. In a world that could not possibly get better before Jesus comes, attempts at social reconstruction were fruitless and a serious waste of time and energy.

The critics of premillennialism often portrayed its advocates as non-involved and little-concerned Christians who folded their arms in anticipation of the Lord's return and let the dying world pass them by.

> There is a danger that by fixing his thought upon the glorious fact of Christ's return, and by assuming that it may come during his lifetime, the [premillennialist] Christian may think there is no urgent need to work against the evils which are about him in the world, and thus fail to keep the real spirit of Christ's exhortation to be watchful. We have those among us who say that the church has nothing to do with reforms in

society. Its only business is to preach the gospel, exhibit holy
and unspotted lives, and thus bear witness to the grace of
God. . . . They announce that to work for the destruction
of the liquor traffic, the suppression of the social evil, the re-
moval of political corruption, the cleansing of the slums, the
improvement of the industrial situation, or any other philanthropic undertaking is but a waste of time and energy and
an interference with the supreme duty of the church. They
say the iniquities which vex society can never be cured till
Christ returns to do this in person, and ask why Christians
should dabble unprofitably with these matters in view of the
fact that Christ will soon come back and summarily dispose
of everything hostile to his Kingdom.[1]

Premillennialists did not always conform to such common
stereotypes, however. While they all could agree that society
could not be reformed in any real sense before the return of
Christ, they did not all agree about what Christians could or
should be doing for it in the meantime. Some premillennialists
condemned all reform efforts as unsuitable for those who expected Christ momentarily; but others believed that until Christ
does appear, Christians should engage in certain kinds of reform
activity and do whatever possible to slow down the inevitable
decline and breakdown of the social order.

Regardless of what side of the reform issue they supported,
all premillennialists seemed to have a real stake in the unraveling
of modern life. They were convinced that the Bible taught that
the "last days" would be characterized by wars, lawlessness, un-
paralleled social upheaval and disorder, the breakdown of morality and family life, persecution of the righteous, and growing
apostasy in the churches. As far as premillennialists were concerned, the turbulent and troublesome decades after the Civil
War were proof positive that everything was right on schedule.

People at every level of society felt the passing of the old order
and sought in various ways to restore for themselves some kind
of power, order, security, and personal meaning under fast-

changing conditions.[2] Even those who still had high hopes for America admitted that society was going through some difficult and potentially destructive times. Josiah Strong, general secretary of the American branch of the Evangelical Alliance, surveyed conditions in *Our Country* in the mid-1880s and concluded that if American Protestants were to take full advantage of their opportunities they would have to deal with a number of "perils." The problem of the cities headed the list.[3]

Between 1860 and 1900, the United States experienced explosive urbanization. Cities grew at a phenomenal rate. During those four decades, for example, Detroit and Kansas City increased fourfold, Memphis and San Francisco fivefold, and Cleveland sixfold. Los Angeles grew twentyfold during the same period, while Minneapolis and Omaha each increased fiftyfold and more. Even already established urban centers such as New York, Baltimore, and Philadelphia more than doubled in size. Chicago, incorporated in 1837 as a frontier outpost with seventeen houses, was the fifth largest city in the world by the turn of the century, with a population of nearly 1.7 million.

Such rapid concentrations of people meant trouble. City services, already overstrained, could not possibly meet the increasing demands. Very quickly, cities offered their inhabitants non-breathable air, horrendous traffic jams, deplorable housing conditions, unsafe food and water, and increasing crime rates.[4] To make matters worse, people who moved to the cities were suddenly cut off from family ties and whatever influence their home-town churches had exerted.[5] Alone, isolated, and bewildered by new sights and temptations, novice urbanites frequently got more than they bargained for.

Many Americans wanted to blame the problem of the cities on the immigrant masses who settled there. Between 1820 and 1900, over nineteen million people immigrated to the United States. Of those, over thirteen and a half million arrived after 1865. After the 1880s most of the immigrants came from eastern and southern Europe and were Roman Catholics, Jews, Eastern Orthodox Christians, or "secularists." Some people believed that traditional American values could not endure such a massive assault. The immigrants congregated in city slums; they refused to keep the Sabbath according to evangelical standards; they preferred to send their children to parochial schools. In countless ways, it seemed, the immigrants resisted "Americanization" and thus threatened the American way of life.

When it became known that in 1900 40 per cent of the population in the nation's twelve largest cities were foreign-born and another 20 per cent were their American-born children, many if not most "old Americans" wondered if the society could escape their corrupting influence.

As if things were not bad enough, Americans were forced to face up to the new problems which came with rapid industrialization of the economy. Cycles of boom and bust affected more people than ever before. Skilled craftsmen were forced to sell their labor and became slaves of the wage system. Farmers lost control over their own produce to railroaders and middlemen. Unskilled laborers worked unbelievably long hours for incredibly low wages. More and more economic power fell into the hands of fewer and fewer financiers. Acute observers knew that things could not continue in the same way for long.

They did not. Frequent depressions and labor conflicts tore the country apart after 1873. Violent strikes, complete with pitched battles between workingmen and federal troops, rioting, arson, and bomb-throwing, were commonplace in the 1880s and 1890s. As a result, many people felt that something solid had gone out of American life. The old unity, if it had ever really existed, seemed gone forever; the future no longer looked as bright as it once had. A growing number of people honestly believed that things were not going to get any better and probably were going to get a lot worse.[6]

During such unsettled times, the churches could not avoid

their share of difficulties. As we have already seen, many evangelicals believed that the old faith could not endure under these new conditions. Evolutionary thought, higher criticism of the Bible, comparative religion studies, and the new social sciences led many evangelicals into various forms of theological liberalism.

When evangelicals were not arguing over the virtues of the New Theology, they were dividing over whether the church should concentrate on saving souls or trying to salvage the crumbling social order. For much of the nineteenth century most evangelical Protestants had never felt compelled to choose between those two enterprises. They had seen them as complementary parts of the Christian gospel. To decide for one against the other would have seemed unnecessary. The church engaged in evangelism to bring people into the kingdom of God. Once converted, Christians were expected to extend the rule of Christ through the social order by applying his teachings to all of life.

Under the deepening crises of the times, the old balance was becoming harder to maintain. More traditional evangelicals believed that social problems would be solved by heavier doses of revivalism, and the growing ranks of the social gospel movement urged the church to recognize the nature of social sin and take steps to change social structures. In time, American evangelicalism divided into a "two party system" over these issues. The "public party" believed that the churches should concern themselves with the great social needs of the day in order to Christianize the social order. The "private party" wanted the churches to concentrate on preaching the gospel to individuals, convinced that when enough people turned to Christ, the social problems would take care of themselves.[7] Eventually, each party claimed that the other had missed the main idea of the gospel completely and was next to worthless.

The premillennialists were disturbed by those developments, but they were far from being surprised by them. Their interpretation of biblical prophecy told them that troubles will increase before the end, and, in a sense, dispensationalists were relieved to see them coming to pass as the Bible had predicted.

As might be expected, premillennialists made use of the growing social discontent to show that their eschatology had been right all along. They frequently noted the bitter and often violent friction between capital and labor and hinted that it could not be alleviated until Jesus' return.[8] They mentioned the corrupting effects of city life on personal morality and society at large.[9] They joined just about everyone else in worrying about the evil consequences of permitting millions of foreigners to invade the cities.[10] In short, premillennialists used the universally recognized problems in American society as clear-cut proof that things were beginning to come apart at the seams, just as the Bible had predicted they would.

In the same way, dispensationalists interpreted the turmoil in the churches as evidence of the apostasy of the end times. The New Theology became the symbol and source of everything that was wrong with American Protestantism. I. M. Haldeman called it the "apostasy of the faith," the "Devil's lie," and "Jericho Theology"—evidently because he expected it to topple to the ground as soon as the trumpets of the second coming were sounded.[11]

James M. Gray denied that the New Theology was even remotely related to historic Christianity and blamed it for the rise of communism, nihilism, anarchism, socialism, theosophy, and Christian Science.[12] William Blackstone identified it as one of the sure signs of Christ's imminent return.[13] If the professing church of God began denying its distinctives, there could be little hope for the rest of the world. Once the church lost its bearings, then the degeneration of the social and political order could not be far behind.[14]

Premillennialists did not stop there. Everywhere they looked were further "signs of the times" to indicate the nearing end of the age. In his analysis of the "signs of Christ's speedy coming,"

Blackstone suggested that the increase in knowledge and the relative ease and extent of travel were fulfillments of Daniel 12:4: "Shut up the words and seal the book even to the time of the end: many shall run to and fro and knowledge shall be increased."

As Blackstone was careful to document, at the end of the nineteenth century knowledge certainly seemed to be on the increase. The proliferation of public and private educational institutions, the availability of books and newspapers, the decline in illiteracy, the widespread postal and communications systems, and even the growing interest in Bible study and prophetic inquiry were clear signs that Daniel's prophecy was being fulfilled.

Similarly, Blackstone reminded his readers of the extensive railroad construction which had gone on in years not long past. Railroad tracks covered the land like iron spider webs. In later years premillennialists pointed to the invention of the automobile and the airplane as further proof of Daniel's accuracy.

Other premillennialists read the same signs. Lewis S. Chafer believed that modern inventions, the spread of knowledge, and the increase of wealth and prosperity were all part of a larger prophetic fulfillment. And William Bell Riley came to many of the same conclusions.[15]

It would be unfair, however, to assume that premillennialists had a "the world is getting worse, praise the Lord" attitude.[16] They neither welcomed nor longed for the decline of human society with sadistic anticipation. They wished things could be otherwise, but knew that they could not. God's eternal plans were not easily changed. There was, however, a certain security in knowing that everything was happening according to the divine blueprint. In 1919 William Pettingill told a prophetic conference audience that "it is a great thing to know that everything is going on according to God's schedule. . . . We are not surprised at the present collapse of civilization; the Word of God told us all about it."[17] They were honestly horrified at what lay ahead for the majority of mankind; but they were also relieved that it was not going to happen to them and that God's plan was being carried out according to the Bible's exact specifications.

Naturally, not everyone agreed with the premillennialist interpretation of things. Some people who were living and working in the same society concluded that things were improving, not getting worse. Postmillennialists, for example, expected the millennium before Christ's second coming and believed that there was ample evidence that things were headed in that direction. In much the same way as the dispensationalists, they felt pressured by their interpretation of biblical prophecies to show that the world was developing along those lines.[18]

In fact, one did not even have to believe in a coming millennium to believe in earthly progress. Most theological liberals and social gospelers rejected explicit millennialism but nevertheless argued that the world was gradually turning into the kingdom of God. William Newton Clarke, whose *Outline of Christian Theology* was evangelical liberalism's most popular textbook, accused both pre- and post-millennialists of reading the Bible selectively and superficially, and he denied any possibility of a millennial reign of Christ.[19] The liberals awaited no apocalyptic intervention of God to usher in a new age. Their kingdom of God would come through the ordinary agencies of human life, not on the clouds of heaven. In contrast to premillennialists, liberals and social gospelers felt more at home in the world and believed that, despite the many problems of the day, time and God's cosmic plan were on the side of progressive goodness.

These optimists could assemble their own evidence to prove that the world was getting better. Speaking as an historian, Shirley Jackson Case did not see how anyone could deny that "history exhibits one long process of evolving struggle by which humanity as a whole rises constantly higher in the scale of civilization and attainment, bettering its condition from time to time through its greater skill and industry."[20]

Their evidence, like that of the premillennialists, seemed overwhelming. Modern civilization had abolished slavery, had outlawed infanticide and human sacrifices, and had made long strides in eradicating other forms of inhuman treatment. It had reformed its prisons and legal systems. It had begun to replace cruel and despotic governments with democracies which were more sensitive to human needs and aspirations. Despite the social and economic turmoil in American life, the plethora of reformers and social gospelers was proof positive that people really believed that something could be done about the situation and were willing to work for lasting improvements.

What were "signs of the times" to premillennialists were interpreted as signs of real progress to others. Modern inventions had certainly made life easier and more fun. Telephones, telegraphs, electric lights, rapid transit, fast and comparatively safe travel by rail and steamer, and, of late, the automobile and airplane were vast improvements over what people of the past had had to contend with.

Even in the religious realm, the optimists argued, things were getting better. The New Theology demonstrated Christianity's ability to adapt itself to changing intellectual conditions and hold the allegiance of modern people. The churches had responded reasonably well to the crisis of the situation: revival campaigns, Sunday schools, specialized work among the young and the immigrants, institutional churches, and a new array of social and welfare services. Social gospelers were putting pressure on Christians to apply the principles of Christ to every area of life. Missionaries covered the globe, with more going overseas every year in the service of Christ and the kingdom.[21]

Taking in the whole picture, one observer concluded that

> these and a host of other things which any intelligent person can discern are evidences of a growing concern for human welfare which aims at nothing less than that redemption of society which was so gloriously prophesied by the ancient Hebrew seers. The world is growing better by the hour.[22]

Who was closer to the truth? It all depended on where one chose to look. As in most historical eras, it was both the best of times and the worst of times, depending on one's perspective. In retrospect, both sides seemed too simplistic and selective in their use of historical evidence, and too quick to discount the obvious validity of the other side. For example, whenever premillennialists were forced to admit by the sheer weight of evidence that at least certain things were improving, they invariably pointed out that such improvements were only of secondary significance and really did not affect their final appraisal of the over-all situation. Anyway, in the dispensational scales, the only things that carried weight were *spiritual*. Therefore, advances in art, science, and culture were hardly sufficient to change their minds about the downward course of the world. As William Blackstone pointed out, art and culture frequently had nothing to do with spiritual matters, and more times than not were detrimental to spiritual development. Such cultural "improvements" were usually accomplished by infidels and skeptics whose spiritual contributions were nil. Therefore, Blackstone concluded, "no matter how refined and polished is their garb or the delicacy with which they may be set forth, still they are only poisonous deceptions of him who can appear as 'an angel of light.' "[23]

Furthermore, and with considerable realism, the premillennialists pointed out that progress never came easily, that cultural and social advances frequently had injurious side effects. Though some things appeared to be improving, their negative aspects canceled out their value. Modern science was unlocking the secrets of the universe, but often at the expense of orthodox religion. Education was available to more people than ever before, but frequently the schools were teaching things that parents did not want their children to learn. Some people were living better than ever, but often at the expense of someone else's poverty. As A. J. Gordon suggested, the ship that carried missionaries overseas also might be carrying rum and opium; the printing press that produced Bibles and hymnbooks also printed the works of infidels and pornographers. At every turn, he noted, the advancing kingdom of God was countered by the kingdom of Satan. The Devil always found a way to undermine even the most beneficial and God-sent blessings. Every miracle of mercy had its corresponding Satanic miracle of perdition.[24]

Given that view of the world's present and future predicament, one is not surprised to learn that premillennialists were not exactly wholehearted participants in the great social movements of their day. In fact, some premillennialists were opposed to any involvement whatever. As usual, they justified their position on purely biblical grounds.

Premillennialists believed that the key to the situation could be found in the vision of King Nebuchadnezzar (Dan. 2). According to their interpretation, the "times of the Gentiles," which had begun at Babylon's ascendancy over the ancient Jews, would remain until the Lord Jesus returned to break Gentile power and restore his Messianic kingdom. Since that situation was part of God's plan, premillennialists had no right to try to change it. Social turmoil, political corruption, and economic exploitation were all natural results of Satan's control over the present age. Until the second coming God had pretty much given everything over to the Devil, and all the reform activity in the world could not change it. The church, therefore, must bide its time and let things run their course.

> Our God . . . keeps His covenants. He gave the government of this world into the hand of the Gentile nations at the time of Nebuchadnezzar. Therefore, the New Testament says, "The powers that be are ordained of God," and the King of Kings Himself could consistently advise Israel to pay tribute to Rome. The function of government includes police authority and the maintenance of law and order. The Church was told to obey the civil powers and not attempt to usurp their authority during the present age. "Judge nothing before the time, until the Lord come." If those to whom God has

committed this duty are negligent or corrupt in administering it, the Church, as such, must not interfere. It must not try to help the Christ-rejecting world make a success of its job. It must wait until the world's "inning" is over, when the Church's time will come. The world is to fail at the last in its efforts to produce good government without God. Then, at the "consummation of the age," the long-delayed kingdom will come and our Lord will show, through His Church, what good government really is when He rules over the whole earth.[25]

It was as though God had wound up a cosmic clock: until the Devil's time ran out, the world was his to do with as he pleased. Christians who had been called out of the world were best advised to keep completely out of the entire sordid affair.

In 1880 James Brookes admitted that he was saddened whenever he saw a Christian involved in politics. "Well would it be," he said, "if the children of God were to keep aloof from the whole defiling scene. . . . [We] can do more for the country . . . by prayer and godly walk than by being 'unequally yoked together with unbelievers.'" He suggested that those who are dead to the world and alive to Christ should avoid the polling place, because "dead men do not vote."[26]

Whether they knew it or not, social reformers and social gospelers were actually playing into the Devil's hands. It would be to Satan's advantage to have people believe that they could make a bad world better. In their feverish effort to turn the kingdom of Satan into the kingdom of God, they would be wasting their time, diverting effort from the only activity open to God's people in this age—evangelism. In contrast to past evangelicals who had looked on social reform as a natural outgrowth of personal conversion to Christ, premillennialists saw it as the clever tool of the Devil:

> Sociology, or social service as generally emphasized is, in its final outworking, a black winged angel of the pit. . . . Satan would have a reformed world, a beautiful world, a moral

world, a world of great achievements. . . . He would have a universal brotherhood of man; he would eliminate by scientific method every human ill, and expel by human effort every unkindness; he would make all men good by law, education and social uplift; he would have a world without war. . . . But a premillennialist cannot cooperate with the plans of modern social service for these contemplate many years with graduate improvement through education as its main avenue for cooperation, rather than the second coming of Christ.[27]

Arno Gaebelein put the same idea in a different way: "The world, to which we do not belong, can do its own reforming without our help. Satan, I doubt not, wants to reform his world a little, to help on the deception that men do not need to be born again."[28]

As a result, premillennialists often used their reading of biblical prophecy to undermine the activities of reform-minded evangelicals. Taking their cues from Daniel 2, dispensationalists noted that the "times of the Gentiles" would consist of the passing of four successive world empires (Babylon, Persia, Greece, and Rome) and an increasing deterioration of monarchial and imperial control until political democracy gained the upper hand. The resulting chaos would pave the way for the world's turning to Antichrist in order to restore peace and security in a world gone mad with unrestrained mob rule.[29]

It is therefore not surprising that some premillennialists viewed the Progressive Movement as a direct and undeniable fulfillment of Daniel 2. The Progressives, who peaked between 1900 and World War I, openly sought to reform American society through a safeguarded political democracy, a more even-handed regulatory state, and a compassionate and equitable welfare state.[30] Philip Mauro, a New York attorney and a prolific writer on prophetic themes, recognized the Progressives' intention to change a nominal democracy into a real one and concluded that the movement was "the carrying out, in actual human history, of the prophecy of Nebuchadnezzar's image, which foreshadowed the descent of governmental authority." Theretofore, the ruling classes had been willing to allow democracy in name only, but now there was a real transference of power.[31]

All this did not mean that premillennialists were elitist or lacked sympathy with the working classes. They often pointed out that one of the signs of the end was the way the rich were greedily heaping up for themselves vast fortunes (James 5:1–6). Arno Gaebelein noted that among the causes of unrest were the extravagant and luxurious practices of the rich, who thought nothing of spending incredible sums of money on frivolous parties and social affairs while the poor were starving to death. He referred specifically to a party which some "grand dames" purportedly had catered for their dogs at an expense of $25,000. "Such an affair creates the most bitter feelings among the poorer classes and feeds the smouldering flames of rebellion and anarchy. Some day there will be an outburst of lawlessness which will deal a fearful blow to the rich. . . . 'Come now, ye rich, weep and howl for your miseries that shall come upon you.' "[32]

Yet such justifiable cause did not lessen the fact that the response of the laboring classes to such abuse was preparing the way for Antichrist. When they, understandably, tried to improve their condition and gain concessions from their greedy employers, laboring people were unknowingly playing the Devil's game. Albert Sims of Toronto, expressing a rather extreme position, claimed that the trade union movement was a direct and obvious step closer to the time when Antichrist would gain control over the world's economic system. During the tribulation, Sims noted, no one would be able to buy or sell without the mark of the Beast (Rev. 13:16–17). Even then, he was quick to add, "union-made" labels were showing up on products everywhere, "as if to point out the world-wide influence of Antichrist's mark." Already in many places men could not find work unless they joined a trade union, and men who could hardly afford it were forced to strike whenever their union bosses told them to. Since such coercion was clearly a forerunner of Antichrist, no Christian should join a union.[33]

What was true of the unions was doubly true of radicals and socialists. Premillennialists denied strongly any assertion that Jesus was a socialist and condemned the lawlessness of such radical groups as the International Workers of the World (I.W.W.). Socialists were Satanically inspired men who borrowed from Christianity its vision of the millennium and then stripped it of its coming Christ and Christian content. Socialists would have their "paradise," premillennialists guaranteed, but it would come through the auspices of the Antichrist.[34]

Such extremism led some premillennialists to repudiate some of the reforms which had traditionally been the special concern of Christians. One premillennialist claimed that despite the fact that intemperance was an unmitigated evil, it should not be opposed because it was one of the predicted signs of the times. Prohibition was an issue trumped up by the Devil "to hinder Christ's return and extend his own probation." Since drunkenness was a sign of Christ's near approach (Matt. 24:37–39), reformers were preventing Christ's return.[35]

One should not be led astray by such extreme anti-reform sentiment, because not all premillennialists were willing to go along with it. Even though many dispensationalists argued that the logic of their eschatology precluded any social action, some of their brethren sought and found ways to become involved in some of the pressing social issues of their day. Though they shared the same world view, these more moderate premillennialists refused to wipe their hands of their own age and turn their backs on human need. They wanted to find a way to sincerely long for Christ's return and participate in certain reform activities.

There may have been a number of reasons for their tentative cooperation in the social order of their time. As self-styled preservers of the American evangelical tradition, they would have inherited an enormous Christian compassion and an almost irresistible desire to remake society according to Christian standards. Despite the second thoughts of later revivalists, revivalism before the Civil War had helped pave the way for the social gospel movement at the end of the century. As Timothy Smith has pointed out, pre-Civil War revivalism went hand in hand with progressive theology and humanitarian concern. The benevolent empire that evangelicals built was established in the conviction that converted people should express their new life in Christ through acts of love and social involvement.[36]

Critics of the new premillennialism offered a second explanation for the social action of moderate dispensationalists: sometimes premillennialists simply refused to accept the logic of their position and gave in to their feelings of Christian love and concern. Writing in the liberal *Biblical World* in 1919, T. Valentine Parker argued that in times of moral crisis, such as World War I, people forgot their eschatological beliefs long enough to pitch in and meet the demands of the crisis.

> The believer in the imminent return of Christ is not necessarily a cold-blooded individual but may be a man of earnestness and compassion, who burns with anger and sorrow as he reads of the terrors of the war. He would not stand aloof if he could. . . . Whatever may be a man's eschatological opinions, his duty in a moral crisis is not altered thereby. Is it morally justifiable to refuse assistance to the right because it is sure to be defeated? To the honor of premillenarians be it said there are thousands who answer, "No. The times are in God's hands, and though the end is near, our duty is still to fight for righteousness."[37]

A third explanation for the more moderate position may be found in the nature of the new premillennialism itself. As previously stated, its unwillingness and inability to set a definite date for Christ's return placed its adherents in perpetual tension: expect Christ at any time, yet live in the world in case he postpones his coming. The extreme position of total separation and withdrawal from the world would be justifiable if one could know that Christ's coming was imminent. But without that assurance, most premillennialists did not believe such action (or lack of it) was justified or even wise. As premillennialists the moderates knew that the world could not possibly get essentially better before the Lord's return, but as Christians they could not help but feel some responsibility for it in the meantime.

James Gray knew that while total separation might be preferable, it was hardly possible under the conditions of the day. Christians might try to withdraw from all contact with the worldly system, yet "we cannot absolutely separate ourselves from its society, its literature, its politics, its commerce, but we can separate ourselves from its methods, its spirit, and its aims."[38] Since contact with the world was inevitable, premillennialists should be true to their calling as children of God and "occupy" until the Lord's return.

In the moderate position, then, premillennialists were able to preserve some of the earlier evangelical commitment to social righteousness. On one level, they admitted, the issue of reform was separate from questions of eschatology. Premillennialists could be interested in matters of social reform simply on the basis of their common humanity with others. In 1910 the editors of The Institute Tie separated the call to reform society from any eschatological considerations. Just as they would kick a potentially dangerous banana peel off the sidewalk, they declared their opposition to the liquor traffic, gambling, and white slavery, as well as political graft and other forms of social injustice. Similarly, evangelist Bob Jones claimed his "love for holiness" would naturally drive him to oppose the same things.[39]

The enemies of premillennialism pointed out that all this was hardly enough. While Progressives and social gospelers fought against evil institutions, powerful trusts, and insidious political power, premillennialists followed the older evangelical style of dealing with individual problems and sins. Their enemies said they were dealing with symptoms, not causes. The premillennialists, on the other hand, said they were doing the best they could, given the nature of the dispensation in which they lived.

It might not be much, said the premillennialists, but it was an essential rear-guard, harassing action against Satan and the "Gentile powers" before Christ's return. The church, despite its minority position, was still called upon to be the salt of the earth and the light of the world.

> The Church does not expect to conquer this world in the present dispensation or with present methods, but it expects to remain on earth as its saving light and its preserving salt until Jesus comes to take it away and substitute other agencies for the execution of His will. In the meantime, let us continue to shine and to hold corruption in check.[40]

The editors of the *Christian Workers Magazine* declared that just "because our politics or 'citizenship' is in heaven is no reason why we should let the rogues in some city hall steal our money, or the rum-seller or the procurer debauch our youth. It is admitted that we are not undoing the works of Satan very fast, but we are giving him all the trouble we can till Jesus comes and that is something."[41]

As long as they remembered the ultimate nature of the present dispensation and kept their social work secondary to old-fashioned evangelism, some premillennialists did what they could to hold corruption in check and slow down the world's slide toward Armageddon.

Despite what some extremist premillennialists were saying about drunkenness being an important sign of the end of the age, other premillennialists believed they were within their rights in trying to stop the evil effects of alcohol. James Gray knew that Prohibition was not a cure-all for every social ill, but he thought it was a worthwhile reform, nonetheless.

It is said that we carry our heads so high in the air, that we are so absorbed in our heavenly citizenship as to have no interest in the citizenship of earth. But this is not so. We love God, but we love our brother also; and while we believe that the highest expression of love to our brother is to seek the salvation of his soul, yet we would not keep back from him the good, if he will not have the best. We will preach the gospel first, last, and all the time, but we will work and vote against the saloon, and urge others to do the same, on every opportunity.[42]

Gray practiced what he preached. During his pastoral days in Massachusetts Gray had been active in the state Prohibition party, stumping the state for the cause, editing the party's journal, and attending its conventions. Later, as head of Moody Bible Institute, Gray remained outspoken against the liquor traffic and even led students in a temperance parade in 1908.[43]

Reuben A. Torrey, just as much a Prohibitionist as Gray, preferred to deal with the problem in another way. In his revival campaigns he frequently held special meetings for "drunkards." After the regular evening service was over Torrey sent out his associates into the saloons and alleys to gather in those men and women who might need to hear a sermon on temperance. At one such midnight service in Birmingham, Alabama, Torrey spoke to 3000 persons—most of whom, reportedly, were obviously under the influence at the time. Over 180 of them made professions of faith in Christ, thus, according to evangelical expectations, taking a giant step toward rehabilitation.[44]

In some cases, premillennialists became prominent spokesmen for civic reform and the elimination of vice. Henry P. Crowell, long the president of Moody Bible Institute's Board of Trustees and president of the Quaker Oats Company, was also the head of the Chicago Committee of Fifteen, which in 1915 secured the passage of a law closing down scores of houses of prostitution in that city. Revivalists Sam P. Jones, J. Wilbur Chapman, "Gypsy" Smith, William E. Biederwolf, and Billy Sunday were all premillennialists who acquired reputations as "reformers": they denounced liquor, prostitution, and other forms of vice, and they frequently portrayed themselves as champions of "social service."[45]

Similarly, as we have already seen, the Christian and Missionary Alliance was actively involved in what Norris Magnuson calls "evangelical social welfare" work. Melvin Trotter, who was converted in Chicago's Pacific Garden Mission in 1897, strongly believed in the imminent second coming and founded sixty-seven rescue missions to meet the physical and spiritual needs of urban derelicts.[46]

That type of reform was ideally suited to the premillennialist world view. It dealt with individual needs, could be related directly to evangelism, and did not require any long-term commitment to social reconstruction.

How, then, should one evaluate the premillennialist attitude toward social reform? Its opponents were at least partially correct when they labeled it pessimistic and fatalistic. Premillennialists *were* pessimistic about the possibility of transforming the social order for the better before the second coming. Yet they constantly insisted that they were the world's greatest optimists. C. I. Scofield spoke for his fellow dispensationalists when he declared that "I am no pessimist; I am the most inveterate optimist because I believe the Bible."[47]

Reuben A. Torrey went further in capturing the premillennialist's blend of open-eyed realism about the world's current condition and his unbending hope in the brighter day ahead:

> The writer . . . is an optimist. He is absolutely sure that a golden age is swiftly coming to this earth. But he is not a blind optimist. His optimism is not the result of shutting his eyes to unpleasant facts: his eyes are wide open to the awful injustices that rule in human society as at present constituted. He is fully aware that there is a storm coming. He does not question that we are facing the wildest, fiercest, most ap-

palling storm this old world ever passed through, but the
storm will be brief and beyond the storm there is a golden
day, such as philosophers and poets never dreamed of. The
writer is an optimist because he has deeply pondered and believes with his whole heart what the Bible teaches concerning the Second Coming of Christ. If he did not believe that,
he could not but be a pessimist, knowing what he does of
social conditions and the trend of human society today. In
the return of our Lord is the perfect solution, and the only
solution, of the political and social and commercial problems
that now vex us.[48]

By this strange twist of irony it becomes evident that Progressives and premillennialists were not so different after all. They
both looked for a millennium. The Progressives believed that the
perfect order would come through hard work, dedicated service,
and the often disappointing striving to undo the evil which has
already been done. The premillennialists believed that the perfect
order would come through the personal intervention of Jesus
Christ. The means were remarkably different, but the end was
the same.

In fact, given the witness of history and the state of society, it
is not surprising that many evangelicals preferred the premillennial vision to that of the Progressives and social gospelers. Their
millennium was in no way dependent on the success of human
effort or the completion of human strategies. No one could prevent its arrival: let the nations rage, let the liberals distort and
undermine the faith, let the dictators rule, let the power of Satan
increase. In the end, they will all be cast feebly aside by the
word of Christ. Premillennialists acknowledged that they did not
even have to work for the millennium, to their immense relief.
The returning Lord would fight the battle and win the victory.
Premillennialism was clearly the "perfect solution" for those who
had become disillusioned with or disappointed by human efforts
to bring about the perfect social order.

That premillennialism was occasionally the haven for the disillusioned can be seen in the experience of Christabel Pankhurst, the fiery leader and strategist of the militant woman suffrage movement in Great Britain before World War I. Like many revolutionary leaders, she looked at the world in simplistic terms. The problems of British and international society could be solved by extending the franchise to women. The solution to all problems hinged on getting women the vote. The struggle was long, bitter, and, thanks to her masterful strategy, often violent. But with victory came terrible disillusionment.

Toward the end of World War I, Pankhurst began to analyze the results of her work:

> Like so many others, I had lived in an atmosphere of illusion, thinking that once certain obstacles were removed, especially the disfranchisement of women, it would be full steam ahead for the ideal social and international order. . . . But when, in 1918, I really faced the facts, I saw that the war was not a war to end war—but was, despite our coming victory, a beginning of sorrows.

Upon further reflection she became convinced that the problem was not so much in institutions, but in the people who ran them. Her depression grew until she made an accidental discovery of biblical prophecy.

> Just then, by what seemed a chance discovery, in a bookshop, I came across writings of Prophecy which pointed out in the Bible there are prophecies foretelling and diagnosing the world's ills and promising that they shall be cured. . . . What did I read? That God foreknew and has foretold in the Bible the evils of this age and their gathering and darkening as the age draws to its close—above all that He has reserved the Imperial Sceptre of the world. Thus, world-power and rule will cease to be the cause of fratricidal human strife, and will be exercised in divine love and wisdom by the Son of God.

> "Ah! that is the solution." My heart stirred to it. My practical political eye saw that this Divine Programme is absolutely the only one that can solve the problems of the world.

She went on to say that this discovery had seemed too good to be true at first and that she had therefore ignored it for a time. "But the hope of the promised return of Jesus as King of Kings and Lord of Lords was there as a refuge from the concerns and cares of the world."[49]

Within a few years, however, Christabel got over her doubts and became a traveling speaker for the premillennialist cause.[50] In her messages she invariably noted how she had found the ultimate and foolproof solution for the world's ills. She had clearly not given up on the ends for which she had worked during her years of political activism, only the means to those ends which she had found so inadequate and impotent. She assured her audiences that the perfect society was coming, but "it has to be remembered, however, that all this will come to pass irrespective of any human wishes, of any human and thus imperfect conception of justice and righteousness." To her immense relief, the coming millennium would arrive no matter what obstacles people placed in its way. Its arrival was guaranteed by the sure word of prophecy, the virtual promise of God. Nothing or no one could stop it.[51]

In premillennialism, therefore, many evangelicals found the perfect solution to the world's social and economic crises. While other evangelicals were forced to revise their visions because of the historical realities around them,[52] premillennialists could maintain theirs, oblivious to their opponents' calls for more effort, more commitment, more hope. Premillennialists had all the hope they needed in the second coming of Christ. Though they rejected the reformer's methods, they had borrowed his dream and placed it beyond the possibility of failure. Though things were bad now and getting worse, premillennialists could afford to be optimistic. Despite everything, they knew the golden age was coming. They had Jesus' word on it: "Fear not, little flock; for it is your Father's good pleasure to give you the kingdom" (Luke 12:32).

5

Wars and Rumors of Wars

And ye shall hear of wars and rumours of wars: see that ye be not troubled: for all these things must come to pass, but the end is not yet.

Matthew 24:6

No event in the fifty years after 1875 did more for the morale of American premillennialists than World War I. There at last was indisputable vindication of their dire predictions about the inevitable decline of the age. Since an event of such enormous and catastrophic proportions was bound to have prophetic significance, premillennialists searched the Scriptures with what they believed was outstanding success. Premillennialist journals ran articles on the war's place in biblical prophecy, often speculating on the significance of the last battle or the latest peace proposal. Countless books, pamphlets, and tracts were published on the same themes. Two large and well-attended prophetic conferences were held in Philadelphia and New York near the war's end. Not since the rise of the new premillennialism after the Civil War had dispensationalists felt so sure of themselves or received such a wide hearing for their views. Though times were tragic, things were never better for American premillennialism.

It would be a serious mistake, however, to assume that premillennialism merely adapted itself to the times. Rather, it looked as though the times had adapted themselves to premillennialism.

Dispensationalists did not change their views to fit the events of World War I; the war seemed to follow an already existing and well-formulated premillennial script for the last days.

As we have already seen, premillennialists believed that God's prophetic clock had stalled in the "times of the Gentiles," which Scofield had defined as "that long period beginning with the Babylonian captivity of Judah, under Nebuchadnezzar, [which shall] be brought to an end by the destruction of Gentile world power . . . [at] the coming of the Lord of glory."[1] That period would be dominated by the rise and fall of four Gentile powers (Babylon, Persia, Greece, and Rome), of which the last was most crucial, since it would be exerting its formidable power when "one like the Son of Man" comes to break once and for all the Gentile powers and establish the messianic kingdom.[2] Consequently, premillennialists studied the Scriptures until they could piece together an elaborate jigsaw puzzle of the conditions and events of the end times.

According to their reckoning, the last Gentile power will be a revived Roman Empire consisting of a ten-nation confederacy which would be headed by a powerful king who had crushed three of his confederates in his rise to power.

> After this I saw in the night visions, and behold a fourth beast, dreadful and terrible, and strong exceedingly; and it had great iron teeth: it devoured and brake in pieces, and stamped the residue with the feet of it: and it was diverse from all the beasts that were before it, and it had ten horns. I considered the horns, and, behold, there came up among them another little horn, before whom there were three of the first horns plucked up by the roots: and behold in this horn were eyes like the eyes of man, and a mouth speaking great things.
>
> . . . The fourth beast shall be the fourth kingdom upon the earth, which shall be diverse from all kingdoms, and shall devour the whole earth, and shall tread it down, and break it in pieces. And the ten horns out of this kingdom are ten kings

that shall arise: and another shall rise after them; and he shall
be diverse from the first and he shall subdue three kings
(Dan. 7:7-8, 23-24).

Premillennialists were certain that this "little horn" of Daniel's
prophecy was the "Beast" of John's Revelation and Paul's "man
of sin"—the Antichrist.[3] As head of the revived Roman Empire,
he would wield tremendous power over the confederacy and be
the central figure in the events of the end.

The deeds of the Antichrist would center in his relationship
with the newly restored nation of Israel, re-gathered in Palestine
for the first time since its captivity by Nebuchadnezzar in late
6th century B.C. Antichrist and Israel would make a mutual defense pact, which would permit the Jews to reconstruct their ancient Temple and to restore the old sacrificial system. Three years
after signing the treaty, Antichrist will break it, enter the Temple, suspend all sacrifices, declare himself to be God, and demand
worship.[4]

In order to carry out those blasphemous demands, Antichrist
would delegate much of his authority to a false prophet who
would compel worship of the Beast through force, clever utiliza-
tion of miraculous powers, and economic coercion. For three and
a half years, he would oversee a reign of terror against all those
who refused to give their allegiance to Antichrist.[5]

Despite the enormous strength of Antichrist, premillennialists
went on, there would be spheres of political power not directly
under his control. Sometime toward the end of his reign his su-
premacy will be threatened by a northern confederacy of nations,
which premillennialists believed would be under Russia's control.[6]
Doubting the Antichrist's willingness or ability to defend Israel,
the northern confederacy would join with a king of the south
(i.e. Egypt) to attack the Jewish state. When the Antichrist
counterattacked he would provoke certain kings of the east, who
evidently would fear the growing power of the new Roman Empire. Raising an army of two hundred million men, the eastern

nations would easily ford the Euphrates and speed to engage the massing forces in Palestine.[7]

With the nations of the world gathered in Israel, history would have reached its climax. Although the situation had begun as a conflict between Antichrist and the northern confederacy, it would then become a united war to destroy the people of God. When the armies began their final assault, Jesus Christ would return and destroy the combatants in Armageddon, a valley northwest of Jerusalem. With Antichrist, the false prophet, and their allies destroyed, Jesus would set up the kingdom.[8]

Premillennialists had agreed on the essentials of that prophetic outline long before war broke out in 1914.[9] Dispensationalists were not personally threatened by these predicted events, however, because they believed that Christ would rapture the church before Antichrist was revealed and the tribulation began. They expected all those events to take place, but they did not expect to be here to see them.

Most dispensationalists did believe, on the other hand, that the church would remain long enough to see events moving in that direction. Exactly how the nations of Europe would come together into Antichrist's empire was not known. At the beginning of the twentieth century, Europe's political boundaries did not come close to what was envisioned for the end. But World War I suddenly provided a way through which the maps of Europe might be redrawn. One month after the war began Arno C. Gaebelein excitedly told the readers of *Our Hope* that "it is possible that out of the ruins, if this universal war proceeds, there will arise the predicted revival of the great confederacy of Europe. . . . If our Lord tarries still for us, we shall have more to say in our October issue."[10]

Thankfully, the Lord tarried, giving Gaebelein and his fellow premillennialists ample time to focus their attention on the war and speculate on its prophetic meaning. How would the war affect the national boundaries of the warring nations? What would happen to the existing alliances? Could this be the beginning of the end?

Before one could answer any of those questions, he had to deal with one more basic: to what extent would the boundaries of the new Roman Empire coincide with those of the old? Some premillennialists argued that since its religious authority would extend far beyond its borders, the new empire would be much larger than the original. Most premillennialists, however, preferred strict biblical literalism and insisted that the new Rome would stay within the original territory.

Even a casual glance at a prewar map of Europe reveals premillennialism's predicament. The national boundaries in 1914 showed little resemblance to what they had expected. Ireland had never been under Roman control, but now it was joined to England which had. Contemporary Germany had been Roman only in its territory west of the Rhine and south of the Danube rivers. While parts of Austria-Hungary had been under Roman jurisdiction, nearly all of its territory north of the Danube, an area equal to about half its holdings in 1914, had not. Before any new Roman Empire could arise, some drastic changes would have to be made.

Consequently, with maps and prophetic Scriptures in hand, premillennialists formulated a number of predictions about the possible state of affairs at the end of the war. Since Germany had not been a member of the original empire and did not seem to figure prominently in the prophetic future, except as part of the northern confederacy which would oppose the new Rome, it would probably lose the war, suffer national humiliation, and give up some of its western territory which had originally belonged to Rome. The Austro-Hungarian Empire will have to be broken up so that some of its Slavic provinces north of the Danube will be free to fall under the influence of Russia and its northern confederation. Russia, though now closely allied with powers formerly within the Roman Empire, would end that association with

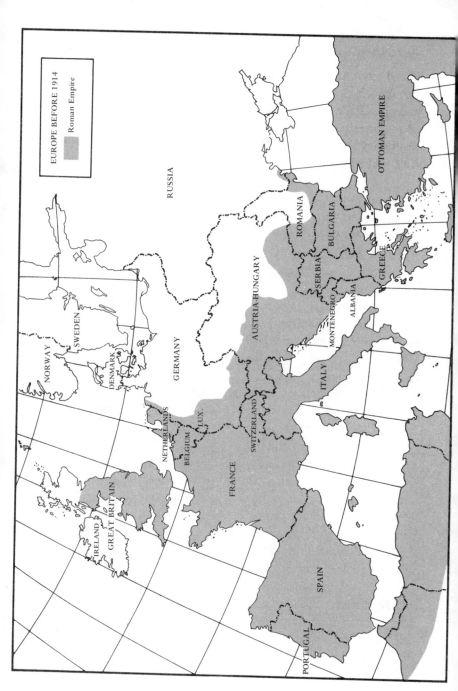

EUROPE BEFORE 1914

Roman Empire

NORWAY

SWEDEN

RUSSIA

DENMARK

GERMANY

NETHERLANDS

BELGIUM
LUX.

IRELAND

GREAT BRITAIN

FRANCE

SWITZERLAND

AUSTRIA-HUNGARY

ROMANIA

SERBIA

BULGARIA

MONTENEGRO

ALBANIA

ITALY

GREECE

OTTOMAN EMPIRE

SPAIN

PORTUGAL

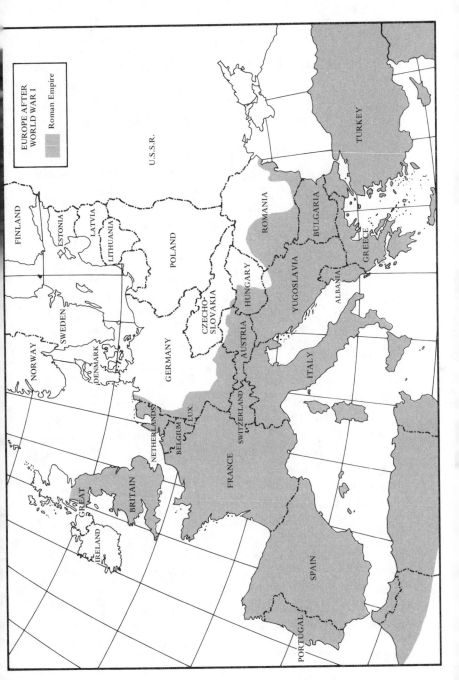

EUROPE AFTER
WORLD WAR I

Roman Empire

NORWAY
SWEDEN
FINLAND
ESTONIA
LATVIA
LITHUANIA
DENMARK
GREAT
BRITAIN
IRELAND
NETHERLANDS
BELGIUM
LUX.
GERMANY
POLAND
U.S.S.R.
CZECHO-
SLOVAKIA
FRANCE
SWITZERLAND
AUSTRIA
HUNGARY
ROMANIA
YUGOSLAVIA
ITALY
BULGARIA
ALBANIA
GREECE
TURKEY
SPAIN
PORTUGAL

III

the West and eventually develop as an independent power with influence over other nations in northern and eastern Europe. The Ottoman Empire, whether as a result of the war or some later series of events, would relinquish control over Palestine or at least allow the re-gathering of the Jews there. Ireland would gain its independence from Great Britain.[11]

As one can easily see, the premillennialists came extremely close to the mark. Germany lost the war, was forced to accept full blame for the conflict, was loaded down with reparations, and lost some of its western territory, Alsace-Lorraine, to France. Austria-Hungary was partitioned into Yugoslavia, Austria, Hungary, and Czechoslovakia, and gave up additional territory to Rumania, Italy, and Poland. Russia suffered two revolutions in 1917, made a separate peace with Germany, and terminated its alliance with the western powers. The Ottoman Empire simply dissolved after the war, with Palestine passing to British control. Ireland won its independence from England three years after the war. By any standard of measurement, the premilliennialists' record was extraordinary.

Clearly, as some of their detractors might have pointed out, one did not have to be a premillennialist to arrive at similar predictions about the war. Anyone familiar with the recent past knew that France and Germany had quarreled for decades over Alsace-Lorraine. Likewise, long-standing antagonism between the different nationalities in the Austro-Hungarian Empire made some kind of reorganization inevitable.

But the premillennialists' claims had not been based on any careful study of political, social, or military history. As they so frequently pointed out, they had come to their amazingly accurate views through the use of the Bible alone. The unfolding events in Europe fit well into the scheme which they had reconstructed by biblical prophecies long before the war began. The significance of their predictions was their source, not just their accuracy. Premillennialists knew both what was going to happen and why.

To say the least, such a record was bound to be noticed by other evangelicals. Here was a biblical approach which had been empirically demonstrated by events reported in the morning newspapers. In light of such success, some premillennialists could not resist the temptation to venture into more speculative territory. It is one thing to predict what might happen next, but quite another to become dogmatic or too precise in one's predictions. Too detailed prophecies could backfire, and many of them did.

Some rather overenthusiastic premillennialists clearly went too far. Seeing no end to the war through normal means, F. C. Jennings predicted that the rapture alone will bring the war to a close. Shocked and bewildered by the sudden disappearance of millions of Christians, the warring nations would no longer be able to carry on. Into the confusion would step a great leader who would restore order and establish a new political unity in war-torn Europe—the Antichrist. Even though Jennings hedged his bets a bit by saying that God might choose to end the war in some other way, such speculation inevitably worked against the movement's growing respectability.[12]

Other premillennialists fell back into the old besetting sin of date-setting. Dispensationalism supposedly had eliminated that temptation, but some dispensationalists forgot their basic principles. William Blackstone unexpectedly resorted to the useless year-day theory and predicted the end of the time of the Gentiles sometime between 1916 and 1934. He denied that he was date-setting, because his calculations applied to Israel and not the church and thus did not strictly predict the return of Christ. But other premillennialists rightly saw that to set a date for the one was to establish an indirect date for the other. Seven months after Blackstone's analysis appeared, W. J. Erdman wrote a disclaimer and warned against adopting old methods which had proved so fruitless in the past.[13]

Still other dispensationalists violated the spirit of their system by promising that the end would "occur in our generation. That is to say, that the man of average age now living, and all younger, barring the usual accidents of sickness and death, [would] witness this tremendous climax and transition."[14] In light of all that happened, that statement did not seem altogether out of line in 1919; but it still committed premillennialists to a vaguely defined time limit which in the end worked against them.

Wisely, most premillennialists showed remarkable reserve and stuck to the main outlines of their program. In fact, all during the war years leaders in the movement warned against reading too much into the events of the day. When the British captured Jerusalem in December 1917, James M. Gray, one of the more levelheaded premillennialist leaders, reminded his fellow believers that the capture of the city did not necessarily mean that the nation of Israel would be restored immediately. The permanent state might be years in the future. At any rate, premillennialists should

> beware of fanaticism, beware of letting down the bars of restraint in any direction whatever. . . . The kind of watching the Lord desires is quite consistent with the care of our households, the proper conduct of our business and especially just now the support of the government.[15]

As most premillennialists soon realized, the closer they stayed to the outlines of their prophetic script, the safer they were. Was the war the biblical Armageddon? James M. Gray denied it, since the battle would occur in Palestine, not along the trenches of the western front, and it would be between the Gentile powers and the returning Son of Man, not the central powers and the western allies. Naturally, things could change rapidly, but until the church was raptured and the Antichrist formed his empire, it was foolish to identify the war with Armageddon.[16]

Was Kaiser Wilhelm II the Antichrist? As much as American dispensationalists disliked the man, they had to admit that he failed to fulfill the prophesied qualifications. He was not from the old Roman territory, he did not rule over a ten-nation confederacy, and he had not declared himself to be God.

If the war was not Armageddon and the Kaiser was not the Antichrist, then what was the war's significance? In 1916 Gaebelein observed that "the only thing a Christian can safely say about these unprecedented conditions among the nations is that these events fully confirm the characteristics of the age and its predicted end as revealed in the Bible and that all that is happening in a way prepares for the very end of the times of the Gentiles and the coming of the King."[17] As bad as things were, the war was just the first of many even more horrible conflicts. As Jesus had said, "And ye shall hear of wars and rumours of wars: see that ye be not troubled: for all these things must come to pass, but the end is not yet" (Matt. 24:6).

Despite their considerable success and the constant temptation to say more, most premillennialists did not predict more than Gaebelein had in 1916. The war confirmed their interpretation of the Bible, indicated a definite realignment of nations in anticipation of the rise of the Beast, and marked a beginning of more wars in the future. The war earned the premillennialists the best reception they had received since the rise of dispensational premillennialism.

As hard as it was to deny or disparage their enviable achievements, some people tried. But as the fortunes of premillennialism rose, the credibility of its critics declined. Those who had promised good times ahead suddenly had to account for the slaughter of millions of people, the apparent blood-lust of the nations, and what looked like the imminent collapse of European civilization.

Despite everything that had happened, a few never-say-die optimists refused to make any concessions to the premillennialists. Postmillennialists, for example, did not let even a world war dampen their convictions about the coming millennium. James Snowden compared the war to the Protestant Reformation. Just as the Reformers had acted to break the power of ecclesiastical tyranny, the Christian soldiers of the allied powers were wielding the sword of Christ, ridding the world of its last imperial tyrant, Kaiser Wilhelm II. The war was not a serious setback to the millennium; it was an essential, God-sent means to that very end. The war was God's way of bringing the millennium one step closer.[18]

Not everyone shared Snowden's "every mustard cloud has a silver lining" approach, but still they did not want to admit that the premillennialists were right. In the middle of 1915 the editors of the liberal *Biblical World* asked their readers not to "paint the present situation . . . in too dark colors." While millions of people were fighting across the trenches, millions more were carrying on life as usual. Taking solace in the growing peace movement, the editors claimed that while "we have not made the world into the Kingdom of God, we have made it much less the Kingdom of Satan." There may be tares in the field, but there was still more good seed than bad. "Let us count our liabilities if we must, but as sensible folk, let us count our assets as well."[19]

As the war entered its fourth year, even such balanced optimism was hard to maintain. By war's end, the United States had lost 48,000 killed in action, 2900 missing, and a staggering 56,000 dead from disease. Equally serious was the massive disillusionment which followed the peace talks. The United States had fought to make the world safe for democracy; but evidently the nations of Europe had fought to acquire as much land and lucre as possible. President Wilson returned from the peace conference, his Fourteen Points compromised and rejected by his former allies. As one American historian has observed, World War I and its aftermath was the end of American innocence.

Shailer Mathews, a leading modernist at the University of Chicago, reflected the great disillusionment after the war:

the outbreak of war in 1914 shattered all optimism. Human nature was still untamed. A state could command the loyalty of its subjects in the face of interests that extended beyond the frontiers. It is easy now to be contemptuous of the optimism of pre-war liberalism, but when one recalls the elements of the world situation, it is not strange that we should have suffered illusion. . . . All seemed to insure the maintenance of peace. The outbreak of war did more than excite horror for itself. It argued a breakdown of forces which we believed were shaping up a new world order.[20]

Liberals may have been shattered by the war, but they were not about to take the rise in premillennialism's popularity without a fight. Before the war the liberals had not seemed overly concerned about the existence of a few dispensationalists, but by the war's end they were obviously worried and threatened. As a result, they launched an unprecedented counterattack.

The liberals' counteroffensive began in earnest in 1917. In his *When Christ Comes Again*, George P. Eckman attacked premillennialists as eccentrics who maintained their views out of some kind of "strange perversity." He denounced their "proof-texting" and rejected what he thought was their gross mishandling of biblical prophecies in their original contexts. Even though dispensationalists claimed they were upholding the Bible against the higher critics, Eckman warned that "the influence of the Bible can be injured by those of its alleged friends who either purposely or unwittingly pervert its teachings."[21]

In the same year Shailer Mathews published *Will Christ Come Again?* Distributed by the thousands by the University of Chicago's American Institute of Sacred Literature, the booklet argued, in an early form of "de-mythologizing," that

historically-minded students of the Bible distinguish between fundamental Christian truths and the method and language used by the early Christians in expressing those truths. They believe that in order to realize these truths, the conceptions of those ancient men of God have to be translated into modern conceptions, exactly as the Hebrew and Greek language has to be translated into English.

In that way Mathews passed off the apocalyptic sections of the New Testament as "the mistakes of early Christians" and no longer binding on modern believers. When premillennialists argued that everything in the Bible was inspired and therefore required belief for all time, Mathews said that "this logically ought to include belief in a flat earth, the perpetuation of slavery, the submission to rulers like Nero." No, Mathews counseled, modern Christians should rise above such "Judaistic hopes."[22]

In 1918 the controversy heated up considerably. Shirley Jackson Case, also of the University of Chicago, issued a book, *The Millennial Hope*, in which he traced the history of millennialism and concluded that apocalyptic movements tend to gain strength during crises. Thus, to use the book's subtitle, the current wave of premillennialism in America was "a phase of war-time thinking." A year later Case took a more exegetical approach, in *The Revelation of John*, in order to show that the Apocalypse was an outgrowth of specific socio-political problems at the end of the first century and could not be taken in the manner of the premillennialists.[23]

In 1919 two more important anti-premillennialist polemics were published. James Snowden refuted the premillennial world view in his *Is the World Growing Better?* and attacked dispensational methods of biblical interpretation in *The Coming of the Lord: Will It Be Premillennial?* The premillennialist view of the millennium, with its restored Temple and blood sacrifices, was militaristic, Judaistic, pessimistic, and totally detrimental to the social dimensions of the Christian gospel.[24]

In 1920 George Preston Mains left no question about his views in his *Premillennialism: Non-Scriptural, Non-Historic, Non-Scientific, Non-Philosophical*. He called premillennialists devout but misguided Christians who appealed to the unlettered and gullible who appreciated a wooden literalism. He called dispensationalism pessimistic, detrimental to the mission enterprises, essentially Jewish in its view of the millennium, and mysteriously well-endowed for its massive propaganda campaign. Evidently himself fully recovered from the shock of World War I, Mains condemned premillennialism's false "psychology of history" which saw only decay and decline ahead for the human race.[25]

In the same year Harris Franklin Rall, professor of systematic theology at Garrett Biblical Institute in Chicago, published a study entitled *Modern Premillennialism and the Christian Hope*. Rall accused the premillennialists of every fault which has arisen during the history of biblical study—literalism, spiritualizing the text when it suits one's purposes, unrestrained fancy in the use of typology and allegory, and an arbitrariness which pays little attention to the original historical setting of biblical passages. Premillennialists, he concluded, had a higher loyalty to their system than to the Word of God.[26]

The liberal attack demonstrated the growing credibility of the premillennialist movement. That liberals took the time to refute them shows that they were starting to make considerable inroads in the evangelical churches. Mathews, Case, and Rall did not waste their time on unimportant fringe movements. It was obvious that as soon as the liberals began attacking it openly, premillennialism had arrived.

One wonders if the liberal attacks did anything to stem the premillennialist tide. Premillennialists themselves for the most part ignored it. Liberals might protest all they wanted about the nature of intertestamental Jewish apocalyptic literature or the necessity of reinterpreting ancient cosmologies in modern terms, but they could not wish away the accuracy of premillennialism's predictions about the war. Yet the critics of premillennialism did manage to find one chink in the dispensationalist armor: if they were true to their principles, premillennialists could not be wholehearted supporters of the American war effort. During the super-patriotic and militaristic war years, some people accused premillennialists of being unpatriotic and anti-American.

In the midde of 1918 Shailer Mathews edited a series of anti-premillennialist articles in the prestigious *Biblical World*. To varying degrees, all of the articles attacked the movement as out-moded, anachronistic, and naïve,[27] but one article in particular made the charge of national disloyalty. Shirley Jackson Case called premillennialism "a serious menace to our democracy" and hinted that its advocates preferred a German victory because it "would bring us nearer to the end of the present world." Sooner or later the enemy would recognize "that to aid and abet the pre-millennial movement is one of the safest and most subtle forms of activity in which he can engage."

A few months before the article appeared, Case had suggested to the *Chicago Daily News* that $2000 a week were being spent to spread premillennialism around the country. "Where the money comes from is unknown, but there is strong suspicion that it emanates from German sources. In my belief, the fund would be a profitable field for governmental investigation . . . for if the belief spreads many would not be able to see the need of fighting for democracy."[28]

Case repeated that foolish charge in his *Biblical World* article and concluded by saying that "of course the premillennialist does not oppose the war; what he opposes—always in principle and sometimes by overt act—is any hopeful effort to win this war and thereby so reconstruct international relationships that warfare may henceforth be eliminated as a factor in human experience." When a person becomes a premillennialist, he warned, "he be-comes a pronounced enemy of democracy and a serious menace to the nation's morale in this hour of its need."[29]

Although in normal times such charges would have been too ridiculous to even acknowledge, in the emotion-charged atmos-phere of World War I America premillennialists had to take steps to refute them. Fellow Chicagoan James Gray responded to

Case's charges by citing the patriotic efforts of his Moody Bible Institute. On the day war had been declared, he said, the American flag had been run up on the institute's flagpole, there to remain until the victory was won. The school gladly opened its doors for the sale of Liberty Bonds, and Moody students regularly canvassed to raise money for the Red Cross. Many students joined the army and a number of them had been killed. The Institute stood firmly for dispensational truth, but it also felt its "duty to be the support of the government to the last dollar and the last man."[30]

Two months after Gray's defense, Reuben A. Torrey added one of his own. Case's witch-trial tactics had gotten one "faithful brother . . . arrested and put in jail because of preaching the return of our Lord. The accusation brought against him was that of treason, or disloyalty to the President." Torrey denied all charges that premillennialism was unpatriotic, then added that "while the charge that the money for premillennial propaganda 'emanates from German sources' is ridiculous, the charge that the destructive criticism that rules in Chicago University 'emanates from German sources' is undeniable." However, Torrey did not believe that the liberals at Chicago should be called traitors because of it.[31]

Gray and Torrey's defense notwithstanding, the liberals were correct in saying that premillennialists could not give unflinching support to America's ideological war aims. President Wilson had called on Americans to fight to make the world safe for democracy; but, according to dispensationalism's reading of biblical prophecy, the growth and spread of democratic governments were a sign of the end of the age. When viewed eschatologically, democracy was sinful man's ultimate attempt to have things his own way. Furthermore, the rise of modern democracies was God's way of showing that mankind was incapable of governing itself. People who put faith in democratic institutions would soon discover that the problem with governments is not necessarily their form, but the sinful people who run them. Change the system, ensure equal access to political power, put government in the hands of the people, and the problems that arise in all human governments are actually compounded. Handing the reins of government to larger numbers of sinful people could only make things worse, not better. According to biblical prophecy, the premillennialists observed, the increase of democracy toward the end of the age would result in the breakdown of all authority and social order and lead to such anarchy that the world would gladly turn to an authoritarian leader who could guarantee law and order.[32]

If pressed, premillennialists had to admit that the very foundations of America's democratic government were corrupt. From the biblical standpoint, the only kind of government worth having was absolute monarchy—under the King of Kings. In 1915 the editors of the *Christian Workers Magazine* declared that the idea that "governments receive their just powers from the consent of the governed" was false. "Democracy (self-government) is the antithesis of autocracy—God's ideal of government. . . . Self-government whether in an individual or in a nation is abhorrent to God's order for the creature." When "Scripturally viewed, the basis on which our government rests is false, that the ideal government is an absolute monarchy where Christ is the monarch," and that it was inconsistent for a Christian "to make himself part of a system whose principle is the apotheosis of man."[33]

Such a statement did not mean that dispensationalists were calling for the overthrow of the American government. They were speaking in eschatological terms, as though the age to come was so close that they could not help comparing it with the obvious limitations of their own age. Even though premillennialists longed for the ideal government under King Jesus, they realized that in the meantime they had to do the best they could. Therefore, in the same article, the editors advised that "when a Christian finds himself one of a democracy, his duty to God . . . requires that he fulfill his obligations as a citizen whether it be in depositing a ballot or shouldering a gun. He may do both these things, and yet in spirit not be a part of that system to which they belong."

When living in light of their own principles, then, premillennialists were always potentially dangerous to the age and to its values. Reuben A. Torrey frequently demonstrated the difficulty of living in two ages at the same time. In 1914 he urged his fellow premillennialists to be cautious in the midst of a growing jingoism:

> To love a country simply because it is one's own country and to stand by it no matter of what injustice it is guilty towards other and weaker nations is radically and thoroughly un-Christian. The sentiment, "My country, may she always be right, but my country whether right or wrong," has been quoted and requoted until some almost seem to think it a portion of the Word of God. It is a thoroughly vicious statement. It justifies the most unjustifiable wars and the most devilish conduct in war. We should love our country . . . but we should not love our country at the expense of other countries. We should not justify our country when she is in the wrong. We should not join hands with the multitude of our countrymen to do evil to other nations. We should seek the peace and prosperity and welfare of other lands as well as our own. We should not seek to always put the best construction on our own acts and the worst construction on the acts of other nations. The law of love should be the law of nations as well as the law of the individual. The fair-sounding word "Patriotism" is often used as a cloak for the basest and meanest conduct. In Christ Jesus there is neither Jew nor Greek, Barbarian, Scythian, German, Englishman, Russian, or American, we are all one in Him (Gal. 3:28, Col. 3:11).[34]

In the years following his statement on the dangers of national chauvinism, Torrey argued against making military training mandatory in the public schools, counseled against the "war madness" that leads to a massive buildup of the armed forces, and, when war seemed inevitable in early 1917, sadly conceded that "no real Christian can relish the suffering that will come to real Christians on both sides."[35]

When Wilson announced that Americans were fighting to make the world safe for democracy, Torrey said that "this may sound well for a Fourth of July celebration and as an appeal to thoughtless people," but "there are many Americans who would refuse to fight for Wilson's ideals."[36] In the same way, an editorial in the *Christian Workers Magazine*, in July 1917, stated that "we are with [President Wilson] in considering this to be the present duty of the nation. But we are reminded by the inspired prophets that the ascendancy of democracy, though certain, is not lasting." Eventually even the democracies will turn themselves gladly over to Antichrist and make war on the returning Christ.[37]

These views show that when premillennialists were true to their eschatology, they could give only tentative allegiance to their government and the American war effort. In fact, had they been entirely honest, premillennialists would have admitted that, in the long run, America will be part of the Gentile powers destroyed at the second coming. Despite their personal love of country, consistent premillennialists acknowledged that, apart from Israel, God was committed to no nation. Like it or not, the United States was a part of the worldly system that was passing away. Since they could not find America explicitly mentioned in biblical prophecy, they did not have to publicize it; but every honest dispensationalist knew that it was true.[38]

Despite those basic premillennialist principles, many if not most dispensationalists caught the war fever by the end of 1917. For example, there was an abrupt change in the editorial policy of the *Christian Workers Magazine*. At one time the editors thought nothing of presenting various views on the wisdom of American involvement. A pro-war piece or an exposition of the just-war theory might be published back-to-back with an article by a Mennonite pacifist.[39] But as the attacks on premillennialists' patriotism increased, there was a tightening up in the magazine's pro-war stance. By early 1918 an editorial urged Christians to continue their support of the government in the conflict by not "giving any unlawful encouragement to pacifists and slackers who are operating in some cases as an enemy in the rear." After Case's pointed charges, the *Christian Workers Magazine* did everything possible to show that premillennialists were just as militaristic as everyone else.[40]

Similarly, no one attending the two large prophetic conferences in the spring and fall of 1918 could have missed the surging patriotism. Speakers at the Philadelphia meeting in May spoke about "cheerfully submitting to the powers that be" and their "absolute patriotism, absolute loyalty" to the American government.[41] The leaders in the November conference in New York wanted it clearly understood that they would not permit "any sentiment not in fullest loyalty to our country and her allies." One of the aims of the meetings, they went on, was to call "attention to the great doctrines of the Gospel as a bulwark and a protest against the subtle skepticism of the German-made theology."[42]

Once America had defended its national honor and won the war, premillennialists could once again afford to apply their doctrines consistently. As the peace talks continued, dispensationalists chose up sides in accordance with their eschatological views. How should devout premillennialists respond to the proposal for a League of Nations? Applying already established expectations, they reacted according to form: the League of Nations, noble in its intent, would utterly fail to bring peace to the world. The course of the age had already been established by God himself. The world war had only been the beginning of troubles. In the November 1918 prophetic conference Torrey stated that while many people were placing their hopes in the League, "such hopes are delusive, they will end in disappointment and dismay." The

League might bring about a deceptive, temporary respite from war, but "then the most awful universal war that this old world has ever seen will follow."[43]

Whereas premillennialists all agreed that the League would eventually fail to bring lasting peace, they were divided about its ultimate prophetic significance. Arno C. Gaebelein did not believe that the League figured prominently in biblical prophecy at all. For one thing, it contained too many nations to be the vehicle of Antichrist. To meet prophetic specifications, Gaebelein argued, the League will have to expel all the nations not originally a part of Roman territory. I. M. Haldeman, on the other hand, believed that the League was unconsciously fulfilling prophecy by helping to restore the old Roman boundaries and by "preparing the way for the final and desperate revival of Rome under the form of ten confederate nations, with its last kaiser, that dark and woeful figure, the man of sin, the son of perdition, the Antichrist."[44]

Regardless of where they stood on the particulars of the issue, the majority of premillennialists agreed that the League was one more step toward the realization of the new Rome and the rise of Antichrist. Therefore they sided with Senator Henry Cabot Lodge against Wilson's attempt to commit America to the League, hoping against hope that non-participation might make things easier on America when Christ returned to judge the Gentile powers. Furthermore, in light of the continuation of "wars and rumours of wars," the United States would be ill-advised to consider any form of disarmament.[45]

The future, according to premillennialists, was not bright. The World War was only the beginning of grief. All attempts to make a lasting peace would fail. No matter what men of good would do, Europe would inevitably realign itself along the old Roman borders, move into a ten-nation confederacy, and fall under the spell of the last dictator. All of those things would take place "not because we wish it to be so, nor because of any prophetic insight given to us, but because we believe the statements of a very old and very much neglected book called the Bible."[46]

As usual, despite the dismal outlook, the premillennialists looked on the bright side. While they saw no hope within the historical process, they were still optimistic about the ultimate outcome. "Then is there not hope? Yes, there is hope, a hope both sure and steadfast, a hope that is absolutely certain, a hope that is built upon the inerrant and infallible Word of Him that cannot lie."[47] Jesus was coming and when he did, he would "speedily produce the end of the last war."[48]

World War I, therefore, was highly significant for the development of the new premillennialism. The apparent apocalyptic character of the conflict provided premillennialists with an unprecedented opportunity to share their views on a much wider scale than ever before. The unfolding of wartime events demonstrated, they believed, that their views could stand the test of time and history.[49]

The war years also demonstrate how the premillennialists used their eschatological perspective to make sense out of the events of their time. Their prophetic program gave them a general superstructure on which to place the events which seemed chaotic and meaningless to other people. By having a pre-existing script, premillennialists were able to explain the events of their time and, as dispensationalists understood so well, once a historical event was placed somewhere within God's eternal plan, it lost its ability to terrorize. That is why premillennialists could be so calm and so hopeful in the face of a dismal and catastrophic future.

6

Hath God Cast Away His People?

Hath God cast away His people? God forbid. . . . God hath not cast away His people which He foreknew. . . . For the gifts and calling of God are without repentance.

Romans 11:1, 2, 29

For I would not, brethren, that ye should be ignorant of this mystery . . . that blindness in part is happened to Israel, until the fulness of the Gentiles be come on. And so all Israel will be saved.

Romans 11:25–26

Since the modern state of Israel was founded (1948) American premillennialists have been firm and unwavering supporters. Their enthusiasm does not arise out of guilt for past persecutions nor even from sympathy for Jews who suffered through the Holocaust. Premillennialists as a whole support Israel because they believe that the Jewish state will play a major role in the prophetic events at the end of the age. Although that conviction lies buried in the premillennialist understanding of the Bible, it was strengthened and affirmed by the events that took place during the decades surrounding World War I. Those years made premillennialists more confident than ever that the present dispensation was nearing its end.[1]

As the Great War entered its final year, the attention of all premillennialists shifted to Palestine. When the British changed the thrust of their eastern operations from Mesopotamia to Palestine, premillennialists were confident that the fall of the Ottoman Empire was imminent and that prophecy was about to be fulfilled.

At the end of 1917, fast-moving events heightened their expectations. On November 2, Lord Arthur Balfour, the British foreign secretary, wrote to Lord James Rothschild, a leader in the international Zionist movement:

> His Majesty's Government view with favour the estabishment in Palestine of a national home for the Jewish people, and will use their best efforts to facilitate the achievement of this object, it being clearly understood that nothing shall be done which may prejudice the civil and religious rights of existing non-Jewish communities in Palestine or the rights and political status enjoyed by Jews in any other country.[2]

Barely five weeks after the Balfour Declaration, the Turks surrendered Jerusalem to British forces under General Allenby. Those events, although eagerly expected by premillennialists everywhere, sent shock waves through their growing ranks. Here was the most substantial proof yet that the "times of the Gentiles" were drawing to an end. For the first time in over two millennia the way was open for the re-establishment of a Jewish state in the Holy Land.[3]

British premillennialists hurriedly organized a number of prophetic conferences to deal with the biblical implications of those events, and their American counterparts were not far behind. In the spring of 1918 a group of Philadelphia businessmen, largely motivated by the events in the Middle East, called together a prophetic conference which was widely publicized and well attended. One of the high points of the three-day conference was the address of the Reverend A. E. Thompson, who had been, until his expulsion by the Turks, the pastor of the American Church in Jerusalem. In part, he said that

> the capture of Jerusalem is one of those events to which the students of prophecy have been looking forward for many

years. Even before Great Britain took possession of Egypt, there were keen sighted seers who foresaw the day when God would use the Anglo-Saxon peoples to restore Jerusalem. When the war broke out, there were some of us who were convinced that it would never end until Turkish tyranny was forever a thing of the past in the Holy City. When the city was captured, we felt very confident we could put one hand upon this great event which had stirred the heart of the whole Christian world, and laying open our Bible at many places in the Prophets say as confidently as Peter on the day of Pentecost, "This is that which was spoken by the prophets."[4]

As Thompson and the other conference speakers indicated, the capture of Jerusalem and the issuance of the Balfour Declaration were in full accord with long-standing premillennial expectations. With few exceptions, all nineteenth-century premillennialists looked for the eventual restoration of the Jews in Palestine and tied their return to the second coming of Christ.[5]

As we have already seen, premillennialists of the dispensationalist variety believed that God had two distinct peoples, Israel and the church. Because of their disobedience to God and their rejection of Jesus Christ as Messiah, God had suspended his dealings with the Jews and had turned his attention to the Gentiles and the building of the church.

That situation would not endure forever. At the end of the age, God would again make Israel the center of his concern. Daniel's seventieth week would begin, leading up to the coming of Messiah and the setting up of the long-promised kingdom. But those who would reign with Messiah Jesus in the coming kingdom must first be purged by suffering for past sins. After the partial re-gathering of the Jews in Palestine and the re-establishment of the state of Israel would come the ill-fated pact with the Antichrist, betrayal at his hands, immense suffering for those Jews who accepted Jesus as Messiah before his coming, and the final invasion by hordes of Gentile armies.

Though intense, the suffering would be brief. When the Gentile powers had the Jews close to total annihilation, Jesus Christ would return to earth, slaughter Antichrist's armies, and finally establish the kingdom that he had originally offered to the Jews at his first advent. After witnessing his majestic display of power, the Jews would acknowledge Messiah Jesus and once again bask in the blessings of God.

As one can plainly see, the entire redemptive plan of God hinged on the restoration of the Jews. Without a restored Jewish state in Palestine, God's cosmic program would not succeed. Consequently, from the beginning dispensationalists insisted that someday, somehow, the Jews would return to the Holy Land and set up their own nation.[6]

Much to their gratification, at about the same time they began preaching the eventual restoration of the Jews there was a revival of nationalism among the dispersed Jews of Europe. The Zionist movement, which arose in the last decade of the nineteenth century, had had many forerunners. By the 1850s such men as Judah Alcalay, Avi Hirsch Kalisher, and Moses Hess had agitated for Jewish colonization of Palestine, but with little success. Many Jews had believed that they could assimilate themselves into the dominant culture without too much trouble. As fully accepted and contributing members of European society, they had seen no need for a separate Jewish state.

Many of their hopes were shattered in the 1880s. In 1881 a wave of anti-Semitic violence swept Russia. In its wake blatantly discriminatory laws were passed, and they were followed by officially sanctioned pogroms, making it clear to everyone that Russia wanted to rid itself of its Jews.

The response to such a frightening outburst was varied. Some Jews became political radicals, while others worked harder at assimilation, hoping against hope that by making themselves indispensable, they might avoid the same fate as their brethren in Russia. Other Jews, however, fanned the flames of nationalism. Thanks to such books as Dr. Leo Pinsker's *Auto-Emancipation* (1882), growing numbers of Jews realized that under existing conditions they could not consider themselves a distinct people because they lacked all the characteristics of modern nationhood—a common language, common customs, and common territory. Unless Jews could obtain those things, even the most well-intentioned concessions by their host countries could not change their essential status. True equality could exist only when Jews had established their own nation.

Jews had talked that way before, but now things began to happen. Within two years after the publication of Pinsker's book a Jewish congress was held in Kattowitz, Prussia, to define goals, raise money, and begin taking steps for the practical realization of a Jewish homeland. Though Pinsker had never specifically mentioned Palestine as the site of the proposed state, the delegates to the congress insisted that no other location could be considered. To demonstrate their commitment to the Holy Land, they adopted the name "Lovers of Zion" (*Hoveve Zion*). Within a decade, the "Love of Zion" (*Hibbat Zion*) movement had spread throughout Europe and as far as the United States.

Though they were never able to forge a unified philosophy, they did bring about the first modern Jewish migration to Palestine. Between 1882 and 1903, about twenty-five thousand Jews settled there, forming mainly agricultural communities. Those settlements were not overwhelming successes because of the difficulty of manual labor: most of the freshly transplanted Jews were clerks and intellectuals, and they received a rather cool reception from the Jews of Jerusalem, who distained their unorthodox religious practices. Despite such obstacles the Lovers of Zion prevailed, and they served as the forerunners of the restoration which they hoped would surely follow.

In the 1890s another incident prodded reluctant Jews to doubt any remaining hopes of assimilation. In 1895 Captain Alfred Dreyfus, a Jewish officer on the French General Staff, was accused and convicted of spying for Germany. When the General Staff refused to act on evidence which proved Dreyfus's innocence, a storm of protest erupted across France. In retaliation, anti-Semitic riots broke out and the army moved to purge its ranks of pro-Dreyfus sympathizers. Although Dreyfus eventually was pardoned by the French President in 1899, the damage had already been done. Increasing numbers of Jews gave up on assimilation.

Among those Jews thoroughly shaken by the Dreyfus Affair was Theodore Herzl, a Hungarian-born journalist. After viewing at first hand the humiliation of Captain Dreyfus and doing extensive research into the "Jewish Question," Herzl published his *Der Judenstaat* (*The Jewish State*) in 1896. His thesis was that although Jews culturally and psychologically were a distinct people, they do not have any of the attributes of nationhood. Statelessness, according to Herzl, was the root cause of Jewish problems and anti-Semitism. The only way for Jews to assert themselves was to establish a political state which would guarantee Jewish survival and ensure a continuing Jewish contribution to the rest of the world.

There was nothing in Herzl's original plan that suggested where the Jewish state should be established. In the beginning, Herzl would have been just as happy with Argentina as with Palestine. But Herzl was soon persuaded: nowhere but Palestine. Whereas most of his predecessors had called for the slow colonization of Palestine by Jewish pioneers, Herzl himself sought the support of the great powers of Europe, which, he hoped, would endorse a mass migration of Jews from their lands and officially recognize the new Jewish state.

When Herzl failed to interest very many wealthy and apparently assimilated Jews in western Europe, he concentrated his efforts on the Jews in eastern Europe, where the love of Zion ran deep. In 1897 the first Zionist Congress was held in Basel, Switzerland, where the best approach to secure the goal of a political state was discussed. Although the Congress agreed to work for common goals, most of the actual work seemed to fall to Herzl. Traveling from capital to capital, he tried desperately to win support for the Zionist cause. When sensitive negotiations with Turkey broke down in 1902, Herzl almost despaired. But then British Colonial Secretary Joseph Chamberlain offered the Zionists Uganda, in British East Africa, as a possible site for settlement. When Herzl offered the plan to the Zionist Congress in 1903, the controversy almost tore the gathering apart. Though Herzl almost immediately reaffirmed his commitment to Palestine, the controversy lasted beyond his death—he died in 1904, at the age of forty-four.

In the decade following Herzl's death, the Zionist movement was torn by dissension. "Politicals" doubted whether the time was right for the establishment of the state; "practicals" urged that Jewish colonies be planted immediately as beachheads for the new Israel. Outside the movement, socialists questioned its purposes; the ultra-orthodox frowned on any attempt that might usurp divine prerogatives; and the Reformed Jews rejected any idea of forsaking their hard-earned status in European society for a sentimental dream about the land flowing with milk and honey. On the eve of World War I, membership in the Zionist organization numbered only 130,000, a small percentage of world Jewry. The Lovers of Zion had established only fifty-nine colonies in Palestine. Zionism may not have been a huge movement by 1914, but it had laid the foundation for the eventual establishment of the Jewish state in 1948.

While Zionism was hard at work in Europe during these years, its reception among American Jews was initially poor. Jews in the United States seemed to have little in common with the plight of European Jews. European-style anti-Semitism was virtually unknown in America, and although there was an occasional outbreak of vicious American nativism, American Jews had no fear of a sudden pogrom or a knock on the door at midnight. Consequently, any movement based on protection against the ravages of anti-Semitism seemed pretty much beside the point in the American context.

The first noticeable wave of Jewish immigration to the United States had occurred in the 1840s. Those German-speaking Jews had been quickly assimilated into American life to a great extent. And even the next wave of Jewish immigrants from eastern Europe, which began in the 1880s, found adjustment, though difficult, quite successful. Although most Jews still might retain some emotional ties to the ancestral lands in Palestine, few saw any need to leave the freedom and relative tolerance of the United States for a strange and barren land where prospects were not nearly as good. For most Jews in the New World, the United States was the land of promise.

Even the early Love of Zion societies that were founded in America in the 1880s were organized as bulwarks against total assimilation, not as catalysts for Jewish immigration to Palestine. Most of those groups were content to study Hebrew and Jewish history and send money to aid the colonies in Palestine. In fact, if it had not been for the publication of Herzl's *Der Judenstaat*, the Lovers of Zion movement might have died out completely in the United States. Herzl's book quickened the wavering nationalistic spirit among American Jews, but petty rivalries and personality clashes among Jewish leaders in America tended to undercut any substantial growth.

The Reformed rabbinate in the United States felt that the Zionist movement was ridiculous. America is our Zion, they proclaimed, and they warned that loyalty to any future state in Palestine would put a condition on their loyalty to America. The Orthodox Jews, on the other hand, insisted that if God wanted to restore the Jews to Zion, he could do it without the help of unorthodox Zionists. Despite their reaction against the religious laxity of Zionists, Orthdox Jews maintained a soft spot in their hearts for the land of Abraham and hoped, along with most Conservative Jews in America, that God would bring about the restoration that Zionists were trying to realize through human efforts. As a result of such divisions, by the start of World War I only about 20,000 of America's 1.5 million Jews belonged to Zionist societies.[7]

While American Jews were vacillating, American premillennialists were watching these developments with great interest. Any movement dedicated to the restoration of the Jews was, naturally, crucial to their prophetic expectations. For decades they had been predicting the return of the Jews, so when the Jews themselves started taking steps in that direction, premillennialists gave them their full attention.

Premillennialist journals kept close watch on anti-Semitism in Europe and commented on how such treatment fed the ancient Jewish longing for Jerusalem.[8] Premillennial reporters and conference speakers noted the founding of the Lovers of Zion movement in Russia and filed frequent stories on their newly established colonies in Palestine. They also kept statistics on the slow but steady growth of the Jewish population there and often speculated about when the Jewish immigrants would start contemplating the construction of a new temple in Jerusalem.[9]

The publication of Herzl's *Der Judenstaat* in 1896 was praised in the premillennialist press, and when Herzl held his second Zionist Congress in Basel in 1898, premillennialists were there taking notes, which were reported to the rank and file back home.[10] Subsequent congresses were also covered in the premillennialist press and judged by how they conformed to biblical prophecy.

In general, most premillennialists viewed Zionism as a probable fulfillment of end-times prophecy. Some even went so far as to suggest that Zionism was the ultimate fulfillment of the prophecies concerning the Jewish restoration, but most observed that Zionism was primarily a political and nationalististic movement, not a religious revival. In 1905 Arno Gaebelein warned that

Zionism is not the divinely promised restoration of Israel.
. . . Zionism is not the fulfillment of the large number of
predictions found in the Old Testament Scriptures, which relate to Israel's return to the land. Indeed, Zionism has very
little use for arguments from the Word of God. It is rather a
political and philanthropic undertaking. Instead of coming together before God, calling upon His name, trusting Him, that
He is able to perform what He has so often promised, they
speak about their riches, their influence, their Colonial Bank,
and court the favor of the Sultan. The great movement is one
of unbelief and confidence in themselves instead of God's
eternal purposes.[11]

At that point, Gaebelein and other premillennialists sounded
like Orthodox Jews on the matter of the religious indifference of
many Zionists. But while they knew that Zionism would not
bring the ultimate restoration of Jews back to Palestine, premill-
lennialists did claim that it was probably the beginning of the
movement which would bring enough Jews back to the Holy
Land "in unbelief" to start the prophetic countdown to the end
of the age. As such, Zionism was a valuable link in the chain of
events which will lead to the revelation of Antichrist and the end
of the "times of the Gentiles" at the glorious return of Jesus
Christ. If Zionism was not the end, it was at least the beginning
of the end.[12]

Some premillennialists were not satisfied to be mere observers
of the Zionist movement. A few became strong supporters and
actually gained recognition within the movement for their aggressive advocacy. No American premillennialist earned more ac-
claim among Zionists than W. E. Blackstone, the author of *Jesus
Is Coming*, probably the most widely read premillennialist book
of its time.

William Eugene Blackstone (1841–1935) was born in Adams,
New York, into a Methodist home and was converted at the age
of eleven. After failing to qualify for active military duty during
the Civil War, he served with the United States Christian Com-

mission, a religiously oriented service organization. After the war, he married and moved to Oak Park, Illinois, where he started a successful business in building and property investments.

It is not clear when or how Blackstone became a premillennialist, but by the 1880s he was an associate of D. L. Moody and had published his book on the second coming. It is also not clear when Blackstone developed his intense concern for the Jews. In *Jesus Is Coming*, he noted the initial movements of Jews to resettle Palestine. His interest must have been increased in 1888, when he and his daughter toured the Holy Land.

On his return, Blackstone organized and was the chairman of the first conference between Christians and Jews in Chicago. At that initial meeting, held in the First Methodist Church, Blackstone advocated the Jewish restoration in Palestine and saw to it that resolutions of sympathy for Russian Jews were passed and copies forwarded to the Czar.

During the following year (1891) Blackstone's concern for the oppressed Jews in Europe led him to sponsor an amazing "memorial" on behalf of Russian Jews. On March 5, 1891, Blackstone sent his memorial to President Benjamin Harrison and Secretary of State James Blaine. The memorial began with a simple question: "What shall be done for the Russian Jews?" After briefly discussing the situation in Europe, Blackstone offered his own answer:

> Why not give Palestine back to them again? According to God's distribution of nations, it is their home—an inalienable possession from which they were expelled by force. . . . Why shall not the powers which under the treaty of Berlin in 1878 gave Bulgaria to the Bulgarians and Servia to the Servians now give Palestine back to the Jews? . . . We believe this is an appropriate time for all nations, and especially the Christian nations of Europe, to show kindness to Israel. A million exiles, by their terrible sufferings, are piteously appealing to our sympathy, justice and humanity. Let us now

restore to them the land of which they were so cruelly de-
spoiled by our Roman ancestors.[13]

The memorial was signed by 413 prominent Americans, including Melville Fuller, Chief Justice of the United States Supreme Court; Chauncy Depew, United States Senator from New
York; Thomas Reed, Speaker of the House of Representatives;
the mayors of Chicago, New York, and Boston; and a number of
other elected officials and judges. Leading journalists from the
Chicago Daily News, *The New York Times,* the *Washington
Post,* the *Philadelphia Times,* and the *Chicago Tribune* signed the
document, as did a number of the nation's most recognizable business leaders, including Cyrus McCormick, John D. Rockefeller,
and J. Pierpont Morgan.

In October of the same year Blackstone wrote an article entitled "May the United States Intercede for the Jews?" which received wide circulation around the country. In it he wrote that

> there is one spot toward which the eye of the Jew has turned
> . . . his loved Palestine. There is room there for two or
> three millions more people, and the ancient scriptural limits
> of the country would largely increase its capacity. The rains
> are returning, agriculture is improving, its location promises
> great commercial possibilities, and only an independent, en-
> lightened and progressive government is needed to afford a
> home for all of Israel who wish to return.[14]

Blackstone's memorial, it must be remembered, was written one
year before the first Lovers of Zion societies were formed in the
United States, five years before Herzl's *Der Judenstaat,* and six
years before the first Zionist Congress.

Blackstone continued to have an active interest in Zionist affairs
after 1891. When Herzl showed a lack of commitment to Palestine as the site for the Jewish state, Blackstone sent him a marked
copy of the Old Testament, showing, in typical premillennialist
fashion, those passages which indicated that the Jews must return

to the Holy Land.[15] In 1916, a year before the Balfour Declaration, Blackstone sponsored another memorial, this one addressed to President Woodrow Wilson. Reminding the President that the first memorial had received no official attention, the second memorial urged more concerted action. The 1916 memorial was endorsed by Andrew White, president of Cornell University and former United States ambassador to Russia; businessman John Wanamaker; the Federal Council of Churches; the Presbyterian Ministerial Association; the Baptist Minister's Conference; and Shailer Mathews of the University of Chicago, who, two years later, would share leadership in the liberal attack on the premillennialist movement.[16]

Zionists sincerely appreciated Blackstone's efforts on their behalf. At a 1918 Zionist Conference in Philadelphia, Blackstone was acclaimed a "Father of Zionism." In the same year, at a Zionist mass meeting in Los Angeles, Blackstone addressed the assembled crowd:

> I am and for over thirty years have been an ardent advocate of Zionism. This is because I believe that true Zionism is founded on the plan, purpose, and fiat of the everlasting and omnipotent God, as prophetically recorded in His Holy Word, the Bible. . . . There are only three courses open to every Jew. . . . The first is to become a true Christian, accepting Jesus as Lord and Saviour, which brings not only forgiveness and regeneration, but insures escape from the unequaled time of tribulation which is coming upon all the earth. . . . Second—become a true Zionist and thus hold fast to the ancient hopes of the fathers, and the assured deliverance of Israel, through the coming of their Messiah, and complete national restoration and permanent settlement in the land which God has given them. It is true that this leads through unequaled sorrows, as prophesied notably by Jeremiah. . . . [Third—] these are the *assimilants*. They are the Jews who will not be either Christians or Zionists. They wish to remain in the various nations enjoying their social, politi-

cal, and commercial advantages. . . . Oh, my Jewish friends,
which of these paths shall be yours? . . . God says that you
are dear unto Him . . . He has put an overwhelming love in
my heart for you all, and therefore I have spoken thus plainly.
Study this wonderful Word of God . . . and see how plainly
God Himself has revealed Israel's pathway unto the perfect
day.[17]

Despite the call for conversion, Blackstone retained a cherished
place in the history of the early Zionist movement. In 1956, on
the seventy-fifth anniversary of Blackstone's memorial to President Harrison, the citizens of the state of Israel dedicated a forest
in his honor.[18]

As Blackstone's Los Angeles address indicates, premillennialists
were not only concerned about monitoring the Zionist movement;
they also cared about converting Jews to Christianity. Certainly
there was nothing new about Christians trying to convert Jews
in America,[19] but premillennialists had a different slant on reaching them with the gospel. Unlike other Protestants, premillennialists believed that God was not finished with the Jews as a national
entity. Most evangelicals believed in a vague sort of way that
somehow at the end of God's redemptive purposes "all Israel
shall be saved" (Romans 11:26); but only premillennialists expected a national restoration in Palestine and a powerful Jewish
state under the returned Messiah as part of the saving process.
Thus, premillennialists were able to stress the evangelization of
the Jews while at the same time they supported Jewish nationalistic aspirations.

In fact, premillennialists were sure that they alone had the key
to successful Jewish evangelism. While nonpremillennialist evangelicals tried to convince Jews that they were wrong to expect a
political kingdom in their future, premillennialists agreed with
those Jews who demanded literalistic fulfillments to Old Testament prophecies. They assured the Orthodox Jews that they were

perfectly correct in expecting the restoration of David's throne, adding only that the Bible promised the Messianic kingdom at Christ's second coming, not at his first.

Premillennialists believed that evangelists who could not make the same assurances were doomed to have meager results among the Jews. James Brookes once claimed that "no man is fit to preach to the Jews unless he believes in the personal coming of the Messiah." Since "most Jews, except those who have been utter infidels, confidently expect to be restored to the land of their fathers," he argued, "it is most important to show them that their hope is founded upon the coming of Messiah."[20] Some time later, Arno C. Gaebelein stated that

> a Christian who does not believe in the second coming of Christ is therefore wholly unfit to deal with the Jews. More than that, the church-missions among the Jews which are run with the un-scriptural post-millennial argument, are a dead failure. The true way to present the Gospel to the Jews is to show them the truth of the two advents in the Old Testament, and also how the New Testament looks forward to the second coming of Christ and the establishment of the Kingdom.[21]

If denominational missions were not using the proper approach in Jewish evangelism, premillennialists would have to establish their own. The first and probably the most typical premillennialist interdenominational Jewish mission was that founded by William E. Blackstone, among others, in Chicago in 1887. First called the Chicago Committee for Hebrew Christian Work, the mission changed its name to the more manageable Chicago Hebrew Mission in 1889. Two years later it was incorporated as the first Jewish mission in the state of Illinois.

The mission moved frequently during its first few years, for a time occupying space in Jane Addams's Hull House before Miss Addams could fully develop her own settlement work on Halsted Street. Eventually the mission had its own reading room, industrial school, temporary home for new Jewish converts, and day nursery for the children of working mothers, all of which were located in different places around the Jewish section of Chicago. In 1906 the mission had a staff of twenty-three, and they conducted preaching services, mothers' meetings, a kindergarten, house-to-house visitation, and literature distribution.[22] The mission eventually had its own publication, *The Jewish Era*, and sponsored regular Conferences on Behalf of Israel in which noted premillennialists analyzed Jewish aspects of biblical prophecy. The 1915 conference was held at Moody Church, Chicago, on November 16–19; it drew 17,000 spectators. Familiar premillennialist speakers such as James M. Gray, Robert McWatty Russell, A. E. Thompson, A. B. Simpson, John Timothy Stone, B. B. Sutcliffe, and William E. Blackstone participated.[23] The mission maintained its strength and supporters long after many of the other premillennialist missions despaired of the cause.

Another successful premillennialist mission to the Jews was New York City's the Hope of Israel Mission, which, after 1892, was under the leadership of Arno C. Gaebelein. Although it was originally affiliated with the Methodist Church Extension Society, Gaebelein eventually severed all relationships with the society. That mission conducted preaching services on Saturday afternoons on New York City's Lower East Side, published a Yiddish monthly paper (*Tiqweth Israel*) and a monthly magazine in English (*Our Hope*), and tried to provide free medical services for the poor whenever possible. The real strength behind the mission, however, was Gaebelein.

Arno C. Gaebelein (1861–1945) immigrated from Germany in 1879 and became a minister of the German Conference of the Methodist Church. He attended some of the early Niagara Bible Conferences and became a premillennialist in 1887. His work among the Jews of New York seems to have been part of the reason behind his acceptance of dispensationalism. Though he was not formally educated, Gaebelein taught himself enough Hebrew and Yiddish to debate with the rabbis on the Lower East Side. When he joined the work of the Hope of Israel Mission in the early 1890s he conducted spirited lectures on Saturday afternoons, and in them he agreed to answer any questions on the Messiahship of Jesus or the future of Israel according to biblical prophecy. In fact, he acquired such an expertise in the Talmud and other rabbinic literature and spoke such flawless Yiddish that he often had a difficult time convincing many in his audiences that he was not a Jew trying to "pass" as a Gentile.

Despite considerable success at the mission, by the turn of the century Gaebelein left his work there to devote full time to editing, writing, and speaking.[24]

Eventually, nearly every major American city that had a substantial Jewish population had some kind of evangelistic witness to the Jews, most of which were either founded or at least heavily supported by premillennialists.[25] For the most part they all used the same methods of outreach. In many ways, the methods used in Jewish evangelism paralleled those used among other immigrant groups: they had reading rooms, social centers, kindergartens, day care centers, sewing and home economics classes, English tutorials in which the New Testament was the only textbook, public lectures, door-to-door visitation, literature distribution by hand and through the mail, and open-air meetings. But missions to the Jews were much more difficult and required a much higher sensitivity than evangelistic efforts among other newcomers.

As one might expect, Jewish immigrants who had just come from pogroms and strangling anti-Semitism in Europe were none too eager to confront Christian missionaries in the United States. Memories of forced baptisms and convert-or-die commands were too fresh for the Jews to give Christian evangelists warm welcomes. Some Jews considered any evangelistic effort another form of anti-Semitism. Consequently, Christian missionaries to the Jews had an extremely difficult task.

Missionaries who conducted open-air meetings in the ghettos

had especially hazardous duty. At one street meeting in Chicago conducted by students from the Moody Bible Institute, things got out of hand. Using a standard evangelical approach, the students tried to conduct their street service from the back of a "gospel wagon." Soon over a thousand irritated Jews gathered, shouting "disconcerting questions" and hurling insults. Charles Meeker, the director of practical work at MBI, had "told the speakers not to get into any wrangles over these questions, but to adhere closely to their testimony and lay the claims of Christ upon the audience with all the power at their command; and no matter how much they disliked or resented it, they should not hesitate to use the name of Jesus freely." But the more the missionaries stuck to their program, the angrier the crowd became. Meeker sent two of his students to look for a policeman to provide some protection from the "rabble," but no peace officer could be found.

Finally, after about an hour of trying to shout above the crowd, Meeker and his brave band started their strategic withdrawal, amidst "an avalanche of watermelon rind, banana peelings, over-ripe tomatoes, and other edible fruit." Such treatment might have deterred lesser men, but Meeker testified that the encounter "in no way dampened our ardor or quenched our desire to give the gospel to the Jew." Despite everything, Meeker claimed, some Jews were converted. In no time, Meeker's students were on the streets again.[26]

For those who wanted to avoid such abuse, there were lessons to learn. When speaking of Jesus of Nazareth, the prudent were best advised to use "Messiah" instead of "Christ" because the latter term had so many horrible connotations for Jews throughout their history.[27]

One lad who assisted his father's mission learned a valuable lesson on how *not* to distribute Christian handbills in a Jewish tenement. The first few times he passed out the literature, he started at the bottom of the tenement and worked his way to the top. But by the time he reached the upper floors, the tenants below had absorbed the nature of the material. With cries of "Meshumed" (apostate), the tenement dwellers let go a barrage of hot soup, pots and pans, and assorted garbage. "Thus I learned that the next time I went into a tenement house, I must start on the top floor and work down."[28]

Frequently, tactically minded missionaries argued about who had the best chance for results among the Jews, the sympathetic Gentile or the converted Jew.[29] But the most sensitive spot in premillennialist missions to the Jews was probably the matter of evangelism among Jewish children. As evangelicals had learned from decades of revivalism, the young are easier to reach with the gospel than are the old. And Jewish children, often embarrassed by the Old World ways of their parents and eager for something new, seemed especially ready candidates for conversion.

Unquestionably, there were times when Christian missionaries camouflaged their evangelism behind sewing, cooking, or singing classes, without letting the children or their parents know exactly what was going on. On one such occasion, at least, that strategy backfired. In one mission the somewhat clandestine session was opened with a hymn. Then something rather unexpected occurred:

> As soon as we expressed in the hymn the word *Jesus,* the children simultaneously, as though done by magic placed their fingers in their ears and refused to sing or to listen. Some of them began to hiss, and some of them decided not to stay. They were shocked, they were horrified, and some were ready even to weep and to run home. Their teachers were puzzled and perplexed. But we kept on singing; and after a little, the children would gradually withdraw their fingers from their ears and listen. When they recognized that the word *Jesus* was not being expressed, they would keep their fingers out till we came to that word, and again that performance was gone through with.[30]

A few months later, however, those same children sang "What a Friend We Have in Jesus" at the top of their lungs as they rode in open trolleys through the Jewish ghetto on their way to a mission-sponsored outing in the country.

Some of the opponents of child-evangelism among the Jews argued that Christian missionaries taught children to deceive their parents openly, or else purchased parental acquiescence through some kind of financial assistance. More scrupulous missionaries, however, advised those who worked with Jewish children to always secure parental permission before taking their children to evangelistic meetings. If everything was aboveboard, some missionaries discovered, parents were sometimes so impressed by the honesty of the evangelists that they gave their permission for their children to attend.[31]

As though those built-in problems were not enough, premillennialist missions to the Jews occasionally suffered the embarrassment of public controversy, even scandal.

A case in point is the controversy surrounding Leopold Cohn, founder of the Williamsburg Mission to the Jews in Brooklyn, New York. According to his autobiography,[32] Leopold Cohn was born in Hungary in 1862 of Orthodox parents. After becoming a rabbi at the age of eighteen, Cohn began to study Old Testament prophecy, without any knowledge of Jesus of Nazareth or the New Testament. The more he studied the Talmud, however, the more confused he became. In 1892 he arrived in New York to work among the Jewish immigrants, hoping to pursue his own studies of Messianic prophecy. Shortly after his arrival, he attended a meeting conducted by a missionary who spoke about the coming of the Messiah. Cohn obtained a New Testament in Hebrew and absorbed it, claiming at first that he did not make the connection between the Yeshua (Jesus) of the Gospels and the Christ of Christianity. When a fellow rabbi pointed out the connection, it was already too late. Cohn soon converted, and he was baptized in June 1892. After traveling to Scotland for theological

training, he had a painful reconciliation with his family, then
returned to New York in 1893, intent on sharing the gospel with
fellow Jews.

After three years of struggling on his own, Cohn obtained the
support of the Baptist Home Missions Society (BHMS) and the
Church Extension Society, at an annual salary of $1000 and $600
for rent. With that modest support, the mission prospered. Cohn
eventually expanded his operation into the Williamsburg section
of Brooklyn, where he conducted Bible studies, evangelistic lectures, child evangelism, and a free medical dispensary. In time his
work spread even beyond New York, into Coney Island, Philadelphia, Pittsburgh, Los Angeles, and Buffalo.[33]

Cohn's troubles began in 1907, when he began feuding with the
Baptist Home Missions Society. As might be expected, there are
conflicting accounts of what actually happened, but it seems that
the BHMS was reluctant to increase its yearly support and resented Cohn's attempts to broaden his work without first clearing
all details with his official supporters. The dispute finally broke
into the open when Cohn solicited funds without the BHMS's
approval and secured a $10,000 donation from a Miss Frances J.
Huntley. Members of the BHMS argued that the money right-
fully belonged to them, since Cohn was under their official aegis.
Cohn agreed to turn the donation over to the Society if Miss
Huntley so directed, but she preferred to leave it with Cohn.
The BHMS then accused Cohn of trickery and deceit, broke off
all support, and warned its constituents that Cohn "has alienated
some of his best supporters by his refusal to have any supervision
of his work in any way whatever. . . . His insulting language
and his bad temper and general management of the work have
alienated many of his best friends." Potential supporters were
therefore advised to keep their money.[34]

In 1913 Cohn found himself embroiled in an even larger controversy. In May of that year Yiddish newspapers in New York
reported that Cohn had lied about being a rabbi in Hungary and

that Cohn was not even his real name. According to the news-papers' sources, he had been an innkeeper in his native land and had had to flee when he had been accused of murder. Cohn's supporters claimed that Jews in New York had raised $10,000 "to get Cohn" because of his missionary successes and had hired a young man to go to Hungary and bribe Cohn's home-town sheriff into making the false accusations.[35]

On top of these charges, which in retrospect look totally fabri-cated, during an appearance in the Brooklyn Municipal Court in December of the same year Cohn admitted that he owned a coun-try estate in Connecticut, another home in New York City, and other real estate holdings. Those disclosures by someone who had made repeated impassioned pleas for money to finance his budg-eted work was extremely disturbing to some of his most faithful supporters.

By 1916 Delavan Pierson, the son of A. T. Pierson, had grown sufficiently suspicious of Cohn that he wrote James Gray, editor of the *Christian Workers Magazine*, demanding that he stop printing advertisements for Cohn's mission. Realizing that Cohn's entire future ministry was at stake, Gray urged the formation of a special investigatory committee to look into the allegations. The committee, made up of Reverend John Carson of Brooklyn; Hugh Munro, vice president of Niagara Lithograph Company; E. B. Buckalew, secretary of Moody Bible Institute's extension program; Roy Hart, an attorney; and Delavan Pierson secured rooms in the Williamsburg YMCA and hired two lawyers to help in the cross-examination of witnesses and the investigation of charges that Cohn had mishandled funds. Public announcements of the sessions were made, and any and all witnesses were invited to appear. After seven weeks, the committee reported its findings: "As a result of these weeks of painstaking inquiry, the committee has found no evidence which could be substantiated which affords a reasonable basis for any of the charges made by his accusers."[36]

Shortly after that conclusion was reached, Gray reported to

his own readers that Cohn was innocent of all charges and had been completely within the law in his activities. Cohn had been persecuted and accused falsely, Gray concluded, and deserved full support.[37] Despite the committee's giving him a clean bill of health, such scandal did not help the image of Christian missionaries among the Jews.

On occasion there was even worse publicity associated with Jewish missions. Jewish converts frequently repudiated Christianity and returned to the faith of their fathers. None, however, did so with more bravado than Samuel Freuder.

Born in Hungary, Freuder had immigrated to the United States in 1883. He met Rabbi Isaac Wise and eventually was graduated from Hebrew Union College (1886). After a brief period as a rabbi in Georgia, Freuder left the rabbinate, discouraged and disillusioned with Judaism. By 1891 he was in Chicago and had come in contact with the Chicago Hebrew Mission. He soon converted and was baptized, and, despite the charge that he had received money to convert (he had not), he enrolled in the Chicago Theological Seminary. Following graduation he was ordained into the Christian ministry. In 1894 he became a missionary to Jews in Boston, but he quit after five months to go into secular business. After working at a series of jobs, Freuder decided to return to the comparative security of lecturing on prophetic and evangelistic themes. Eventually he transferred into the Protestant Episcopal Church and joined the staff of Grace Episcopal Church in New York City. By 1908 Freuder was extremely unhappy and disillusioned, this time with Christianity, so he resolved to break from it and publically repudiated his conversion.[38]

In June 1908 Freuder was scheduled to speak on "Christ and the Talmud" at a Hebrew Messianic (i.e. Hebrew Christian) Conference in Boston's Park Street Church. Instead of speaking on his assigned topic, Freuder declared to a stunned audience that he was leaving the Christian faith and ministry. He told the gathering that "you don't know what it means and costs for a Jew to be baptized—the rended soul, the disrupted family, the desertion of friends, the loss of respect." He then advised fellow Jews that if they were satisfied with their faith, they ought to stick to it. In conclusion, he pronounced a curse on himself if he ever preached in a Christian pulpit again. In his letter of resignation to his bishop, Freuder stated that missionaries to Jews would lose their jobs if their manipulative techniques were widely known and would then have to "turn their faking abilities into some business channels less destructive of true manhood and morality."[39]

When Freuder published an exposé of Christian missions to the Jews, the picture was not very flattering. He stated that, in order to retain the support of their contributors, missionaries were forced to falsify the results of their work. They also frequently took advantage of their new "converts" by dragging them around like spiritual trophies and thrusting them into situations in which they were forced to deliver canned testimonies on how miserable their Judaism had made them until they rejected it for Jesus. Most of the missionaries in Freuder's portrayal appeared to be thoughtless and exploitative manipulators who did not know the first thing about what it meant for a Jew to become a Christian. Freuder's analysis was obviously overdone, but it did reflect the prevailing Jewish view of Christian evangelism.[40]

As a whole, Christian missionaries to the Jews were much more sensitive than Freuder suggested. While some of the missionaries were less than honest or even overly aggressive, the majority were sincerely concerned about the spiritual condition of Jews and desired them to experience the same religious satisfaction that they themselves had had.

To say the least, the role of the Christian missionary to Jews was not easy. Eager to lead Jews to Christ, such missionaries were occasionally victimized by less-than-sincere Jewish "converts." By their own admission, some Jews came to Christian missions for financial assistance. A feigned interest in the missionary's message and a hard-luck story usually brought some kind of monetary aid.

In some cases, dishonest "inquirers" passed the word about a soft-hearted missionary to all their friends before he caught on to the ruse.[41] Gaebelein confessed to being fooled on occasion by "converts" who suddenly backed out of baptism when they discovered that there were no direct financial benefits for the convert.[42]

Despite their basic honesty and sensitivity, most Christian missionaries could do nothing about easing the culture shock of their converts. To most Jews, conversion to Christ meant a total repudiation of one's identity, family, and friends. Accepting Christ had many more radical implications for a Jew than it did for the average unchurched Gentile. Jews who responded to the Christian gospel were frequently expelled from their homes and considered dead by their own parents and spouses.[43] In such situations missionaries provided homes for the new converts and found them new jobs with Christian employers. None of those efforts could change the fact, however, that Jewish converts usually found themselves isolated and lonely.

Some Christian missionaries were deeply concerned about the cultural crisis which many of their converts had to undergo and wondered why they could not retain some of their Jewishness after accepting Christ. Other missionaries believed that unless a total break was made with the past, the converts might be induced to reject Christ and return to their old lives.

In 1914 the Hebrew Christian Alliance of America was organized to create a better working relationship between all the Jewish mission agencies in the United States. In their third annual conference the delegates took up the matter of the cultural identity of converted Jews. By an overwhelming majority, the conferees rejected a resolution allowing Jewish Christians to retain some of their Jewishness by observing the feast days of Judaism. The delegates voted to close "the doors once for all to all Judaizing propaganda," and recommended that the pure gospel of grace be preached.[44]

When the conference took this stance, other missionaries thought that its ruling was a serious breach of biblical principles. Citing the events recorded in Acts 15, one premillennialist noted,

> when the Christian church was founded at Jerusalem, these first Jewish Christians were nationally so narrow-minded that they believed that the Gentiles must first become Jews and be circumcised before they could gain admission to the church of Christ. It would be the same narrowness of opinion now, at the end of the church age, if Christians were to demand that the Jewish people must first enter one of the churches before they could have part in the Kingdom of God.[45]

Arno C. Gaebelein also supported the right of Jewish converts to observe parts of their traditional religious practices. When outlining the principles of his Hope of Israel Mission, Gaebelein insisted that

> the Jew has no need whatever of the organization or institutions of historical (i.e., Gentle and denominational) Christianity. All he needs is personal, saving faith in his own Jewish Messiah, the Christ of God, nothing more. And all that was divinely given him through Moses he has full liberty to retain and uphold as far as possible when he becomes a believer in Jesus Christ.[46]

Such convictions were easier to express than to carry out. Since converted Jews were despised by other Jews, they found little fellowship in old quarters. On the other hand, they were often shunned by Christians if they accentuated their Jewishness.[47] As a result, they had three alternatives: reject Christ and return to Judaism; reject all parts of Judaism and assimilate into Gentile churches; or create their own Jewish-Christian congregations, such as the Chicago Hebrew Christian Assembly, in which they tried to maintain their new Christian commitment in their own distinctive Jewish style.

The last alternative proved to be the most difficult. Too few converted Jews had the desire to remain "Jewish Christians." Recently converted Jews needed the fellowship of the larger Christian community. Consequently, most efforts to develop a Jewish kind of Christianity failed miserably.

Even though Christian missionaries tended to turn Jewish converts into Gentiles, for the most part they were sincerely and deeply concerned about them. They recognized them as the people of God who, as premillennialists pointed out, would one day in the future receive all of the divine promises made to their fathers. Premillennialists, therefore, were fierce opponents of anti-Semitism in any form, and they frequently called themselves the friends of Israel.

Yet there was an ironic ambivalence in the premillennialist attitude toward Jews. On the one hand, Jews were God's chosen people and heirs to the promises; but their rejection of Jesus as Messiah placed them in open rebellion against God and ensured their eventual rendezvous with Antichrist during the great tribulation. The glory of Israel was still in the future; in the meantime, Jews were under the power of Satan and were playing their assigned role in the decline of the present age. From that perspective, Jews deserved the scorn of premillennialists as well as their sympathy.

Accordingly, at times premillennialists sounded anti-Semitic. Despite their claims that anti-Semitism was a gross and unexcusable sin against God, some leaders of the movement acted like representatives of American anti-Semitism.

This can be seen in their reactions to the *Protocols of the Elders of Zion,* an alleged series of secret proceedings in which Jews plotted to take over the world. The manuscript outlined an elaborate conspiracy to undermine civil government, disrupt international economy, and destroy Christianity.[48] Whatever their source, the *Protocols* created a sensation when they appeared in the west after World War I.

When Henry Ford published exerpts of the *Protocols* in his

Dearborn Independent, Arno Gaebelein welcomed the disclosures, remarking that "all true Jews will be grateful for an exposé like the one published by the *Independent.*" Observing that "there is nothing so vile on earth as an apostate Jew who denies God and His Word," he noted how many Jews owned liquor trusts and how many robbers and lawbreakers had Jewish last names. Gaebelein declared that such activity was clearly predicted in the Bible, but added that not all Jews were involved.[49]

In an article entitled "The International Jew," which appeared in the premillennial Bible Institute of Los Angeles' *The King's Business,* Charles C. Cook sadly concluded that the *Protocols* were authentic.

> The Jewish race is morally fully capable of doing all that is charged against it. It is at present rejected of God, and in a state of disobedience and rebellion. . . .
> As a race Jews are gifted far beyond all other peoples, and even in their ruin, with the curse of God upon them, are in the front rank of achievement; but accompanying traits are pride, overbearing arrogance, inordinate love for material things, trickery, rudeness and an egotism that taxes the superlatives of any language. Oppressed are they? Indeed, and subject to injustice more than any other race, and yet never learning the lesson of true humility. . . .
> These cheap adulations [of editors, ministers, and politicians] are usually based on no better foundations than self-interest, for the unregenerate Jew usually has a very unattractive personality. There is a reason for his being persona non grata at resorts and in the best society; who can deny it?[50]

Moody Bible Institute's James M. Gray took a more even-handed position, but he still believed that "the *Protocols* are a clinching argument for premillennialism and another sign of the possible nearness of the end of the age." He admitted that "anti-Semitism is evil and has no place in our Christian civilization" and offered sincere condolences for anyone stirring up more persecutions for the Jews. But he also felt constrained to add that the prophets of the Old Testament said worse things about the Jews than any modern anti-Semite did. Despite the persecutions which might fall on the Jews because of the publication of the *Protocols*, Gray had to admit that they sounded authentic and were "Satan's counterfeit of God's purposes" for the end of the age.[51]

Some years later, William Bell Riley, one of fundamentalism's most colorful and forceful spokesmen, by the end of the 1920s admitted that while at first he thought the *Protocols* were fraudulent, after watching the events in postwar Europe and the United States, he was convinced that they were amazingly accurate. Claiming that there was absolutely no racial or religious prejudice behind his assertions, he argued that the "finger prints" of the *Protocols* could be found in every nation on earth, that the advocates and participants of the conspiracy were at the side of every great ruler on earth, dictating national policies, and that 80 per cent of Russia's communist leaders were Jews. The plan outlined in the Protocols, Riley concluded, was being carried out in the international communist conspiracy.[52]

Although that kind of anti-Semitism was not inherent in the premillennialist position, it seemed compatible with its view of the end of the age.

In the last analysis, premillennialists had a somewhat ambivalent attitude toward Jews. Their expectations of the end of the age made them strongly interested in and occasionally aggressive supporters of the Zionist cause and also enthusiastic participants in Christian missions to the Jews. But their fraternal feelings for Jews as co-heirs of the promises of God could not alter the Jews' present position as rejectors of Christ and the eventual tools of Antichrist. At that time, Jews were blinded and hardened to the gospel, but someday, on the other side of the tribulation, after one last period of intense suffering for their rejection of Messiah and their continual disobedience, Jews would finally attain the promise, and reign with Messiah Jesus. Despite their status as pilgrims and exiles, at the end of the age they would shine forth as the sun, ablaze with glory as fully restored children of God.

In the end, the premillennialist vision for the Jews was positive, and their support for Israel was uncompromised. Somehow, "all Israel shall be saved."

7

The Faithful Remnant

When the Son of Man cometh, shall he find faith on the earth?

Luke 18:8

The new premillennialism greatly affected the actions and attitudes of those evangelicals who accepted it in the half-century after 1875. On the personal level, the doctrine of the imminent return of Christ increased the expectancy and urgency of daily life and placed people in the difficult position of being ready to meet Christ at any time, while still preparing for the future in case his arrival was delayed. The possibility of the rapture likewise aided evangelists in the battle for souls and helped premillennialists shore up slipping evangelical social mores.

In a variety of ways, the new premillennialism altered the way people viewed the world around them and their responsibilities in it. The imminent return of Christ led many premillennialists to volunteer for foreign missionary service or give liberally to the missionary enterprise. Similarly, their beliefs about the inevitable decline of the social order and the futility of reform led many premillennialists to substantially modify the earlier evangelical commitment to social action and reform.

Premillennialists were able to show, at least to their great satisfaction, that their view of biblical prophecy was being vindicated by events of the day. World War I especially gave them ample evidence that they had read the Scriptures correctly. Time after time, their views seemed to be verified in the morning newspapers. Likewise, their beliefs about the re-gathering of the Jews in Palestine were borne out by the rise of Zionism. At a time when other Protestants did not seem to care too much, premillennialist eschatology led some evangelicals into becoming fierce supporters of Jewish nationalism—and aggressive missionaries to the Jews.

But how did the acceptance of premillennialism affect church life within the evangelical denominations? During the five decades between 1875 and 1925, American Protestantism was decimated by internal strife and schism. As we have already seen, there was a seismic shift in evangelical theology during that period, and many evangelicals refused to accept those fundamental changes in the way church people viewed the world, the Bible, and even Jesus Christ himself. What role did premillennialists play in the disintegration of evangelical unity in the churches? To what extent were premillennialists involved in the fundamentalist/ modernist controversy, and how was their participation a direct result of their eschatology? If scholars can determine the connection between premillennialist beliefs and fundamentalist behavior, they will have come a long way toward understanding at least part of the ethos of fundamentalism.

As with all historical analysis, one must guard against the simple answer or the facile explanation which tries to account for too much. From the outset, it is clear that not everyone who called himself a fundamentalist believed in the premillennial coming of Christ and that not every premillennialist took an active part in the fundamentalist controversy. Clearly, then, the turmoil can not be studied in terms of a conflict between premillennialists and non-premillennialists. Sometimes premillennialists opposed each other over ultimate goals and strategy in the fight against modernism. At times temperaments and personalities seemed more important than common beliefs about the second coming of

Christ. While rejecting the temptation to overstate the role of premillennialism in the fundamentalist/modernist controversy, one should not fail to see its real significance.

In his study on *The Roots of Fundamentalism*, Ernest Sandeen argued that premillennialism "gave life and shape to the Fundamentalist movement."[1] In order to correct a serious oversight, Sandeen distinguished between the fundamentalist *movement* and the fundamentalist *controversy*. While the controversy arose over the spread of modernism in the churches and evolutionary theory in society after World War I, the movement began shortly after the Civil War in the conservative Bible conference movement in which certain evangelicals banded together to affirm the old verities in the face of the New Theology. The prophetic conferences which spread the doctrine of the premillennial second coming of Jesus Christ were also a part of the conservative movement, many of its leaders having played an important role in the more ecumenical Bible conferences. From the first prophetic conference in 1878 to the two major prophetic conferences in 1918, premillennialists consciously considered themselves the rightful heirs of the conservative evangelical tradition and firmly placed themselves against all who tried to lessen its impact or subvert its theology.

The fundamentalist/modernist controversy of the 1920s, then, had its roots much earlier. Conservative and liberal evangelicals had been opposing each other for decades by the time open and bitter hostilities erupted after World War I—and premillennialists were involved from the beginning.

Sandeen made a good case for the central role of premillennialists in the beginnings of the fundamentalist controversy. The bitter attacks on premillennialists at the end of World War I and their often equally acrimonious replies did much to set the mood of the disputes which followed. Certainly, one can detect a growing combativeness on both sides during the war years. During the Philadelphia prophetic conference in the spring of 1918, one of the participants called on fellow premillennialists to "make war against foreign innovation into our religious world." German theology "has been forcing its way into the veins and arteries of all our religious life. We ought to fight it to the finish."[2]

By 1918 premillennialists were beginning to realize that the crisis at hand demanded less emphasis on eschatology and more vigorous defense of the whole evangelical gospel. During the Philadelphia prophetic conference, its organizers made plans to hold a similar meeting the following year. But within a few months the leaders of the conference were summoned to R. A. Torrey's summer home in Montrose, Pennsylvania, to consider a change in plans. Someone suggested that the times required a world-wide fellowship of conservative Christians to lead the battle against modernism. After a few days of discussion, the premillennialists shelved their original plans and announced that, instead of holding another conference on prophecy, they would sponsor a World's Conference on Christian Fundamentals to consider the formation of a more permanent organization to fight modernism.[3]

Over six thousand people from forty-two states and Canada responded to the call: they gathered in Philadelphia between May 25, and June 1, 1919. There they heard a systematic exposition of the fundamentals of the evangelical faith and a fervent call to their aggressive defense. Such familiar speakers as Riley, Gray, Griffith-Thomas, Torrey, Chafer, Pettingill, and Munhall affirmed the inspiration of the Bible, the evangelical doctrines of God, Christ, Satan, sin, atonement, sanctification, grace, redemption, the church, the premillennial second coming, resurrection, and future punishment.

In the long run, however, what the leaders did was far more important than what they said. In order to stem the rising tide of modernism, the premillennialist-led conservatives at the conference founded the World's Christian Fundamentals Association (WCFA). Five standing committees were formed to carry on the work of the convention, including those on Bible conference, missions, religious publications, an accrediting agency for Bible schools and colleges, and a committee to correlate the work of colleges, seminaries, and academies. The association established its own publication, *Christian Fundamentals in School and Church,* under the editorship of William Bell Riley, and adopted its own "creed," which included a strong statement on the premillennial second coming.[4]

Though the WCFA remained active for over thirty years, it failed to purge modernism from the churches and schools of America. As the organization grew, it was forced to compromise its premillennialist position to some extent and to adapt its thrust to more popular issues of the day. The important thing about the WCFA for the purposes of this study is that it grew out of the prophetic conference movement, was dominated by premillennialists, and even included a premillennialist article in its organizing creed. Sandeen was not overstating the case when he claimed that "as a result of the 1919 World's Conference on Christian Fundamentals, the millenarian movement had changed its name. The millenarians had become Fundamentalists."[5]

In much the same way, premillennialists played an important role in the denominational disputes which eventually split two of the major evangelical churches, the northern Baptists and Presbyterians, in the 1920s.

From the turn of the century, conservative Northern Baptists had been uneasy about the growth of liberalism within the Northern Baptist Convention. At first the conservatives focused their attention on Baptist schools. Few Northern Baptists failed to detect the acceptance of critical biblical methodology and liberal theology at the University of Chicago Divinity School. In 1913, when one of the Divinity School's leading professors, Gerald B. Foster, was forced out of the Chicago Baptist Ministers Conference for his heterodox work, *The Finality of the Christian Faith,* conservatives organized the Northern Baptist Theological Seminary in Chicago as a more orthodox alternative to the Divinity School.

In time conservatives realized that Chicago's Divinity School was only the tip of the liberal iceberg and that providing a conservative seminary was no way to stem the growth of liberalism in other Baptist institutions. Conservative discontent was obviously on the increase, but until 1919 it lacked the focus and direction to mount an aggressive movement.

The catalyst was provided by the annual Northern Baptist Convention of 1919, which met in Denver, Colorado. The convention speaker that year was Harry Emerson Fosdick, a gifted preacher from New York City who was well known for his liberal sentiments. His presence and prominence in the convention angered a number of conservatives, who had already identified Fosdick as part of the problem in the Northern Baptist Convention. To make matters worse, delegates voted to approve *The Baptist* as the new convention magazine and placed it under liberal control. The most shocking action of the Denver convention as far as conservatives were concerned, however, was the vote which made the Northern Baptist Convention a participant in the ecumenical Interchurch World Movement, an interdenominational fund-raising organization that lacked any real doctrinal boundaries.[6] Curtis Lee Laws, a leading conservative Baptist, voiced the concerns of many when he criticized the Interchurch World Movement for emasculating

> Christianity by eliminating all doctrinal emphasis from its pronouncements and appeals. It had no doctrinal basis, and yet it sought to explain to the world the meaning of Christianity. Because it represented everybody, it was under obligations to offend nobody. The movement represented the compromising spirit of the age, and yet Northern Baptists were foremost among its promoters! Within our fold we hail as leaders men who deny the miraculous birth of Christ, the vicarious death of Christ, and the promised second coming of Christ.[7]

Aroused by the events in the 1919 convention in Denver, the conservatives got organized. A month before the next annual convention convened in Buffalo, one hundred and fifty conservative ministers and laymen issued a call for a pre-convention meeting in Buffalo on "Fundamentals of Our Baptist Faith." Two days before the regular convention began, 3000 Baptists crowded into Buffalo's Civic Auditorium to hear speakers, half of whom were premillennialists, condemn the spread of modernism in the Northern Baptist Convention and its schools. Finally stirred into action, the conservatives founded the National Federation of Fundamentalists of the Northern Baptists, which in time was popularly known as the "Fundamentalist Fellowship."

When the regular convention convened, the newly elected president of the fundamentalist federation, J. C. Massee, asked for the appointment of a Committee of Nine to look into the theological soundness of Baptist institutions. After a lengthy and noisy debate, the convention voted to establish such a committee and asked it to report its findings at the 1921 convention, which was to be held at Des Moines.

The Committee of Nine discovered exactly what the fundamentalists expected it to: that certain teachers were bringing "strife to our ranks and confusion to the work." The committee advised that "it is the duty of the Baptist communities throughout the country to displace from the schools men who impugn the authority of the Scriptures as the Word of God and who deny the deity of our Lord."[8] Despite the clear verdict of the committee, the convention decided to take no action on its recommendation to dismiss unorthodox teachers.

That approach stymied, the fundamentalists tried another. Although Baptists traditionally resisted the formulation of creeds, many Northern Baptists believed that the adoption of a formal statement of faith might put an end to theological confusion, or at least clearly outline the boundaries of orthodoxy. In their pre-convention conference in 1921 the fundamentalists had tentatively drafted a confession which they eventually wanted to submit to the convention for approval. Early in 1922 representatives from both the Northern and Southern Baptist Conventions met to explore the possibility of issuing a joint affirmation of faith. But when the Northern Baptist Convention met in Indianapolis in 1922 for its annual meeting all hopes for a unified statement of faith vanished.

Part of the blame for the convention's failure to adopt a confession of faith belongs with the fundamentalists themselves. Some of them wanted to wait until a confession of faith could be worked out with the Southern Baptists, but others, led by William Bell Riley, pushed for an immediate campaign. After much discussion, Riley's point of view prevailed and the fundamentalists agreed to submit the New Hampshire Confession of 1833 as the binding statement of faith for all Northern Baptists.

The fundamentalist strategy failed, however, when Cornelius Woelfkin, a former premillennialist who had become a liberal leader among New York Baptists, made a motion "that the Northern Baptist Convention affirm that the New Testament is an all-sufficient ground for Baptist faith and practice, and they need no other statement." Not wanting to vote against the New Testament, the convention passed Woelfkin's resolution by a vote of 1264 to 637.

The bitterness and disappointment over this failure to adopt a statement of faith eventually split the fundamentalist camp. More militant fundamentalists rallied behind W. B. Riley, Frank Norris, T. T. Shields, and A. C. Dixon to form the Baptist Bible Union (BBU), which sought to include members from the Northern, Southern, and Canadian Baptist Conventions. The more moderate fundamentalists remained within the Fundamentalist Fellowship under J. C. Massee's leadership and restricted themselves to members of the Northern Baptist Convention.

By 1924 the two fundamentalist groups began to feud more with each other than with the liberals. When the BBU introduced an ultraconservative statement of faith before the 1924 convention, the Fundamentalist Federation refused to support it. Then, when Massee was appointed to a committee to investigate the orthodoxy of certain Baptist missionaries, he followed a more moderate line than suggested by the BBU, further driving the two groups apart.

Both fundamentalist Baptist organizations were heavily premillennialist, though the BBU probably had a much higher percentage. In fact, there were postmillennialists in the Fundamentalist Fellowship. Whereas it is safe to assume that there were few if any premillennialists on the liberal side of the conflict, it would be misleading to see the controversy as one between premillennialists and non-premillennialists. By the mid-1920s premillennialists themselves were divided on goals and strategy. When the BBU threatened to permanently disrupt the convention, more moderate fundamentalists, many premillennialists among them, decided that more might be accomplished by remaining loyal to the Northern Baptist Convention.[9]

Premillennialists also figured prominently in the controversy within the Northern Presbyterian Church. Since the early 1880s there had been a fairly good working relationship between premillennialists and conservatives who followed the Old School Calvinism taught at Princeton Seminary. At the 1892 General Assembly they cooperated to pass the "Portland Deliverance," which established the inerrancy of the Bible as an "essential" doctrine for all Northern Presbyterians. They also combined forces to oust from the church such liberals as Charles A. Briggs, A. C. McGiffert, and H. P. Smith; and they were successful in getting the General Assemblies of 1899 and 1910 to agree on which "fundamental doctrines" were necessary for the Christian faith.

By the end of World War I it appeared that this conservative alliance might hold out forever, but by the early 1920s the coalition had begun to crumble. In 1923 the General Assembly was forced to act on Harry Emerson Fosdick's rather inflammatory sermon, "Shall the Fundamentalists Win?" Ordinarily, a sermon by a Baptist like Fosdick would have been no concern of a Presbyterian General Assembly, but for the preceding five years he had served as "guest minister" of the First Presbyterian Church of New York City. Conservatives once again joined forces, and the General Assembly ordered the Presbytery of New York to bring the First Presbyterian Church into greater conformity with Presbyterian faith and practice.

In the following year, however, the Permanent Judicial Commission ruled that it had no jurisdiction in the matter, because Fosdick was not a Presbyterian. When he declined the invitation to change his affiliation and thereby face certain charges by conservatives, the matter was closed.

In the same 1924 meeting the conservatives suffered another setback. The same Judicial Commission ruled against the Philadelphia Presbytery's suggestion that the General Assembly require all denominational officials to reaffirm their commitment to the standards of the church. The commission ruled that the General Assembly had no authority to make doctrinal requirements for ministers or elders. Only the local presbyteries had such a right. In effect, the commission had overruled and outlawed all of the previous conservative attempts to establish essential doctrines for all Presbyterians.

The 1925 General Assembly marked the beginning of the end for the old conservative alliance within the Northern Presbyterian Church. At first conservatives were encouraged: the New York Presbytery was condemned for ordaining to the ministry two candidates who had refused to affirm the virgin birth of Christ. But the conservative victory was short-lived. An inevitable showdown between liberals and conservatives which might have permanently split the church was diverted when Charles Erdman, professor of practical theology and moderator of the General Assembly, appointed a Commission of Fifteen to examine "the present spiritual condition of our Church and the causes

making for unrest." When the commission reported back to the
assembly in 1926 and 1927, it virtually undid everything that the
conservative/premillennialist alliance had been working for during the preceding forty years. It noted the history of tolerance
and inclusiveness in the Presbyterian Church and concluded that
the church was big enough for liberals as well as conservatives.

As with the Baptists, there were premillennialists actively involved in the struggle. The Commission of Fifteen, which dealt
such a severe blow to the fundamentalist cause, contained three
premillennialist members: Mark Matthews, pastor of the First
Presbyterian Church of Seattle, Robert Speer, missions executive,
and Charles Erdman. Those men were non-doctrinaire premillennialists who had little desire to force the church to the point
of schism and actually sided with the moderates and liberals.
Many premillennialists like them preferred ecclesiastical unity to
absolute theological purity and openly opposed the militancy of
their own former conservative allies.

Though the conservatives were still free to fight on the presbytery level, the more militant decided that the battle was already
lost. Unity, they thought, was too high a price to pay, and many
took steps to leave the church. When a reorganization of Princeton Seminary broke the domination of the old conservative fac-
tion, four faculty members, J. Gresham Machen, Oswald T. Allis,
Cornelius Van Til, and Robert Dick Wilson, resigned in protest
and helped to establish Westminster Theological Seminary along
more conservative lines. Though the men who left Princeton had
cordial relations with premillennialists, none of them actually believed in the premillennial second coming themselves. Similarly,
when dissidents formed the Presbyterian Church of America,
some of its leaders wanted it clearly understood that they saw
little virtue in dispensationalism, though they were able to find
more common ground with other kinds of premillennialists. Machen, in an unfamiliar role, tried to act as a peacemaker between
the feuding factions within the new church, but by 1937 a schism

occurred, with most of the premillennialists forming their own Bible Presbyterian Church under the direction of J. Oliver Buswell, president of Wheaton College, and Carl McIntire, who later emerged as a leader in the militant crusade against communism.

Once again premillennialists had been unable to present a united front. As with the Baptists, the fundamentalist controversy within the Presbyterian Church was not primarily a conflict between premillennialists and non-premillennialists. Though premillennialists were invariably conservative in theology, they did not always choose a separatist stance when the unity of the church was threatened. Thus, when the time came to choose up sides, premillennialists could be found in both camps.[10]

In none of the other Protestant denominations did premillennialism play such an important role. The Disciples of Christ underwent a fierce controversy over modernism, but they had been almost totally untouched by premillennialism. The Southern Baptists and Presbyterians contained a relatively small number of premillennialists within their memberships and did not have to face any major problems over theological liberalism because of their generally more conservative stance. Though there was some contention, Methodists, Episcopalians, and Lutherans had neither an active nor a large premillennialist party, nor did they have a major or schismatic struggle between conservatives and liberals.

Premillennialists, therefore, were active participants in the fundamentalist/modernist controversy. As members of the conservative evangelical tradition, they naturally opposed the spread of modernism and felt obligated to speak out against it, although they often disagreed among themselves as to the best way to deal with it in the churches. But can one account for their involvement in terms of their beliefs about the second coming of Christ? To what extent were the premillennialists being consistent with their beliefs when they engaged in strenuous efforts to save their churches from religious apostasy?

Sandeen claimed that premillennialists betrayed their basic

principles when they fought to purge modernism from their denominations:

> When a millenarian like Riley said such things as "If Christ delay, the defeat of Modernism is certain," he was falling into the most serious kind of millenarian contradiction. There does not seem to be any way in which a consistent millenarian could have justified the attempt to force "creationism" upon the schools or, for that matter, "orthodoxy" upon the churches. To do so was to forsake one of the basic ingredients in the millenarian world view.[11]

At first glance, Sandeen's point seems well taken. Premillennialists believed that one of the marks of the end of the age was apostasy in the churches. Even before 1850, John Nelson Darby, the Plymouth Brethren who had given shape to modern dispensationalism, had given up on the "professing church" and had declared it "ruined" and "without remedy."[12] Strict dispensationalists made a distinction between the church (the spiritual body of true believers) and Christendom (the apostate body of alleged Christians who knew nothing of the "new birth"). C. H. Mackintosh made the distinction clearly:

> What varied thoughts and feelings are awakened in the soul by the very sound of the word "Christendom!" It is a terrible word. It brings before us, at once, that vast mass of baptized profession which calls itself the church of God, but is not; which calls itself Christianity, but is not. Christendom is dark and a dreadful anomaly. It is neither one thing nor the other. . . . It is a corrupt mysterious mixture, a spiritual malformation, the masterpiece of Satan, the corrupter of the truth of God, and the destroyer of the souls of men, a trap, a snare, a stumbling block, the darkest moral blot in the universe of God. It is the corruption of the very best thing, and therefore, the very worst of corruptions. It is that thing which Satan has made of professing Christianity. It is worse, by far, than Judaism, worse by far than all the darkest forms of Paganism, because it has higher light and richer privileges, makes the very highest profession, and occupies the very

loftiest platform. Finally, it is that awful apostasy for which is reserved the very heaviest judgment of God—the most bitter dregs in the cup of His righteous wrath.[13]

Similar sentiments can be found throughout premillennialist literature in America. In *Jesus Is Coming*, W. E. Blackstone condemned the corruptions of the professing church and saw them as clear indications of the end of the age.[14] In his study on *Christianity and Anti-Christianity in Their Final Conflict*, Samuel Andrews saw the rise of the New Theology and modern biblical criticism as harbingers of the apostasy. From the time premillennialists started speaking out against liberalism in the churches, they predicted and actually expected that it would corrupt the entire evangelical mass. As disturbing as these expectations were, premillennialists grimly accepted them as inevitable. They believed that when Christ returned he would find Christendom completely and compliantly under the control of Antichrist and would destroy it along with the rest of the Gentiles who opposed Israel.[15]

When premillennialists equated the rise of modernism with the predicted apostasy in the churches, they seemed to have but one course of action—separate themselves from the denominations affected. According to their beliefs, all reform efforts would ultimately fail, so that resistance to the rise of infidelity would be futile.

Many premillennialists took that position. In 1922 A. C. Gaebelein called on all Bible-believers to separate themselves from those who had left the historic faith. Two years later he warned fellow fundamentalists not to use "carnal" weapons against modernism. Instead of using propaganda, founding rival religious institutions, or seeking "political" victories within the churches, true Christians should withdraw from apostate denominations and try to persuade others to do the same. By 1925 Gaebelein concluded that "the modernistic cancer is too far gone. There is no more hope." He advised fellow premillennialists not to expect any reformation of the churches nor a general return to the truth. "The apostasy is on," he said, "and when 1925 closes, it will be worse than when the year began. God help us all to be faithful, loyal, and uncompromising."[16]

Not all premillennialists took such an extreme position. Some fought hard to reform their denominations, while others decided to remain within them even though they had to share company with modernists. Were they as inconsistent as Sandeen claimed?

On the contrary. Their interpretation of Scripture allowed them a certain latitude of behavior in reaction to the rise of modernism. Just as some people refused to accept the "logical" premillennialist position which forbade any efforts at social reform, some premillennialists refused to accept the extreme position which called for separation from the churches. Why?

Most American premillennialists had never given wholehearted support to Darby's doctrine of the ruin of Christendom. When Darby had visited the United States during the 1860s and 1870s, he had been somewhat discouraged by his reception and had doubted that he had accomplished very much. He had thought the American churches extremely worldly and had observed that while a number of American evangelicals had accepted his doctrine of the second coming, few had been willing to abandon their churches and form totally independent groups which met "only in the name of the Lord," as Darby's Plymouth Brethren had done in Great Britain.[17]

American evangelicals had more faith in their churches than that. They had developed denominationalism in response to the disestablishment of the churches and had devised a highly functional system to meet the needs of recruitment and evangelism. Few evangelicals were willing to claim that they belonged to the only true church, and most recognized that the other churches were doing much the same work, but in slightly different ways. Although at times denominational competition was fierce, in general the churches had little difficulty cooperating in ecumenical campaigns for the conversion of souls or the reformation of society.[18] For the most part, ecumenical cooperation, not separatism, was the predominant evangelical style in nineteenth-century America. It is not surprising, then, that the first generation of premillennialists after the Civil War worked hard at maintaining their denominational ties and counseled each other about the dangers of severing them.

The second generation of American dispensationalists, on the other hand, showed a marked decline in denominational loyalty. The conservative consensus, which had reigned supreme in evangelicalism before the turn of the century, broke apart. Liberalism, once advocated by only a few, spread quickly throughout schools and churches. What had seemed unthinkable to the first generation of premillennialists—the necessity of leaving apostate churches—did not appear so unthinkable after the turn of the century. To make separation easier, later premillennialists did not seem to need the support of the denominations as much as their predecessors had. Whereas the first generation of premillennialists required membership in good standing in evangelical churches to maintain their credibility, those in the second generation were able to draw on a totally independent base of support if they had to. The Bible institutes eventually acted as quasi-denominational centers for the premillennialists. Those institutions were far more than safe educational centers for evangelical young people. They developed reputations as centers of piety and sound doctrine. Their faculties constantly supplied local pulpits and Bible conferences. They produced a steady supply of pastors, teachers, and missionaries who maintained the faith and spread Bible-school loyalties. In short, the Bible institutes provided everything a premillennialist needed to get along. Moody Bible Institute, for example, was a magnet for premillennialist activities in the Middle West. It educated the young, sponsored numerous Bible and prophetic conferences, published periodicals and countless books on its own presses, and saw that they were distributed through its well-organized colportage association. Such activities produced tremendous loyalties among its constituents and friends, many of whom had deeper ties to the Institute than they did to their own denominations.[19] As a parody of a popular gospel song put it, "My hope is built on nothing less / Than Scofield's notes and Moody Press."

Similarly, drawing on the examples of such independent evangelicals as D. L. Moody, some premillennialists discovered that they could function successfully with little or no denominational support by establishing their own ecclesiastical empires. William Bell Riley, despite his active participation in the conflicts within the Northern Baptist Convention, clearly could go it alone if he had to. He was the pastor of the First Baptist Church of Minneapolis, headed his own Bible institute, and edited his own publication. His following extended far beyond the Twin Cities, and he commanded large forces inside and outside the Northern Baptist Convention.[20] Other premillennialist leaders developed similar personal empires and demonstrated that their denominational ties were expendable.[21]

One can easily see how this rather extreme separatist position might justify certain kinds of militant fundamentalist behavior. If the modernists in the churches were apostates, then there was no need to consider them Christian brothers or sisters or treat them with respect. They were playing into the hands of Satan and had become his agents in the destruction of the evangelical churches. Since their rise had been predicted in Scripture (e.g. II Tim. 3), there was no use in trying to lessen their influence or win them over.[22] In those circumstances, a person had only one alternative—leave.

Not all premillennialists followed this route. As we have already seen, some premillennialists refused to leave their churches or abandon them to modernists, even when they thought that apostasy was inevitable.

Once again, premillennialism could legitimately support more than one kind of response. Though one might be tempted to completely separate oneself from the growing apostasy in the churches, one might also decide to try to "occupy" until the Lord returned by winning back those who had strayed from the fundamentals of the faith, or at least by slowing down the slide to infidelity.

There were plenty of scriptural justifications for that kind of reaction. In his parable of the wheat and the tares (Matt. 13:24–30), Jesus indicated that until his return, the children of God and the children of the Devil would "grow" side by side and would not be separated until the "harvest" at the end of the age. Then and only then would the tares be separated out from the wheat and burned. Consequently, premillennialists could consistently choose to stay within their churches and do everything possible to stop the spread of modernism. Even Gaebelein admitted, albeit before he advised his readers that the modernistic cancer was too far gone to successfully operate, that the inevitability of apostasy was no excuse to be idle or throw up one's hands in despair. God still expected his people to oppose bad doctrine no matter what.

> Complete apostasy is on the way. But that does not mean that God's people should idly stand by and do nothing. Some have said, What is the use, we can not stop it? But we can be witness-bearers, contend for the faith, be used in snatching some out of the fire, and above all by our testimony against error, the Word of God and then our ever blessed and adorable Lord is exalted and glorified. It is pleasing to Him and He will not forget, but reward our faithfulness.[23]

In light of the possible delay of Christ or of his theoretically imminent appearance, one could choose either approach and still be well within premillennialist options.

Clearly, then, Sandeen was correct in criticizing Riley's statement about the eventual collapse of modernism—at times Riley seemed to get carried away with his abilities as a giant-killer. But Sandeen did not take into consideration the immense flexibility of the premillennialist system. Premillennialists acted differently during the fundamentalist controversy in the 1920s depending on their commitment to their denominations, their friendships within all theological parties, and the degree to which they accepted Darby's doctrine of the total ruin of Christendom. Just as some premillennialists were able to justify some involvement in reform efforts ("We're giving the Devil as much trouble as we can until Christ comes"), others were able to justify their forceful efforts to save the denominations. Just as premillennialists dedicated their lives to missionary service when they knew that their efforts could never convert the world, some premillennialists decided to remain within their churches to fight modernism at close quarters, even when they knew that in the end apostasy would have the last word—until Jesus came.

8

The Uncertain Sound

For if the trumpet give an uncertain sound, who shall prepare
himself to the battle?

I Corinthians 14:8

Losing the evangelical denominations to the modernists and their
supporters in the 1920s did not break the spirit of American premillennialism. Angered and appalled by the widespread demise of
evangelical orthodoxy, premillennialists knew that the apostasy of
Christendom had been clearly prophesied in the Scriptures. Once
they became resigned to the fact that liberalism had captured the
bulk of American Protestantism, most fundamentalists withdrew
from the mainline denominations and set about building their own
churches, schools, mission agencies, and publishing houses.[1]

Establishing their own separate religious subculture, however,
did not totally occupy the interests or consume the energies of the
premillennialists. Interpreters of prophecy were hard pressed to
keep up with the fast-changing events in the 1930s and 40s. In their
attempt to read the signs of the times, they often had major difficulty making the details of history fit together into their prophetic
puzzle.

Events in the thirties and forties provided ample grist for the
premillennialist mill: the continuing spread of apostasy, the Great
Depression, the rapid centralization of the United States government under the New Deal, changing mores in American society,

increasing divorce rates, and so on. But nothing riveted their attention more than the rise of totalitarian regimes and the growth of anti-Semitism. As previously indicated, premillennialists believed that to a large extent the coming of Antichrist will be facilitated by the growing popular acceptance of totalitarianism due to the breakdown of democratic political institutions.[2] Fearful of lawlessness, economic collapse, and escalating social chaos, people will gladly accept authoritarian solutions to their mounting problems. Naturally, then, premillennialists interpreted the rise of totalitarian regimes as significant signs along the road to Armageddon.

Since the boundaries of European nations were redrawn following World War I, premillennialists had been looking for signs of the emergence of the revived Roman Empire under Antichrist. For over a decade, Benito Mussolini and his rejuvenated fascist Italian "empire" kept students of prophecy guessing.

Like much of postwar Europe, Italy was in a state of economic, political, and social upheaval. Mussolini organized his first "combat groups" (*fasci di combattimento*) in 1919 and launched them on a campaign of violence and intimidation. Jockeying for power against the Popular (Catholic) party and the Socialists, the Fascists finally got the grudging, though often unenthusiastic, support of conservatives who feared "bolshevism" and of patriots who resented the meager "rewards" that Italy received at the Peace Conference of 1919. Though Fascists held only a few seats in the Chamber of Deputies, Mussolini was appointed premier in October 1922. He was unable, however, to put his program into practice until April 1924 when the Fascists finally obtained a majority in the Chamber, thanks to a rigged election in which terror was freely used. Once firmly in control, Mussolini deprived opponents of their seats in the Chamber, dissolved rival political parties, and stifled dissent.

Premillennialists watched Mussolini's rise to power with considerable fascination. Could he be the prophesied Man of Sin who would head up a new Roman Empire? He seemed to fulfill many, if not most, of the biblical criteria: he was charismatic, hungry for power, militaristic, and obviously intent on expansion. Furthermore, Mussolini was based in Rome, where most premillennialists believed the capital of the new empire would be located; and he had made peace with the largest segment of apostate Christendom, the Roman Catholic church, through the Lateran Treaty and the Concordat of 1929.

Given Mussolini's credentials, it is not surprising that as early as 1925, a few premillennialists began to speculate about the possible revival of the Roman Empire under Mussolini, the Antichrist.[3] Prophecy journals carried a story about an interview between *Il Duce* and Mr. and Mrs. Ralph Norton, Belgian premillennialists who were well known in American prophetic circles. During their meeting with Mussolini, they asked him if he intended to rebuild the Roman Empire. He answered that it would be impossible. "We can only revive its spirit, and be governed by the same discipline." Evidently the Nortons were not satisfied with his answer, so they informed him of the biblical prophecy about the new Roman Empire of the last days. According to the Nortons' report, "Mussolini leaned back in his chair and listened fascinated, and asked, 'Is that really described in the Bible? Where is it found?'"[4]

Despite the considerable evidence that Mussolini might be the Antichrist, most premillennialists wisely decided to remain open-minded until more data were in. Prudence demanded that biblical interpreters not rush to judgment. It was safer to view Mussolini as a prototype or paradigm of the beast, but not necessarily the beast himself. In 1933 James Gray commented on the final outcome of the struggle between Fascists and communists: "If we understand prophecy, it is Fascism that will win in the end, though possibly under another name, for the reason that superman when he appears will be a Mussolini on an international scale."[5] Three months later, Gray was a bit bolder in his evaluation of *Il Duce:*

> Whatever else may be true of Mussolini, he is not the Antichrist as some thoughtlessly imagine. Fascism, as we have said on other occasions, may aid in preparing the way for that superhuman despot, preparing it, that is, from the national or political side. But

> Fascism as Mussolini represents it is the protection of Italy from
> Vaticanism on the one hand, and Communism on the other.
> Therefore, for the present at least, it may be well to wish it
> succeeds.[6]

A few premillennialists continued to speculate about Mussolini
as the Antichrist; but most students of prophecy agreed with Gray
that he was only a "type" or forerunner of the beast.[7] For example,
when Mussolini invaded Ethiopia in October 1935, Leonard Sale-
Harrison argued that he should no longer be considered a viable
candidate for Antichrist. The invasion had so outraged the rest of
Europe that his popularity had drastically declined. Mussolini was
too egotistical, blunt, and undiplomatic, Sale-Harrison believed, to
be the beguiling despot of the last days. Nevertheless, he was serving an important prophetic role.

> Italy has been welded into an armed camp, which will be useful in
> the hands of a stronger and more cunning dictator. In other words,
> the resurrection of ancient Rome, even in the eyes of the most
> superficial observer, is certain of accomplishment, and is rapidly
> moving towards its goal, as prophesied in Holy Writ.[8]

In short, though Mussolini was probably not the Antichrist, he
was preparing the way for his coming. W. D. Herrstrom suggested
that by instituting the fascist salute, Mussolini had already pro-
gramed people to accept the mark of the beast (Rev. 13:16–18). "It is
certain that the people of the world will be required to raise their
right hands with a movement similar to the present Fascist salute, in
order to show the mark during the reign of the beast."[9]

After Mussolini's invasion of Ethiopia, that was about all prudent
premillennialists *could* say. Sale-Harrison had surmised correctly.
Italian expansionism did alienate western Europe. The League of
Nations immediately voted economic sanctions against the aggressor
but could not enforce the only one with teeth, the embargo on oil.
As a result, Italy was not deterred in its imperialism, but it was
politically and morally ostracized from the rest of western Europe.

There was, of course, one major exception to this antipathy toward Mussolini—Adolph Hitler's Nazi Germany. As the "two bad boys" of Europe, it was not surprising that Mussolini and Hitler joined forces. By the summer of 1936 the Rome-Berlin Axis existed in fact, though the formal agreement was not struck until October of the next year. That settled it, as far as most premillennialists were concerned. Germany will belong to the northern confederacy, not the revived Roman Empire. No Antichrist worth the name would make an alliance with Germany because in the end Rome and the nations of the northern confederacy will be enemies, not allies. Once the Rome-Berlin Axis was solidified, most premillennialists who had had high hopes for Mussolini as the Antichrist fell silent. There will be another.

One leading premillennialist teacher continued to look to Mussolini as the probable Antichrist: Louis Bauman, a Los Angeles pastor and part-time faculty member at the Bible Institute of Los Angeles. In 1940 he still believed that Mussolini was the prime candidate for the Man of Sin. "Notwithstanding a present common belief, the mastermind of Europe today is *not* in Berlin. Neither is he in Moscow, nor in London. In our opinion, the mastermind of Europe is in Rome." Bauman believed that Mussolini had cleverly and shrewdly maneuvered himself into a no-lose situation.

> Europe had not space enough for two Caesars. So the Roman Caesar invited the German Caesar down into his domain, tickled his vanity in a glorious parade of honor, formed an "axis" with him, and sent him back to Berlin with all the swell and swagger of a Napoleon ready to "lick the world"! He promptly began trampling beneath his spurred boots the helpless states to the east. None knew better than Mussolini that this would sooner or later involve him in endless difficulties with his powerful neighbors.[10]

When Hitler's adventurism drew England and France into the war, Mussolini held back his troops, waiting for the right moment to make his move. Bauman expected Mussolini to become the protector of the Balkans, then eventually strike an agreement with France and England. The Roman Empire was on the way.

For a while, at least, Adolph Hitler and Nazi Germany also seemed to have major prophetic significance. But eventually they too proved to be a major disappointment for premillennialists. With few exceptions, premillennial students of prophecy expected Germany and Russia to become the backbone of the northern confederacy. This view was based on their interpretation of Ezekiel 38 and 39, probably the most important passage on the battle of Armageddon and its participants. Premillennialists believed that "Gog" and "Magog" referred to Russia and its "prince" and that "Gomer" referred to Germany.[11] Throughout the 1930s, however, premillennialists were faced with an apparently insurmountable problem. Hitler was the sworn enemy of Bolshevism. How could Nazi Germany and communist Russia ever get together?

For the present, at least, premillennialists were willing to bide their time. In 1932, the *Moody Bible Institute Monthly* reported that in the previous year, the deposed German Kaiser had said, "Like the Russians, we cling with all our roots to the East. . . . Germany's next kin is Russia."[12] That was precisely what premillennialists wanted to hear. But the Kaiser's sentiments did not change current reality. During most of the 1930s, the great majority of premillennialists conceded that there was little chance of an alliance between the two countries as long as Hitler was in power. He was dedicated to the destruction of communism, so any agreement with Soviet Russia seemed out of the question.[13]

Consequently, most premillennialists were surprised when the two countries signed a nonaggression pact on August 23, 1939. Only a few interpreters had dared to predict that *Hitler* and *Stalin* would become "allies." But when the deal was struck, many premillennialists claimed prescience. Louis Bauman had hinted at the possibility of such an alliance in 1934:

> Many German editors insist that Germany can never march with the Bolsheviki. But stranger things than that have happened. Strange forces are at work these days in a world more afflicted with revolution and devolution than with evolution. When the

> hour strikes, Germany will tramp, Hitler and his Fascist brown
> shirts notwithstanding, with . . . *Gog!*[14]

Though he had not been nearly as specific as Bauman, Arno Gaebelein reminded the readers of *Our Hope* that he had predicted a
German-Russian alliance in *Harmony of the Prophetic Word* (1907),
more than thirty years before the event.[15]

Most premillennialists were elated by these developments, certain
that their reading of Scripture and current events had been vindicated. Five months before the signing of the nonaggression pact,
Moody Bible Institute announced a prophetic conference in New
York City for November 5–12, 1939.[16] Along with many of his
colleagues, Arno Gaebelein believed that the timing of the conference was providential. He pointed out that before other major
fulfillments of biblical prophecy, God had led him and others to
organize similar get togethers. In 1913, for example, a few months
before the outbreak of World War I, premillennialists gathered in
Chicago to discuss the signs of the times. In 1918, toward the end of
the war, conferences were held in Philadelphia (May) and New York
(November). When organizers scheduled their gathering for November 1939, they had no idea that they would be meeting at such
an auspicious time. God's hand had to be in it, Gaebelein wrote, and
suggested that the November meeting might be the most important
conference of them all: "For all we know, this may be the last
prophetic conference which will be held, for 'our gathering together
unto him' cannot be far away."[17]

Premillennialist euphoria was short-lived. In June 1941 Hitler
launched a massive *blitzkrieg* against Russia. Those who had seen the
Nazi-Soviet nonaggression pact as the beginning of the northern
confederacy were stunned. Students of prophecy seemed confused
and even a little embarrassed by the attack. In his study of the
premillennialist response to the Nazi invasion, Dwight Wilson
found "just one big awkward silence" from the prophetic experts.[18]
One premillennialist journal, however, did own up to its miscalcula-
tion. The *Evangel* acknowledged a certain perplexity at being caught

with prophetic egg on its face: "There are some prophets who are suffering no casualties. They are inspired writers of Bible prophecy. Their words shall be fulfilled. We may err when we forecast just how and when they will be fulfilled, but in God's own time the entire prophetic plan shall be complete."[19]

Soon after the breakdown of the Nazi-Soviet association, premillennialists encountered another problem. When the United States entered the war, Americans found themselves on the same side as the Russians. After the Bolshevik Revolution of 1917, premillennialists viewed Russia as a major center of satanic activity. In 1933 Arno Gaebelein published *Conflict of the Ages*, an elaborate exposé of the development and spread of the spirit of lawlessness in human society. Gaebelein believed that he had uncovered an enormous conspiracy to overthrow all established government, eliminate private property and inheritance laws, destroy patriotism, undermine family life, and obliterate religion. He found the indelible fingerprints of the plot in rationalism, the Illuminati, socialism, and communism. After 1917, he believed, the conspiracy was controlled from Moscow: "This six point program is now functioning in Russia through Communism and its ever-spreading propaganda."[20]

It is not surprising, then, that American premillennialists were not enthusiastic about having Russian allies. Most realized that cooperation with the Soviets was temporarily necessary to defeat the Nazis; but a few openly opposed it. In 1942 Louis Bauman warned that America should think twice about throwing in with the Russians. It would be better for the United States to lose the war than lose its soul by complicity in communist crimes.[21] Others predicted that after the war the United States and Russia would become the most bitter enemies. Though somewhat delayed, Armageddon was still on the way.[22]

For the most part, then, the fortunes of war smashed the early expectations of the premillennialists. Mussolini disqualified himself from the running for Antichrist when he joined forces with Hitler; and hopes for the formation of the northern confederacy were broken when Germany and Russia became enemies and the United States, temporarily at least, joined hands with the Soviets. Premillennialist scholars did not agree on America's place in prophecy, but none believed that the United States would be part of the Russian orbit in the last days.

During the thirties especially, most premillennialists also demonstrated a certain doublemindedness about anti-Semitism. On the one hand, they repeatedly condemned it as sin against God; but on the other, they saw it as an important part of the divine plan for the end of the age, due in large part to the sins of the Jews themselves. This ambivalence can most clearly be seen in the premillennialists' continuing interest in the *Protocols of the Elders of Zion*.

Arno Gaebelein was a master weaver of conspiracy theories. As already mentioned, Gaebelein believed that he could see an intricate web of conspiracies operating in human history. Satan, the great deceiver, had been working in virtually every revolutionary movement in the nineteenth and twentieth centuries. World domination was the Devil's goal; world revolution was his method.

Gaebelein studied the *Protocols* in great depth and concluded that Serge Nilus, the Russian who first published them in 1901, "was a believer in the Word of God, in prophecy, and must have been a true Christian." Though he could not definitively answer questions of authorship, Gaebelein was sure that the document was no "*crude forgery*. Behind it are hidden, unseen actors, powerful and cunning, who follow the plan still, bent on the overthrow of our civilization."[23] The identities of these conspirators, however, were not hidden from Gaebelein. They were Russian communists who were supported by their apostate Jewish allies.

Gaebelein amassed considerable evidence from a variety of sources (including some Jewish) to show that communism had Jewish roots and that the Bolshevik revolution of 1917 had been masterminded largely by a well-trained, fanatical cadre of Jewish agitators. Marx was a Jew; Lenin reportedly had a Jewish mother; and Trotsky, whose real name was Bronstein, had lived for a while in New

York City's predominately Jewish lower east side before he returned
to Russia to become the "main instigator of this program of hell."
Gaebelein cited sworn testimony before a United States Senate sub-
committee by Dr. George A. Simons, a former director of Methodist missions in Russia, and numerous news reports from the London
Times, the French journal *L'Ilustration*, and the *Jewish Chronicles* to
prove the Jewish-communist connection. Even Jews themselves,
Gaebelein observed, admitted the ties between the two: "The ideals
of Bolshevism at many points are consonant with the *finest ideals of
Judaism.*"[24]

For Gaebelein, the *Protocols* provided the undeniable link between
Jews and the international communist conspiracy. "The most
important fact is that throughout the twenty-four Protocols we have
a *very pronounced re-statement of the principal theories of Illuminism and
Marxism*" (italics his).[25] Furthermore, he thought that the current
Jewish-communist conspiracy will eventually lead to the ultimate
confrontation between the forces of good and evil, Christ and Antichrist, at Armageddon. Unlike most of his premillennialist colleagues, Gaebelein expected the Antichrist to be a renegade Jew who
will head up an evil coalition of apostate Jews and Gentiles. Although Gaebelein did not believe that all Jews were involved in
antisocial and lawless behavior, he saw evidence that "bad" Jews
were starting to outnumber "good" Jews.

> Here we must draw attention to the fact that while there is an on-
> sweeping apostasy in Christendom, there is also a corresponding
> Jewish apostasy, or rather infidelity. Any Christian will honor the
> orthodox Old Testament believing Jews, who still cling to the
> hope of a coming Messiah, and who pray for His coming and
> expect him. . . . But they are becoming less. The greater part of
> Jewry has become reformed, or as we call it "deformed." They no
> longer believe in the law and in the prophets. The Messiah and the
> glorious future is looked upon as a delusion. . . . Turning away
> from the hope of their fathers and their own Scriptures, they
> become infidels and finally through their reaching out after mate-
> rial things and power they become a menace. The lower elements

become lawless. As we have shown, these infidel Jews were prominent in the revolutionary propaganda during the nineteenth century. Karl Marx, the author of the "Communist Bible," was an infidel Jew, so was Lasalle and hundreds of others active in the socialistic-anarchistic and communistic activities. Trotsky and at least two score other leaders of the Russian revolution were apostate Jews. They make themselves felt in our country and in other civilized countries. Watching the names of those who were arrested in anti-government demonstrations, we find that a large percentage are Jews.[26]

Gaebelein made a clear distinction between orthodox Jews and their irreligious brethren. The orthodox were "reachable"; their unbelieving fellow Jews were not. During the Great Tribulation, after the church has been raptured, "the orthodox Jews, who have held on to the faith of their fathers, who pray for the coming of the Messiah-King, whose eyes are [now] blinded that they cannot see, from them the veil will be removed." They are the prophesied remnant that will be saved. Most Jews, however, will experience a different fate. "The international Jews, the political-financial schemers, the lawless elements, who ridicule and hate religion of any kind and are atheists . . . these Jews will worship the beast. They reject the true Christ and accept the false Messiah."[27]

Did these views make Gaebelein anti-Semitic? In light of his entire career, his years of service to Jews, and his persistent championing of Jewish rights, it would be misleading and facile to so label him. His writings reveal a sincere love for Jews, especially orthodox ones. Because of their ancient covenant with God, they are God's chosen people. Though they had forfeited their place in the center of God's redemptive plan because of their rejection of Christ, someday God will make them the focus of His activity once again.

Yet there is another side of Gaebelein that must be accounted for. Despite the substantial evidence supporting his positive feelings for Jews, his writings also contain certain negative elements. He sincerely cared for Jews but he deplored what had become of them because of their rebellion against God. Thanks to the corroding acids of modernity, most were now apostates. Because of their unique standing with God, there was something especially loathsome about "fallen" Jews. "There is nothing so vile on earth as an apostate Jew who denies God and His Word."[28] Infidels were often a "menace" to society, a threat to God-fearing and law-abiding people. While he wanted all Jews to be saved, Gaebelein realized that at present they were under a "national blood-guiltiness" that would not be wiped away until the Second Coming.[29] Nevertheless, he hated and condemned anti-Semitism. Before most people knew or seemed to care, he denounced with moral outrage the Nazi persecution of the Jews.[30] But by giving credence to tales of international Jewish conspiracies, he affirmed many of the arguments that anti-Semites used to justify their war against the Jews. In that way, Gaebelein was giving unintentional ideological support to the forces of anti-Semitism.[31]

How can we account for Gaebelein's mixed message? It seems clear that his premillennialism, not his personal feelings, was at the root of his ambivalence. Premillennial eschatology is, after all, a conspiracy theory of cosmic proportions. Consequently, its adherents have been somewhat susceptible to ideas of clandestine plots, sinister forces, and satanic subterfuge. That is why people like Gaebelein who showed authentic affection for Jews could also portray them in negative and even hostile terms. Premillennialism is amazingly adaptable. It can be used to defend Jewish rights, defame Jewish infidelity, or disclose Jewish plots against humanity. Sometimes it does all three at the same time.[32] In his *Fundamentalism and American Culture*, George Marsden observed that between the two world wars, Fundamentalists "could be both pro-Zionist and somewhat anti-Semitic, favoring the return of the Jews to Israel, which would lead eventually to their conversion; yet in the meantime especially distrusting apostate Jews."[33] Though historians might argue over the scope and definition of Marsden's "somewhat," they must finally recognize that both sentiments could and often did exist simultaneously in American premillennialism.

Gaebelein was not the only premillennialist to see a Semitic dimension to the international communist conspiracy. William Bell Riley, a Baptist from Minnesota who commanded a national following, also believed that the *Protocols* revealed Jewish and communist collusion.[34] Yet as convincing as the evidence seemed to men like Gaebelein and Riley, by the mid-1930s many premillennialists were beginning to shy away from using the *Protocols* in their prophetic teaching.

James M. Gray of Moody Bible Institute may serve as a case in point. Like most premillennialists in the 1920s, Gray believed that the *Protocols* were the actual secret plans of Jewish conspirators. In 1921 he called the documents "a clinching argument for premillennialism."[35] Because he believed in their authenticity, he felt he could defend Henry Ford when he published them in his *Dearborn Independent*. In a 1927 editorial in the *Moody Bible Institute Monthly*, Gray claimed that Ford "had good grounds for publishing some of the things about the Jews. . . . Mr. Ford might have found corroborative evidence [of the Jewish conspiracy] had he looked for it."[36]

By late 1933 Gray was under increasing pressure to repudiate the *Protocols*. The evangelical *Hebrew Christian Alliance Quarterly* criticized *Moody Bible Institute Monthly*, *The Sunday School Times*, and Donald Grey Barnhouse's magazine *Revelation* for not condemning the *Protocols* as a forgery and doing more to stem the tide of anti-Semitism. It did not take long for Gray to respond. In an editorial in the Institute's *Monthly*, he affirmed the *Protocols'* validity and pointed out that Moody Bible Institute had always worked for the highest interests of Jews by training people to evangelize them. He warned that anti-Semitism was a horrible sin, but added that Jews will suffer worse things if they do not accept Jesus as their Messiah. Furthermore, he hinted that Jews were at least partly to blame for their ill treatment. To support his views, he referred to an article in the same issue of the *Hebrew Christian Alliance Quarterly* by Max Reich, a faculty member in the Institute's Jewish missions department. Reich mourned the fact that many American Jews were becoming "de-

Judaized without becoming Christian." As a result they posed a major problem. "Without religion, the Jew goes down and becomes worse than others, as a corruption of the best is always the worst corruption." A bad Jew was somehow worse than a bad Gentile. To further substantiate his suggestion that Jews were partially responsible for anti-Semitism, Gray cited Rabbi Elias Margolis, president of the Rabbinical Assembly of New York, who had recently observed that if Jews wanted justice and fair treatment from others, they must be willing to give the same in return.[37]

Needless to say, Gray's defense did not put an end to the controversy. Accusations of anti-Semitism kept coming. By the beginning of 1935, Gray was fending off charges from the *American Hebrew and Jewish Tribune*, the *Bulletin of the Baltimore Branch of the American Jewish Congress*, and even *Time* magazine[38] that persons connected with Moody had been actively distributing the *Protocols*. Gray defended the Institute in an address over MBI's radio station and eventually published his remarks in the Institute's magazine. Gray never categorically denied the charge; but he did say that he deplored their dissemination from any *Christian* source. He called anti-Semitism "one of the most despicable, brutal and dangerous forms of racial hatred and antagonism known to mankind," and added that it had no place in Christian civilization. "It is true that Jehovah has awfully cursed Israel for her sins, and His curse rests upon her today. But it is one thing for God to curse her and another thing for us to do so."[39]

Due to this growing criticism, some of it from fellow evangelicals, Gray was beginning to see that the use of the *Protocols* had become more of a liability than an asset. As long as the *Protocols* seemed to be "a clinching argument for premillennialism," he never thought twice about using them. But when their use brought charges of anti-Semitism, it was time to think again. As an opponent of anti-Semitism in all its forms, Gray decided to do without them. Though he never quite repudiated their reliability, he suggested that the Bible, after all, contained all the information about Jews that Christians needed to know. "Therefore, in the present state of the public mind on this question, my advice to Christians would be this: Let us confine ourselves to the Bible and leave the Protocols alone."[40]

Other premillennialists showed the same kind of uneasiness over using the *Protocols* in their prophetic teaching. In *Shirts and Sheets: or Anti-Semitism, a Present-Day Sign of the First Magnitude*, Louis Bauman admitted that the *Protocols* had become a divisive issue among premillennialists. In light of the controversy, he decided to avoid the question of their authenticity. Even if they were true, he went on, they reflected the views of only a few fanatical Jews and did not represent the whole race.[41] Four years later, when he published a more extensive examination of anti-Semitism entitled *The Time of Jacob's Trouble*, he did not even mention them.[42] Likewise by the mid-thirties, the *Evangel* consistently maintained that the *Protocols* were a forgery, though it recognized that they were still being used in premillennialist circles.[43]

Clearly, then, premillennialists did not need the *Protocols* to substantiate their understanding of the flow of history. They were serviceable as long as they were not so closely tied with organized anti-Semitism; but when using them made premillennialists look bad, most students of prophecy quickly found them expendable. The last thing premillennialists wanted was to appear anti-Semitic.

Consequently, the premillennialist response to growing anti-Semitism in the 1930s is instructive. As already indicated, though they consistently condemned the hatred of Jews, premillennialists believed that increased anti-Semitism was clearly predicted for the last days. Thus, though they dissociated themselves from it, they fully expected it to occur. Earlier than almost anyone else except Jews themselves, premillennialists were cognizant of growing anti-Semitism in the 1930s. Premillennialist authors kept their readers fully informed of the growth of anti-Semitism around the world and tried to put it within their prophetic perspective.[44] In 1938, for instance, long before the rest of the world was aware of such places, premillennialists knew all about Buchenwald.[45]

Naturally, people with their eyes on the growth of anti-Semitism kept their gaze fixed on Germany in the 1930s. Adolph Hitler became German Chancellor in January 1933 and within six months had performed a *gleichschaltung*, a "bringing into line" of the German nation. Thanks to the terrorist campaign of his Storm Troopers, Hitler bullied the Reichstag (German parliament) into passing the Enabling Act of March 23, 1933. This legislation gave Hitler and his Nazi Party the power to rule by decree for four years and turned Germany into a virtual dictatorship. With these new powers, Hitler moved quickly to silence all dissent. By the end of the summer, most of Hitler's opponents were in jail, in hiding, in exile, or in concentration camps.

Premillennialists kept close tabs on these goings on and reported them in detail. Once Hitler's intentions became clear, premillennialists condemned them unswervingly. But until the full import of Hitler's policies were known, many premillennialists were slow to judge Germany's new Chancellor. To a large extent their hesitation grew out of their inability to decide whom to believe about Hitler. Since Christians in Germany were far from united in their appraisal of the Nazis, it is not surprising that American premillennialists were confused.

Hitler knew that if his policies were to succeed, he would either have to woo or neutralize the churches. First the Nazis went to work on German Catholics. On July 20, 1933, a Nazi-Vatican Concordat was signed. In this agreement, Catholics essentially agreed to stay out of German politics in return for Hitler's promise to safeguard the freedom of Catholics to practice their religion. But Hitler had no intention of honoring his pledge. In 1935 the Nazis began a series of vicious attacks against the Roman church. In a sensational propaganda campaign, nuns and priests were accused of smuggling, disloyalty to the state, and sexual immorality. By 1937 these assaults had accomplished their goal. Nearly all Catholic schools were closed; and those that remained open were under constant pressure to conform to Nazi doctrine. In response, Pope Pius XI issued *Mit brennender Sorge* ("with burning sorrow"), a papal encyclical that condemned Nazism for its racial policies, deification of the state, and blatant paganism. Hitler was furious at this show of Catholic independence, but chose to ignore it, confident that he had the support of most Catholic laypeople. Though a few Catholic bishops managed to continue their public criticism of Nazi policies, for all intents and purposes, the Roman church ceased to be a factor in national life.[46]

The Protestant state churches did not fare much better. In 1932, the year before Hitler came to power, a group of pro-Nazi Protestant leaders organized the "German Christians," a group that wanted the churches to serve the aims of the Nazi Party. Thus an intense struggle for control of the Protestant churches began. Before the Third Reich was inaugurated, the "state church" actually consisted of twenty-eight regional Lutheran and Reformed bodies. The "Evangelical Nazis," as the German Christians were also called, wanted to unify these groups into a single national church and put them under the control of a governing synod and a Reichsbishop. After a campaign of propaganda and terror, the German Christians managed to force through a new church constitution and elect a Nazi, Ludwig Mueller, as Reichsbishop. Once in control, the German Christians tried to "Aryanize" the church by excluding from church office all those with Jewish blood. By 1933 the German Christian movement claimed a membership of three thousand out of a total of about seventeen thousand Protestant ministers.

Most German Protestant laypeople and a large number of their pastors were confused by high-level ecclesiastical politics and did not understand at first what was at stake in the conflict. But by the end of 1933, most saw clearly where the Nazi program was headed. In November of that year the German Christians unveiled their program for all to see. They wanted to revise the New Testament to show the German ancestry of Jesus, eliminate the Old Testament from church life, and create a separate church for Jewish Christians. That declaration helped to mobilize and unify the opposition. Pastor

Martin Niemoeller and other evangelical pastors organized the Pastor's Emergency League, which in turn brought into being the "Confessing Church." It refused to recognize the authority of the new church constitution or the Reichsbishop. In its "Barmen Confession" of May 1934 it declared openly its hostility to National Socialism and committed itself to the lordship of Jesus Christ and loyalty to the gospel. When the Confessing Church grew to about seven thousand pastors, the German Christians realized that they had failed in their attempt to unite the Protestant churches under the Nazi banner. But the anti-Nazi Protestants paid heavily for their dissent. In 1935 an anti-Christian Nazi named Hans Kerrl was appointed Reichsminister for Church Affairs. He quickly confiscated the funds of the Confessing Church, forbade its supporters from raising more, and ordered them to stop training new ministers. In addition, the Gestapo arrested hundreds of evangelical pastors and threatened additional thousands. By 1936 most of the Confessing Church's leaders were behind bars, and the rest were forced "underground."[47]

By the end of 1935, Hitler's true intentions toward the churches were clear. But in 1933 and most of 1934 many American premillennialists found it difficult to understand what was actually happening in Germany. They struggled to sift through radically different evaluations of the situation, all purportedly from Christian sources.

In light of the conflicting reports coming out of Germany, James Gray believed that it was wise to present divergent perspectives in the *Moody Bible Institute Monthly*. In the July 1934 issue, for example, he printed a letter from Ernst Modershohn, a German pastor.[48] The German clergyman denied that Christian Jews were being excluded from the churches, that Christians were supporting the boycott against Jewish businesses, and that reading from the Old Testament had ceased in public services, as had been reported.

> This statement is one of the many lies which are being circulated among the different nations in order to find fault with the new republic in which we live, and to arouse suspicions against its

aims. . . . We are very thankful that we now have among our
nation peace and harmony and this in a way as we never had it in
the history of Germany.

Similarly, in the next issue, Gray published side by side pro- and
anti-Hitler pieces. In "The New Germany and the Evangelical
Church," Paul Umlauf of Berlin denied that the new Nazi regime
was hostile to religion. "Chancellor Hitler, in his national socialist
program, has made it clear that he looks upon Christianity as the
cultural foundation on which the new state must be built." Hitler
wanted the churches to run their own internal affairs; but they had
proved themselves to be incapable. Social-Democrats and Marxists
who had been pushed out of the nation's political life had now
infiltrated the church and were trying to use it for their own political
ends.

> Thus the government was compelled to take a stand and to under-
> take the work which it was really the duty of the churches to
> attend to. . . . The ways of Providence are too difficult to under-
> stand; and if God thinks fit to do so, He will call upon the tempo-
> rary powers to adjust any errors that may have crept into the
> government of the church.

Umlauf believed that the crisis in the churches necessitated the election of the Reichsbishop and the appointment of Nazi commissars to
monitor church life.[49]

On the other side, Gray reprinted an editorial from the April 1934
issue of the *Bulletin* of the Federal Council of Churches. It painted a
much different picture of government involvement in church affairs.
It referred to Nazi propaganda, threats, ruthless force, and deception. It condemned the forced election of the Reichsbishop and reported that the selection of students for ministerial training had been
turned over to the Hitler Youth. "The leaders of this frankly nationalistic and increasingly pagan organization make no secret of
their desire to make God salute Hitler if He wishes to have an
official place in German life."[50]

No one should be misled by such evenhandedness. As already stated, in the beginning it was not clear to many Germans, let alone most American premillennialists, where Nazi policies were heading. As Gray stated in late 1934, "We would not be interpreted as holding a brief for Herr Hitler and Nazism, but we always wish to be fair."[51] Despite Gray's desire to be fair, he could be critical of Hitler when he thought that he had his facts straight. In January 1934 Gray attacked the "German Christian" attempt to rid the churches of Jewish converts and the Old Testament:

> Aryanism versus Semitism in government is hardly our business, but to deny that there is neither Jew nor Gentile in Christ touches the very quick. Protocols or no Protocols, the Christian Jew is the brother of the Christian Gentile and a fellow member of the body of Christ. . . . We repeat, we would not interfere with the autonomy of the German nation. The Nazis may or may not have justifiable cause for objecting to what they consider Jewish dominance in the state, but shall the witnesses to Jesus Christ hold their peace when *He* is assailed?[52]

By March 1935 Gray so clearly recognized the Nazi threat to the churches that he even endorsed an appeal for aid by theological liberals. Earlier in the year, the ecumenical Conference on Life and Work made a plea for money and prayer on behalf of the beleaguered German churches. In what seemed slightly out of character in a fundamentalist periodical, Gray declared that though the American representatives of the Life and Work movement were "modernists," evangelical Christians ought to support this worthy cause. In order to give more weight to his argument, Gray added that Moody's new president, Will H. Houghton, had been in Germany the previous summer and fully agreed that the situation was serious. Fundamentalists, therefore, should feel free to pray for and possibly even give money to the liberal-sponsored project. During times of intense crisis, one could temporarily overlook theological differences.[53]

In light of Gray's growing awareness, it is curious that in the fall of 1935 he published without comment a blatantly pro-Hitler letter to the editor from a German national living in Maryland. The writer identified herself as an old woman and devout Christian who prayed regularly for the second coming of Christ. She praised the magazine for not misjudging Hitler and passed along reliable information that the *Fuehrer* "studies the New Testament." She claimed that all her German relatives, who were also devout evangelical Christians, loved Hitler, prayed for him, and refused to believe everything that his enemies said against him. Furthermore, she reported that during a recent trip to the Reich, she witnessed complete freedom in the churches to preach Christ. "We believe that Christ will come soon and that He will be merciful to Hitler too. Hitler's father was a drinker, but Adolph lives with his mother and is a very good son."[54] Either Gray had quite a sense of humor, or he was not as "enlightened" as he should have been in 1935.

Of course, as difficult as things became for Christians in Germany, Jews suffered much more from Hitler's policies. In *Mein Kampf* (1924) Hitler blamed the Jews for almost every ailment in German society. He never deviated from the conviction that Jews controlled the German economy and threatened to "contaminate" the "pure blood" of the Aryan master race. Before gaining power, Nazis had to be content with attacking Jews in the press and occasionally beating and even murdering them in the streets. But after the Enabling Act, they took more organized and ruthless action. In September 1935 the Nurnberg Laws were passed. These regulations forbade Jews from marrying or having sexual relations with Aryans. (A Jew was defined as anyone with at least one Jewish grandparent.) By the end of 1938 Jews were expelled from the civil service and virtually excluded from government positions, the professions, and cultural life. When a Jewish boy assassinated the German diplomat Vom Rath in November 1938, the Nazis used this as an excuse to increase their violence against the Jewish population. Jewish businessmen were forced to liquidate their financial concerns at a loss, and Jews who had not yet emigrated were systematically rounded up.

At first some premillennialists were slow to condemn Nazi policies toward the Jews because they did not understand them. For example, soon after Hitler's accession to power in the spring of 1933, James Gray wanted readers of the *Moody Bible Institute Monthly* "to suspend their judgment about Germany's present dealings with the Jews until both sides have an opportunity to be heard." After stating that he hated anti-Semitism in any form, he referred to evidence that Hitler might not be guilty of all of which he had been accused:

> We learn from private sources, more than one, and worthy of respect at least, that the Jews in Germany are not being persecuted as a race, but that Communism organized by Russian Jews is being punished by Hitler. Former government positions, it is said, were held by Jews, and in every form of business they were given preference over Germans. Jewish artists, for example, always received the prizes in the art exhibits.

Gray went on to quote a letter from a German believer who claimed that the reports of bloody attacks against Jews that appeared in the foreign press were actually circulated by Social-Democrats or communists who wanted to defame the *Fuehrer*. According to Gray's German source, over 90 percent of those alleged anti-Jewish attacks were actually communist attacks against Nazis. Gray noted that "there are Jews and Jews just as there are Gentiles and Gentiles" and that communists are known for using "satanic propagandism" to achieve their ends. He then confessed to being honestly confused by such conflicting reports and to being in need of more information before he could make up his mind about Hitler's treatment of the Jews.[55]

But by 1935 and the passage of the Nurnberg Laws, Hitler's intentions were unmistakable, and premillennialists saw no need to listen to both sides. They followed the playing out of Hitler's genocidal policies with horror. Gaebelein's *Our Hope,* the *Moody Monthly,* and other premillennialist journals carried regular reports on the Nazi campaign against the Jews and tried to make sense of it in terms of biblical prophecy. Premillennialists believed that the holocaust was the harbinger of the predicted "time of Jacob's trouble" (Jer. 30:5–7) and the result of the Jews' rebellion against God.[56] Like Nebuchadnezzar's Babylonians in the Old Testament, Hitler's Nazis were in a sense agents of God's judgment against his rebellious people. But because they dared to strike against Abraham's seed, God will judge them too. Although God intended the Jews to suffer, his wrath was tempered with mercy. Ultimately, God's purposes were redemptive, not punitive. God was using the Nazi horror to bring Jews to faith in Jesus Christ and rekindle their desire for a homeland in Palestine.

Consequently, premillennialists both grieved for the Jews in their suffering and rushed to take spiritual advantage of their plight. Of first importance in their response was prayer. In 1939 a veritable who's who of premillennialist leaders issued a call for an international day of prayer for the Jews. The organizers suggested a full day of activities for December 1, but nowhere did they urge Christians to pray for the persecutions to cease. Instead, they told people to pray for Jewish conversions.

> Workers among the Jews in America, Europe, Palestine, and other lands agree that the hearts of the chosen people are more open and receptive to the Word of God and the gospel message today than ever before. The terrific persecutions in Europe, the troubles in Palestine, and the ever-increasing anti-Semitism throughout the world have softened their hearts and made them long for security and rest of soul.

Thus the prayer-day organizers concluded, the best thing they could do for suffering Jews was to send them more New Testaments and evangelists.[57]

In general that was the message of the Jewish missionary agencies: in the midst of persecution and death, God had given the church an unprecedented opportunity to win the Jews for Christ. Premillennialists had always been extremely interested in Jewish evangelism, and, in return, Jewish missionary agencies advertised heavily in premillennialist journals.[58] In one issue of the *Moody Monthly*, for example, there were advertisements from the Friends of Israel Refugee Relief Committee (Philadelphia), the New York Gospel Mission to the Jews, the Hebrew Christian Alliance of America (Chicago), the New York Jewish Evangelization Society, the Hebrew Christian Mission (Detroit), and the Hebrew Christian Society (Cleveland). In one of its advertisements, the New York Jewish Evangelization Society stated that "these Jewish persecutions may be in God's providence our opportunity to win them to Christ and show that we really care."[59] Almost three years earlier, President Will Houghton of Moody Bible Institute declared that persecution had dramatically increased the longing for the coming of Messiah among orthodox Jews and that this had made them more open to the gospel. In fact, because of the fear of an impending Nazi invasion in the summer of 1939, it was reported that there had been a mass turning to Christ among Warsaw's Jewish youth. "Perhaps that is the reason the Devil saw to it that Warsaw was wrecked and the Jews scattered."[60] Premillennialists never produced any statistics to prove that being persecuted by Gentiles made Jews more open to the message of Christian evangelists. But the assertion appears throughout premillennialist literature.

One should not conclude from all this that premillennialists cared only about converting Jews to Christ. There was an authentic humanitarian concern as well. No one could read, for example, Gaebelein's news reports from Germany in 1937 about Jewish suffering without detecting an authentic concern for their welfare.[61] In early 1939 the *Moody Monthly* carried an article entitled "An Appeal for Persecuted Israel." The article presented an accurate picture of the Jewish situation under Nazism and declared that well over six million European Jews, including at least a million Jewish Christians, were in peril of their lives. The appeal called Christians to action:

> God is calling his people to show forth mercy, sympathy, love, and substantial help to the Jews and to the Jewish Christians of Central Europe. Under no circumstances would we differentiate between races or religions in an appeal for help. All belong to the great suffering human family.

In order to meet this critical need, a number of prominent evangelical leaders organized the Friends of Israel Refugee Relief Committee. Based in Philadelphia and administered by a number of Christian businessmen and ministers, the Committee solicited funds to alleviate the suffering of Jews, regardless of their religious convictions.[62] The Committee was serious about its relief efforts. Subsequent advertisements asked for money to provide emergency food and housing for displaced Jews.[63]

As terrible as the persecutions were, premillennialists were confident that they would not ultimately succeed. "Jew haters never learn anything from history. . . . Anti-Semitism is futile because it is fighting against God. . . . The Jewish people are indestructible."[64] Although the God of Abraham might permit the Jews to suffer severely, he would not allow their extinction. God's entire prophetic program hinged on getting them back to Palestine to reestablish the nation of Israel in preparation for Armageddon and the second coming of Christ.[65] Nazi persecutors, therefore, were accomplishing more than they knew. Not only were they making Jews more susceptible to the gospel message, they were also preparing the way for the greatest fulfillment of biblical prophecy in the twentieth century, the reestablishment of the state of Israel in Palestine. According to Harry Rimmer, "By driving the preserved people back into the preserved land, Hitler, who does not believe the Bible and who sneers at the Word of God, is helping to fulfil its most outstanding prophecy."[66]

In retrospect, premillennialists had shown more enthusiasm than accuracy in their interpretations of the roles of Italy, Germany, and Russia before and during the war. Their leaders were confident *that* biblical prophecy was being fulfilled, but events kept forcing them to reevaluate their interpretations of *how* it was being fulfilled. One is struck by how forgiving and forgetful the premillennialist rank and file must have been during this period. They stuck by their leaders even when they misread the signs of the times. The leaders themselves seemed little deterred by their mistakes. Events were changing so quickly that they had little time for apologies. There were more books to write and more conferences to attend. Many premillennialists were aware of their rather poor track record and were rather sensitive about it. In 1942, after so many early speculations about the new Roman Empire and the northern confederacy proved to be mistaken, William Culbertson, then president of Moody Bible Institute, offered a defense of sorts. He pointed out that while students of prophecy had been wrong in the past, they were not nearly so wrong as those who deny prophetic truth. "Suppose there are some eccentrics in the realm of prophecy. What does that prove? Suppose some sincere enthusiast expressed an opinion made ridiculous by current history. What of it? Scientists have not thrown science on the scrap heap because some theories of other days are now discarded."[67]

Culbertson's attempt to lessen the significance of interpretive errors probably convinced already-committed premillennialists. But it did not adequately address the problem. Some of the movement's most respected teachers, not just a lonely eccentric here and there, had been "made ridiculous by current history." Furthermore, premillennialist Bible scholars were not scientists who were theorizing about the make-up of an obscure and confusing universe. They presented themselves as students of the "sure word of prophecy" who claimed to have an infallible guide for the unraveling of future events. No premillennialist Bible scholar claimed omniscience for his interpretations, but few showed much humility or tentativeness either. It is difficult to attract or keep a clientel with "mights" and "maybes." When times are terrifying and people need assurance that everything is going according to the divine plan, premillennialists prefer "there's-no-doubt-about-its."[68]

Earlier in the century premillennialists had made their case to the American public largely on the basis of their ability to fit together prophecy and current events. Their performance before and during the war years might have undercut completely any claim to credibility had it not been for one thing. Shortly after the war, the most important prophetic expectation of the century was fulfilled. The ancient state of Israel was restored in Palestine. Premillennialists could afford to forgive and forget. That one fulfilled prophecy gave premillennialism a new lease on life and brought it more credibility and visibility than ever.

9

The Sign of Thy Coming

Tell us, when shall these things be? and what shall be the sign of
thy coming, and of the end of the world?

Matthew 24:3

The founding of the state of Israel in 1948 gave American premillennialists the reference point that they had been waiting for. The
existence of Israel revitalized premillennialism and gave it, at least in
its own eyes, undeniable credibility. More than any other event in
the twentieth century, the rebirth of Israel meant that the prophetic
clock was winding down, that premillennialists must press home
their gospel of the near approach of the second coming and the end
of the age. In short, since the late 1940s, premillennialists have
achieved their greatest exposure and their widest hearing. They
have reached more people than ever and have proved themselves to
be adaptable to the times.

As already indicated, premillennialists had been counting on the
reestablishment of the state of Israel from the beginning of the nineteenth century.[1] Therefore they watched and often actively supported the early Zionist movement. When the Balfour Declaration
of 1917 committed the British government to "the establishment in
Palestine of a national home for the Jewish people," premillennialists
were ecstatic. It looked like a fulfillment of Jeremiah 29:14: "And I
will be found of you, saith the Lord: and I will turn away your
captivity, and I will gather you from all the nations, and from all the
places whither I have driven you, saith the Lord; and I will bring

you again into the place whence I caused you to be carried away captive." In the years following World War I, they carefully monitored Jewish immigration to Palestine and felt confident that prophecy was being fulfilled before their eyes.[2]

The native Arab population in Palestine, however, did not share the same enthusiasm. Even though the Balfour Declaration promised that "nothing shall be done which may prejudice the civil and religious rights of existing non-Jewish communities in Palestine," most Arabs were convinced that a Jewish state would mean the loss of Arab rights and property. In the spring of 1920, Arabs rioted over the liberal British immigration policy for Jews. And in 1929 an apparently insignificant incident concerning Jewish practices at the Wailing Wall escalated into bloodshed. As the only thing remaining of Herod's temple, the wall was a sacred place for Jews. They naturally considered it "theirs" and often forgot that they were allowed there out of Arab deference. What had been part of a Jewish temple in the first century was now part of a Moslem mosque in the twentieth, the mosque of Omar, a sacred place for Moslems. On Yom Kippur, 1929, some of the Jews who had gathered at the wall to pray tried to erect a partition to separate male and female worshipers. The Arabs objected, and rioting broke out. When the fighting ended, the Jews had suffered 472 dead and wounded, the Arabs, 348.

Arab/Jewish conflict did not stop there. Throughout the 1930s, tensions smoldered just below the surface, and often erupted into the open. In 1933–34 there were Arab riots against Jews and their British supporters. And in 1936 there were Arab strikes and widespread terrorism. Understandably, by the late thirties, the British were beginning to have second thoughts about their policies. After the 1936 riots, the British government authorized a Royal Commission to review the Palestine situation. In July 1937 the Commission recommended, in the spirit of compromise, that the region be partitioned into Arab and Jewish states.

Premillennialists watched these developments and generally did not like them. They believed that God had given Palestine to the Jews, and though the Jews had been displaced from it because of their disobedience, they still held title.[3] On the basis of Genesis 15:18, premillennialists even suggested that the Jews had a right to more than Palestine proper: "In the same day the Lord made a covenant with Abram, saying, Unto thy seed have I given this land, from the river of Egypt unto the great river, the river Euphrates."[4] By divine decree, Israel's rightful borders extended from the Nile to the Euphrates, from Egypt to Iraq.

Naturally, these sentiments raised the issues of justice and international law. Despite ancient promises to the Jews, Palestine was currently occupied by a substantial Arab population. Arab peoples had been in possession of the land for centuries. What about the rights of the Arab majority? What of self-determination, democratic principles, and simple human fairness? As a whole, premillennialists were not unconcerned about these matters; but they cared more about the fulfillment of biblical prophecy. In 1931 because of growing Arab opposition, the British cut back on Jewish immigration to Palestine. James Gray observed in a *Moody Bible Institute Monthly* editorial that Pharaoh had tried that some time earlier, with disastrous results, and that despite the British effort to keep Jews in a minority position, they will never submit to Arab rule. In a subsequent letter to the magazine, a reader objected to Gray's apparent disregard for democratic principles. Gray answered that when it comes to the Jews in Palestine, "the ordinary rules of statesmanship do not work." They are not obligated to "be governed by the principles that maintain in a democracy like the United States. . . . The Jews were, are, and always shall remain a peculiar people, and the reason why a 'reversion' should be 'sanctioned' in their case, and why it certainly will come to pass, is because Jehovah has so ordained it."[5]

Given this perspective, premillennialists viewed the native Arab population in generally negative terms. Because of their ties to ancestral lands, they were ostensibly impeding the fulfillment of prophecy. Premillennialists were not quite sure how to account for Arab hostility against the Jews. Some viewed it as a modern continuation of the biblical fraternal feuds between Ishmael and Isaac or Esau and Jacob. In either case, the Arabs were the "usurpers," the Jews the true "sons."[6] Others blamed Arab resistance on communist, Nazi, or simply satanic influences.[7]

A few premillennialists cautioned against disregarding Arab rights. In a rare plea for equal treatment, W. F. Smalley published "Another View of the Palestine Situation" in *The King's Business* in 1930.[8] He pointed out that since both Jews and Arabs had obtained the land through conquest, neither side could claim title on that basis alone. He also recounted that before the British issued the Balfour Declaration, they had promised Palestine to the Arab population. Furthermore, Smalley observed, "It is easy to forget that Palestine has, after these years of freedom for Jewish immigration, some 163,000 Jews as over against about 635,000 so-called Arabs. Shall the minority rule?" Hitting close to home, Smalley asked how Americans would feel if their country were conquered by some foreign power that decided that since there were so many other places for them to live, Californians should evacuate their state and turn it over to the Indians who used to inhabit the land. "It is altogether likely that the inhabitants of California would do as much as the Arabs do today." Smalley affirmed his belief in the eventual restoration of the Jews, but questioned whether God would approve of such an unjust program as the Balfour Declaration. "I want to see the Jew given every right that the Arab has, but I do not like to see three-quarters of the population threatened with being ruled by the other one-fourth."

Smalley, however, was in the distinct minority. Premillennialists were convinced that God was fulfilling his promises to the Jews by bringing them back to Palestine. That the present Arab population resented the migration was God's problem, not theirs. The prophecy will be fulfilled, no matter what anybody says or does. Nothing or no one can stop it.

For a while, at least, the British tried. After struggling to fulfill the promise of the Balfour Declaration, they finally gave up. When they failed to bring about a negotiated peace between Arabs and Jews, the British issued a "White Paper" in May 1939 in which they essentially abandoned their pledge to establish a Jewish state. They announced a drastic restriction in Jewish immigration for five years, then promised to let the Arabs decide whether it should be resumed at former levels. Naturally, premillennialists were disappointed, but they were not deterred. "They [the Jews] *shall* go back to their own land. . . . How and when the White Paper will be repudiated we do not know, but that in the end it *shall* be non-effective is a certainty."[9] When the British reaffirmed their restrictive policy in 1944, the *Evangel* confidently stated that "God will reopen the door in His own time, never fear, His prophetic plan for Palestine will be fulfilled in spite of all."[10]

After the war, things got worse, not better, in Palestine. Jews had taken advantage of the war years to arm and train themselves, and Arabs were not about to lose the gains that the British White Paper had given them. So further conflict was inevitable. By 1947 the British were looking for a way out of their Palestinian morass, so they turned to the newly established United Nations for assistance. In August 1947 the United Nations' Special Committee on Palestine recommended that the area be partitioned into separate Jewish and Arab states. In general, American premillennialists were excited by the U.N. plan, though they said that, given God's promises to ancient Israel, the land will not stay partitioned for long. DeCourcy Rayner predicted that "the Jews will eventually be given not a partitioned Palestine, but the whole of the land, and ultimately the whole of Trans-Jordan as well."[11]

Once again the Arabs felt betrayed and called for a general strike. By the spring of 1948, the situation became so serious that the United Nations finally had to abandon its plans for partition. By then everyone knew that there would be no political solution to the Palestine problem. As soon as the British withdrew their forces on

May 14, 1948, the Jews announced the founding of an independent Israel and were immediately invaded by armies from surrounding Arab states. After intense fighting, the better-trained Israeli troops prevailed, and a cease-fire was called in November. In May 1949 Israel was admitted to the United Nations.

Needless to say, premillennialists were almost beside themselves over these developments. Louis T. Talbot of the Bible Institute of Los Angeles reflected the prevailing view when he wrote, "I consider it the greatest event, from a prophetic standpoint, that has taken place within the last one hundred years, perhaps even since 70 A.D., when Jerusalem was destroyed."[12] Now, with Israel back in its rightful home, the rest of God's prophetic plan could be carried out.[13]

From that time on, premillennialists made Israel the center of their prophetic teaching. They believed that it was the one undeniable piece of evidence that God keeps his promises, despite the vagaries of history and the skepticism of sinners. Seemingly, premillennialists could not say or write enough about the rebirth of the Jewish state. It was not only the proof that vindicated their approach to the prophetic Scriptures, it was also the key to the rest of the end-time events. Now that the Jews were regathered in the land of promise, premillennialists could turn their attention to the rest of the prophetic puzzle. With Israel in its proper place, there was nothing to stop the rapid fulfillment of the rest of the prophecies.[14]

Premillennialists kept a close eye on Israel and its neighbors and overwhelmingly supported the Israeli side in any wars or disputes. In 1956 Israel, with the approval and assistance of France and England, attacked Egypt. The Israelis wanted the Sinai; its allies wanted control of the Suez Canal. The United States government immediately lent its support to a United Nations cease-fire resolution, but not so American premillennialists. For the most part, they supported the Israeli attack and urged their government to do the same. They believed that God always blessed those nations that supported the Jews against their enemies and cursed those nations that did not.

George T. B. Davis, for example, argued that God had punished Britain with the dismantling of its empire because of its shabby treatment of the Jews in Palestine and warned that if the United States did not lend its unbending support to Israel in its time of need, God might punish America:

> We are standing at the crossroads at this very moment! Will our leaders believe God's Word and take the road of blessing that will lead our nation to still greater glory and victory; or will we forsake God's Word and take a stand against the Jews and so bring upon us terrible judgments of God as in the case of Egypt, Spain, Germany and Great Britain?[15]

Not every premillennialist, however, gave unquestioned support to Israel's action. Paul S. Allen, president of Simpson Bible College, suggested that "God does not need to use questionable methods in bringing about the fulfillment of prophecy." Even though Israel's return to the land had been prophesied, it is currently a return in "unbelief." "Possibly that unbelief will encourage methods incompatible with the Christian sense of justice." Consequently, Christians must not lose their moral perspective. "The Israel of today must justify its acts, not in terms of its ultimate destiny (which is not universally recognized or accepted) but in terms of the moral conscience of the nations of today." While Christians sympathize with the reestablishment of a Jewish homeland, they must always remember that the ends do not justify the means. "If Israel's reactions to probing along its borders seem out of proportion to the provocations suffered—admittedly a two-eyes-for-an-eye policy of retaliation—the Christian is duty-bound to apply the measuring stick of moral values as he knows them."[16]

Most premillennialists were a bit more fatalistic than that. Questions of morality and international law were not totally beside the point; but they were made rather moot by biblical prophecy. Ultimately it made little difference whether Israel was justified in its policies or not, though most premillennialists believed it was. The important thing was that it was expanding its borders and making the "right" kind of enemies according to premillennialist expectations for the end times.

Premillennialists gave even more enthusiastic support to Israel in the Six-Day War of June 1967. Fearing an imminent attack from Soviet-supplied Egyptian and Syrian forces, Israel struck first. In a matter of days, Israeli troops defeated the Arab coalition and occupied all of the Sinai peninsula to the banks of the Suez Canal, all the territory on the west bank of the Jordan River, the Gaza Strip, and the Golan Heights. From the premillennialist perspective, however, the most important acquisition of all was the city of Jerusalem. According to L. Nelson Bell in *Christianity Today*, "That for the first time in more than 2,000 years Jerusalem is now completely in the hands of the Jews gives a student of the Bible a thrill and a renewed faith in the accuracy and validity of the Bible."[17] The *Moody Monthly* devoted most of an issue to the war and concentrated on the significance of the Israeli capture of the city.[18] To many premillennialists, the Jewish occupation of the city was a clear fulfillment of Luke 21:24: "And Jerusalem shall be trodden down of the Gentiles, until the times of the Gentiles be fulfilled." Now that this milestone in prophetic fulfillment had been passed, premillennialists were more confident than ever that they were living in the last days and that the rapture of the church was imminent.[19]

No premillennialist was more successful at getting these ideas across than Hal Lindsey. Educated at the University of Houston and Dallas Theological Seminary, where he learned his dispensationalism, Lindsey spent most of the 1960s as a minister to students at U.C.L.A. under the auspices of Campus Crusade for Christ. During those years, he began lecturing on prophetic themes to college and church groups. He published his material in 1970 as *The Late Great Planet Earth*.[20] Since then, the book has sold over eighteen million copies, a staggering achievement that prompted the *New York Times* to declare Hal Lindsey the best-selling author of the 1970s. Due to the sales of that one book, Lindsey has become the most widely read writer on prophetic themes in history.[21]

In its basic approach, there was nothing unusual about *The Late Great Planet Earth*. Premillennialists have been writing books like it since the nineteenth century to show that the Bible contained a clear picture of the future and that some current events were prophetic fulfillments. The main difference between Lindsey's book and the others was the historical context in which the books were written. *The Late Great Planet Earth* was published at a time when the pieces of the prophetic puzzle seemed to fit together better than they ever had before.

As with all premillennialist interpreters after 1948, Lindsey believed that the nation of Israel was the most important sign of the coming end of the age. The ultimate biblical clue was found in the "parable of the fig tree" in Jesus' Olivet Discourse: "Now learn the parable of the fig tree; When his branch is yet tender, and putteth forth leaves, ye know that summer is nigh: So likewise ye, when ye shall see all these things, know that it [the return of the Son of Man] is near, even at the doors" (Matthew 24:32–33). In typical premillennialist fashion, Lindsey took the "fig tree" as a symbol for Israel. Thus, Lindsey argued, "When the Jewish people, after nearly 2,000 years of exile, under relentless persecution, became a nation again on May 14, 1948, the 'fig tree' put forth its first leaves." Furthermore, he went on, Jesus connected his second coming to the reestablishment of the state of Israel: "Verily I say unto you, This generation shall not pass, till all these things be fulfilled" (Matt. 24:34).

> What generation? Obviously in context, the generation that would see the signs—chief among them the rebirth of Israel. A generation in the Bible is something like forty years. If this is a correct deduction, then within forty years or so of 1948, all these things could take place. Many scholars who have studied Bible prophecy all their lives believe that this is so.

Consequently, the founding of Israel set in motion other prophetic fulfillments that will lead directly to Armageddon and the second coming. Especially significant were Israel's taking possession of Jerusalem in the Six-Day War and the growing talk of rebuilding the temple. The founding of Israel "has now set the stage for the other predicted signs to develop in history. It is like the key piece of a jigsaw puzzle being found and then having the many adjacent pieces rapidly fall into place."[22]

Lindsey's puzzle was elaborate and up to date. He joined standard dispensationalist expectations with an awareness of current events. That is what made his presentation so convincing to so many people: contemporary history and Lindsey's sometimes imaginative interpretation of biblical texts seemed to flow together nicely. According to Lindsey's understanding of prophecy, the world was ready for Armageddon. Israel was firmly in control of Palestine and seemed intent on expansion. The European Common Market was on the verge of becoming the revived Roman Empire uner Antichrist, who was about to be revealed. Russia and her Arab allies were the sworn enemies of Israel and a constant threat to its security. The Communist Chinese had become a military threat, boasting of their ability to raise an army of 200 million men. Modern military technology had advanced to the point where prophecies could be fulfilled to the letter.

Consequently, *The Late Great Planet Earth* predicted the following scenario: sometime before the fortieth anniversary of the founding of Israel (1988), the Israelis will sign a treaty with the leader (the Antichrist) of the ten-nation European Common Market. The Antichrist will guarantee Israel's security and usher in a period of peace and prosperity, during which the Jews will rebuild their temple in Jerusalem. After three and a half years, the Antichrist will enter the new temple and declare himself to be God, thereby instituting a reign of terror against all who will not worship him and wear his mark. Soon after, an Arab-African confederacy, under Egyptian control, will launch an attack on Israel from the south. The "king of the south" will be joined in his aggression by the northern confederation made up of Russia and its allies, nations from the eastern European communist block (Gomer) and Iran. After the Red Army sweeps into

Israel from the north, it will double-cross its Arab and African allies and subdue them as well, leaving Russia firmly in control of the Middle East. After achieving this swift and treacherous victory, the Red Army will regroup in Palestine to prepare for a counterattack from Antichrist and his western European forces and a new threat, a 200-million-man Communist Chinese army from the east. While awaiting the arrival of these new antagonists, the Red Army will attempt to destroy the remaining Jewish population. At that point, Lindsey argued, God will intervene, pouring out fire and brimstone (or possibly prompting a nuclear attack) on the Russians until they are destroyed. That will leave only the Chinese army and the forces of Antichrist to do battle at Armageddon. The resulting slaughter will be enormous. A nuclear exchange will obliterate the world's major cities and in Palestine the blood will flow as high as the horses' bridles. Just when the nations seem to be on the verge of destroying themselves, Jesus Christ will return, wipe out the remaining armies, subdue Antichrist, and establish his millennial kingdom on earth.[23]

Naturally, as a dispensationalist, Lindsey does not believe that the true church will witness these fulfillments firsthand. It will be raptured before Antichrist is revealed and will return with Christ as part of his victorious army of saints at the second coming at the end of the tribulation. But the Bible clearly teaches these things and current events proved that they were certain of fulfillment.

In the last chapter of *The Late Great Planet Earth*, Lindsey makes some predictions about developments in the immediate future. On the religious side, he foresees a deepening apostasy in the denominations, a speeding up of mergers into "religious conglomerates," and a growing exodus of "real Christians" from institutional Christianity. He expects open persecution against conservative believers, who will establish "a true underground church." He also believes that there will be a movement in Israel to rebuild the temple and an effort to make Jerusalem the religious capital of the world.

On the political and social scene, Lindsey predicts that because of student rebellions and Communist subversion, the United States will forfeit its leadership in the free world to western Europe. "Look for the emergence of a 'United States of Europe' composed of ten inner member nations. The Common Market is laying the groundwork for this political confederacy which will become the mightiest coalition on earth." He forecasts a greater involvement of the papacy in political and economic movements. He also suggests that there will be a limited use of nuclear weapons, probably between Russia and China or against the continental United States, and that this will so terrify the world that it will gladly follow the Antichrist's promise of peace. Finally, he prophesies a massive increase in crime, drug use, and religious cults.[24]

But what does Lindsey expect premillennialists to *do* about these predictions? His suggestions are religious, not political. Like premillennialists in the past, Lindsey's purposes are overwhelmingly evangelistic and spiritual. He wants to bring people to Christ and encourages believers in holy living. After his discussion of Armageddon, he poses the ultimate question: "As history races toward this moment, are you afraid or looking with hope for deliverance [in the rapture]? The answer should reveal to you your spiritual condition. One way or another history continues in a certain acceleration toward the return of Christ. Are you ready?"[25] And in the conclusion of his book, he gives a more extensive appeal:

> If you are not sure that you have personally accepted the gift of God's forgiveness which Jesus Christ purchased by bearing the judgment of a holy God that was due your sins, then you should do so right now wherever you are. . . . Right at this moment, in your own way, thank Jesus for dying for your sins and invite Him to come into your heart.[26]

Likewise, Lindsey advises his readers to submit to the Holy Spirit's direction in their lives, read the Bible regularly, and, in the knowledge that the rapture may occur at any moment, take the gospel to others before it is too late. Finally, Lindsey repeats some old, familiar premillennialist advice: "We should plan our lives as though we will be here our full life expectancy, but live as though Christ may come today."[27]

Throughout the 1970s, premillennialists continued to use their prophetic views for evangelistic purposes. As we have already seen, that has been an important part of the movement's ethos since the days of D. L. Moody. Premillennialist revivalists still conjure up images of the returning Christ to move reluctant sinners to decide for Jesus. Billy Graham, for instance, always includes a sermon on the second coming in his crusades. But now premillennialists have new means of spreading their gospel. Many of the leading figures of the so-called electronic church are premillennialists who often use their television programs to teach prophecy: Pat Robertson of the "700 Club," Jim Bakker of the "PTL Club," Oral Roberts, Rex Humbard, Jerry Falwell, Kenneth Copeland, Jimmy Swaggart, and Richard DeHaan, to name only a few. Hal Lindsey has a regular program on prophecy and the news; it is syndicated throughout the country on a number of "Christian" television networks.

Similarly, in the 1970s premillennialists began producing "prophecy films" to be shown in churches and in other settings. Films with titles like *A Thief in the Night*, *A Distant Thunder*, *Image of the Beast*, *Years of the Beast*, *Early Warning*, *The Rapture*, *Revelation*, *The Return*, *The Final Hour*, and *The Road to Armageddon* are widely used in premillennialist circles, primarily for evangelistic purposes. The message of these films is simple and direct: Armageddon is coming, so if you want to avoid the terrors of the tribulation, then accept Jesus Christ and be raptured with the true church. Those who use the films testify of their effectiveness at prompting decisions for Christ.[28]

Since the appearance of *The Late Great Planet Earth*, part of American premillennialism has become more sensitive to political issues. This has been due in large part to the growing political involvement of fundamentalism in American politics.[29] Though still primarily used for evangelism and spiritual edification, biblical prophecy, some of its advocates have discovered, can be used for other purposes as well. As a result, a number of popular prophecy teachers have rather openly joined their teachings to other blatantly political concerns.

One can observe this tendency in Hal Lindsey by comparing *The Late Great Planet Earth* and his more recent *The 1980s: Countdown to Armageddon* (1980). While the latter book primarily documents how events in the 1970s corroborated Lindsey's earlier predictions, it also contains some rather unprecedented political pronouncements.

Most of *The 1980s: Countdown to Armageddon* consists of a prophetic update. The 1970s contained few surprises for Lindsey. Events either matched his earlier expectations to the letter or fulfilled them in unexpected but completely compatible ways. The Soviet Union drastically expanded its power and influence since 1970. The Middle East, rich because of desperately needed oil, remained a time bomb waiting to explode. The European Common Market reached its full complement of ten nations in 1979 and was just waiting to be taken over by the Antichrist, who, Lindsey stated, is alive somewhere in the world today, possibly even sitting as a member of the Common Market's "parliament." He noted the flexing of OPEC muscles in 1973, the Iranian revolution under the Ayatollah Khomeini, and the Russian invasion of Afghanistan. He had little difficulty fitting the events into his framework. Even the Egyptian-Israeli peace treaty, which potentially could subvert premillennialist expectations of continuing hostilities in the Middle East, posed few problems. Lindsey noted that such an agreement had little chance for lasting success, given the attitudes of the rest of the Arab world, and warned that Anwar Sadat, who was along with Menachem Begin the architect of the peace, was "in constant danger of being assassinated by militant Arabs."[30]

In addition to analyzing contemporary events, Lindsey made some predictions about the early 1980s. In a section on signs of the end of the age, Lindsey predicted that the so-called Jupiter effect would touch off "history's greatest outbreak of earthquakes" in

1982.[31] He also stated that the increased interest in UFOs fulfilled Jesus' prediction that there will be "terrors and great signs from heaven" just before his return (Luke 21:11).

> It's my opinion that UFOs are real and that there will be a proved 'close encounter of the third kind' soon. And I believe that the source of this phenomenon is some type of alien being of great intelligence and power. According to the Bible, a demon is a spiritual personality in a state of war with God. Prophecy tells us that demons will be allowed to use their powers of deception in a grand way during the last days of history (II Thessalonians 2:8–12). I believe these demons will stage a spacecraft landing on Earth. They will claim to be from an advanced culture in another galaxy.[32]

Had Lindsey stopped there, *The 1980s* would have been pretty standard, though sensational, premillennialist fare. But he did not. In the middle of his prophetic analysis of contemporary events, Lindsey included an *apologia* for various right-wing political causes.

As he did in *The Late Great Planet Earth*, Lindsey argued that the United States will play no major political or military role in the events of the end time. "So from the standpoint of Biblical prophecy, the U.S. *must* fade from its place of leadership for the west and its former supreme superpower status."[33] The decline might come about through a communist takeover, destruction by a surprise Soviet nuclear attack, or economic dependence on the Common Market. Decline was inevitable; how and when were still unclear. Because Lindsey believes that this is what the Bible teaches, one would expect him to accept it, however sadly. But Lindsey believes that he has found a way for America to delay the inevitable:

> If some critical and difficult choices are made by the American people *right now*, it is possible to see the U.S. remain a world power. We could become an equal ally of the European confederation, with each dependent on the other. In that way, America could keep much of its sovereignty and freedom.[34]

If American Christians act *now*, then "America will survive this perilous situation and endure until the Lord comes to evacuate His people."[35] In other words, it may be possible for America to retain its present power until the rapture of the church. After that, it evidently will not make much difference to American Christians what happens to their country.

In the political analysis that follows, Lindsey leaves his premillennialism behind; that is, he never demonstrates how his diagnosis of and prescription for American political and social life has anything to do with biblical prophecy. His observations and remedies come out of right-wing political ideology and have nothing to do with premillennialism per se. Among other things, Lindsey decries the weakening of American military power since the 1960s. He bemoans the fact that the United States did not use its superior nuclear might against communism in the late 1940s and early 1950s, when it had the chance.[36] He goes to great lengths to show that the Bible's teachings on love and peacemaking do not apply to military defense against the communist threat. "That's why I believe that the Bible supports building a powerful military force. And the Bible is telling the U.S. to become strong again. A weak military will encourage the Soviet Union to start an all-out war."[37] He condemned the SALT (Strategic Arms Limitation Treaty) agreements and declared that "SALT is finished. There is no more basis for negotiation. It is time to use our vast and superior technology to create the world's strongest military power. Only this will stop the Soviets' insane rush toward nuclear war."[38]

To a large extent, Lindsey blames America's demise as a world power on the influence of hidden forces. He argues that the Council on Foreign Relations, which has been in control of the State Department since the mid-1940s, has had an "unbroken string of defeats and accommodations to the communists." "I believe it is high time for the citizens of this country to clean this 'elite' group out of the Department of State and replace it with some people with common sense and courage."[39] Likewise, he condemns the Trilateral Commission, "an international group of the western world's most powerful bankers, media leaders, scholars and government officials bent on radically changing the world in which we live."[40] The Commission worked behind the scenes to get Jimmy Carter elected president in 1976; and in return Carter packed his administration full of "fellow Trilateralists." Though he refused to assign any evil motives to the people involved, Lindsey stated that "the Trilateralist movement is unwittingly setting the stage for the political-economic one-world system the Bible predicts for the last days."[41]

In addition to rebuilding America's sagging military forces, Lindsey believes that Americans must get back to their traditional political values. "Although no way is perfect, the democratic, capitalist free-enterprise system has produced more freedom, prosperity and financial independence for more people than any other system in history."[42] However, since Franklin D. Roosevelt's "New Deal," Americans have adopted a "free lunch" mentality. They have allowed an enormous, unbiblical welfare system to develop and have permitted the spread of socialistic ideals. "We need to clean house in Washington, and elect a Congress and a President who believe in the capitalist system."[43]

Clearly, Lindsey broke new ground in *The 1980s*. Without showing any essential connection, he incorporated the concerns of the so-called New Christian Right into his traditional premillennialist presentation. Nowhere in the book does he attempt to show that his political program is based on an understanding of biblical prophecy. He took his cues from other sources. An analysis of his footnotes reveals that his understanding of America's current political, social, and military condition comes almost exclusively from Barry Goldwater's *With No Apologies* (1979) and the conservative Coalition for Peace Through Strength.[44] Though his premillennialism led him in one direction, his political commitments led him in another. America will fall from its prominence in world politics, but if Lindsey and other concerned Christians have anything to do with it, its demise will not occur until *after* the rapture.

Why did Lindsey shift his approach? The success of *The Late Great Planet Earth* had opened numerous doors for him and his teachings. He was invited to address Jamaican government officials on prophetic themes, as well as groups of military planners at the American Air War College and the Pentagon. Despite the difficulty of getting Christian books published in Israel, *The Late Great Planet Earth* was translated into Hebrew. "The book caught on like wildfire. A great many copies circulated among military men and government officials as well."[45] These high-level contacts must have set Lindsey to thinking about the political and military consequences of his prophetic views. No other premillennialist has ever had the kind of audience that Lindsey developed in the 1970s. It is not surprising, then, that he took advantage of his influence to address broader concerns. Also, in the late 1970s many religious conservatives like Lindsey decided that it was now permissible, if not imperative, to speak out on political issues in ways that they had been avoiding for decades.

Lindsey was not the only premillennialist to juxtapose, however awkwardly, eschatology and right-wing politics. Jerry Falwell, the founder of the Moral Majority, has done much the same thing. Though Falwell heads a conservative political coalition that cuts across religious lines, viewers of his televised *Old-Time Gospel Hour* know that he is a dispensationalist premillennialist who believes that the world is getting worse and worse and that history is careening toward Armageddon. How, then, can he justify his deep involvement in trying to reform American life? How does he put his premillennialism and his politics together? It is difficult to say, because Falwell does not make his eschatology explicit in his political views.[46] Certainly no one can accuse him of trying to "bring in the kingdom" through political means. He does not seek to usher in the future millennium of peace through his reform efforts, as postmillennialists used to do; he simply wants to put America back the way he thinks it was, to repair its now-disintegrating Christian (or at least moral) foundations. When seen from that perspective, Falwell is not going against his premillennialist principles. He is merely setting them aside or keeping them separate from his politics, where other values and commitments take precedence. In short, premillennialists like Lindsey and Falwell often juggle their eschatology with other concerns. In addition to being believers in the second coming, they believe in certain political ideologies and find ways to hold on to them all.[47]

If Lindsey and Falwell fail to demonstrate how their eschatology relates to their political views, other premillennialists make the connection more explicit. This is clearly seen in the premillennialist-survivalist writings of Jim McKeever, who advertises himself as an international consulting economist, a computer expert, an ordained minister, and a gifted Bible teacher. Unlike dispensationalist premillennialists, McKeever is a posttribulationist who believes that the church will live through the reign of the Antichrist and be rescued by the rapture at the *end* of the tribulation period. Because they will refuse the mark of the beast, Christians will be prohibited from buying and selling and from holding regular jobs. They will experience famine and nuclear war along with everyone else. In light of this terrifying future, what are Christians to do?

No one can accuse McKeever of skirting the behavioral consequences of his views. In his *Christians Will Go Through the Tribulation: And How to Prepare for It* (1978), he stated, "If one believes, first, that Christians will go through the Tribulation, and second, that we are living in the end times, this will change his entire life. It will change his value system, his dedication to God, and the amount of physical and spiritual preparation that he is making for the events of the Tribulation."[48] As a result, Christians must learn how to be self-sufficient and how to bypass Antichrist's various restrictive policies.

> We are considering the time when Christians will not be able to buy and sell, and will want to be independent of the utility systems. Let's now look at the ideal self-supporting house, as I envisage it. It would be at least partially "underground," with the south side in glass for passive solar heating. . . . A twelve-volt wind electrical generating system would run the lights and the refrigeration, and a 110-volt dual system would run the freezer. The 110-voltage would normally be drawn from the utilities, but there would be an emergency 110-volt diesel generator which

could run the freezer and the other power equipment. The stereo, CB and other entertainment equipment would run off of the 12-volt system, and the TV only off of the 110 commercial power. There would be a garden, and chickens, rabbits and other small animals would be raised. . . . For food preservation there would be a root cellar at least, and possibly a springhouse, in addition to the 12-volt refrigerator.[49]

Thus McKeever's book is a veritable handbook for physical and spiritual survival. He tells readers how to build bomb shelters, store food and water, manage without access to public utilities, water, or sewer service, and get in touch with various "survivalist" organizations for equipment, plans, and food supplies. Probably the most controversial part of the book deals with the question of guarding one's food supply.

If I have a nice supply of food stored and famine times occur, what do I do if a bunch of people decide to come and take my food? Do I give it to them? Do I kill them? How far do I go in protecting my food supply? . . . You must do whatever God tells you to do at the moment. . . . I believe that God might lead one Christian family to protect their food with all their might, even to the point of killing those who would attempt to steal it. I also believe that God would lead other Christians to give most or all of it away. (Remember our confidence is not in the food we have stored, but in God!) . . . I must state here that I am in favor of free enterprise and individual effort. The one time when the church tried a communal (communistic) way of living was in Jerusalem right after the ascension of Christ. Everyone sold all that they had and pooled their resources. This inevitably leads to laziness, unequal distribution, and so forth. That experiment failed so miserably that eventually the Christians in other parts of the world had to send food and money to these Christians in Jerusalem.[50]

McKeever's survivalism has caught on in some premillennialist circles, though it is impossible to say just how extensive or popular it has become. On the "700 Club," for example, Pat Robertson has promoted the stockpiling of food and other survivalist preparations for the tough times ahead. He wrote the forward for McKeever's *The*

Almighty and the Dollar (1980), a book that promises to help people take financial advantage of the coming economic collapse.[51]

Though McKeever showed a much closer connection between his beliefs and his suggested behavior than Lindsey did, one suspects that his eschatology is almost secondary to his commitment to personal survival. Apart from the eschatological framework, McKeever's writings are almost indistinguishable from the survivalist books of economic doomsdayers like Harry Browne and Howard J. Ruff.[52] The more customary post-tribulational call to prepare for suffering and even martyrdom gets comparatively little attention in McKeever's writings.[53] His most obvious message is that those who prepare for the coming tribulation will have it much easier than those who do not. With God's help and careful planning, Christians can survive anything, even the Antichrist. Despite his efforts to combine individualistic, every-person-for-himself survivalism and premillennialism, McKeever's works have an air of unreality about them. Nowhere does he explain why the Antichrist and his forces will allow properly prepared believers to sit securely in their solar-powered homes and enjoy the fruits of their foresight.

Another premillennialist who joins eschatology and economic concerns is Mary Stewart Relfe. Within six months of its publication in January, 1981, her book *When Your Money Fails* sold three hundred thousand copies.[54] She asserted that the "666 System" is already well established in the world's economic system. She based her conclusion on the widespread use of the numbers 666 in computer programs, credit-card systems, and the "universal product code," which appears on virtually all products and is "read" by electronic scanners at supermarket checkout counters. She found what she believed was irrefutable evidence for the 666 system in the production codes of Olivetti business machines, NCR computer systems, Boss work gloves, Scotty fertilizer, McGregor clothing, Italian shoes, and parts for Caterpillar tractors. She found evidence that Sears, J. C. Penney, Montgomery Ward, Visa, and MasterCard had all used 666 as a prefix in account numbers. She stated that electronic fund transfers, debit cards, and other computerized bank and financial services were preparing the way for a "cashless society" and Antichrist's takeover of the world economy. Ultimately, she predicted, the United States and other nations will issue for each citizen a national identification card and number that will replace all other credit-card and identification numbers. In order to prevent the theft or loss of this all-important number, Relfe suggested that governments will order people to be "branded," probably by laser beam or the implantation of a computer chip, on their foreheads or hands.

Relfe is a midtribulationist. She believes that the church will witness the rise of Antichrist and his coercive economic system, but will be raptured before God pours out his wrath on the earth and the battle of Armageddon takes place. Since Christians will have to endure the coming of the Antichrist, what should they do? Like McKeever, Relfe is very specific. In order to avoid as many financial transactions as possible during the tribulation, Christians should now work to get completely out of debt; pay off their home mortgages if at all possible; buy an acre of land in the country "and learn to live independent of city conveniences"; give abundantly in tithes to the Lord's work; and pray for guidance to know how to convert one's liquid assets into something more substantial, such as gold or silver.[55] More importantly, she warns that Christians would do well to decide beforehand what they will do when the government issues the "Final Card" to all its citizens. She suggests that they should refuse to accept them.[56]

In summary, premillennialists are convinced that they are living in the last days. The founding of the state of Israel is their assurance that the pieces of the prophetic puzzle are falling into place. More than any other time in history, premillennialists believe that contemporary events prove that the end is imminent. That confidence has put premillennialist leaders under unprecedented pressure. If the end *is* near, then practical issues become more important than ever. How, then, should premillennialists live in the shadow of the second coming?

As we have seen, premillennialists have given different answers to that question. Whereas most of them are content to retain their traditional emphasis on evangelism and holy living, a few of their most "public" leaders are willing to bring their eschatology into line with various political and economic ideologies, with varying success. Hal Lindsey and Jerry Falwell, while obviously believing deeply in premillennialist doctrine, have not been able to show how their eschatology and political ideology fit together. Jim McKeever and Mary Stewart Relfe, on the other hand, have more successfully linked their economic views to their prophetic interpretations, though at times it is difficult to determine which beliefs are primary.

At this point, there is no reason to believe that the premillennialist movement as a whole has become the servant of the New Christian Right. Certainly, the two movements do share many of the same concerns. Both movements fear "apostasies" of one kind or another, detect and deplore the widespread decline of traditional values, and are susceptible to simplistic conspiracy theories of history. But in the last analysis, premillennialism is not essentially "right-wing" any more than it is inherently anti-Semitic. After all, one of America's best-known premillennialist politicians is Senator Mark Hatfield of Oregon, a moderate Republican whose policies are usually at odds with those of the New Christian Right.[57] And a number of the signers of the Chicago Declaration of Evangelical Social Concern (1973) were premillennialists.[58] Being a premillennialist does not preclude one from being involved in moderate or even liberal politics. If the historical survey presented in this book has indicated anything, it has proved that premillennialists are highly adaptable people. Their eschatology coexists with a number of other personal, social, and political concerns. Sometimes their premillennialism takes precedence; sometimes it does not. They can adjust to changing contemporary events, even if it means making major mid-course corrections. And they can "use" other ideologies if they serve their purposes. One thing seems certain: for the time being at least, most premillennialists are more interested in following the fulfillment of biblical prophecy, especially those related to Israel, than they are in joining their eschatology to any given political or social ideology.

Conclusion

How, then, should the new premillennialism be viewed? We have traced it from its beginnings, struggling for recognition and respect as a small movement on the fringes of American evangelicalism. Though it often appeared to its earliest critics as a movement of theological eccentrics, premillennialism has survived and prospered since it gained a wide following after World War I and the rise of the fundamentalist movement. Premillennialism in all its forms currently commands the allegiance of millions of Americans.[1] The descendants of the militant fundamentalists are still almost exclusively dispensationalists, and many people within the more moderate evangelical movement also maintain a strong commitment to their premillennial heritage, though not necessarily in its dispensational form.[2]

Because of the continuing strength of premillennialism in American Christianity, it seems appropriate to take a concluding look at its appeal, note some of its effects, and even hazard a prediction about its future.

As we have seen in our study, premillennialism has always had an enormous appeal for many people. That much is certain, though historians of religion have not always had an easy time explaining why. Until fairly recently, most historians have not been favorably disposed toward millennial movements. They have portrayed pre-millennialists as a collection of lunatics, hypocrites, and fanatics.[3] All that, however, began to change in the late 1950s. Using some insights from anthropology and sociology, many historians began to recognize that millennialism of one kind or another had occurred in nearly every place and period of human history. They recognized that Christianity was not the only religion to have a millennial tradition and took the first steps toward devising a historical model to explain the phenomenon.

Eventually most historians working in the field came to the conclusion that millennialism has appeared most often among certain kinds of people: the poor, the alienated, the disinherited, and the despairing. Relying heavily on theories of "relative deprivation" and "status anxiety," historians have tried to show that many people turn to visions of a glorious, millennial future when they give up hope of ever achieving their dreams in this life, through ordinary human means. Cut off from political and social power, shut out of or alienated from prevailing religious practices, many people give up on history and long for salvation from beyond it.[4] That description does fit many millennialist groups—from medieval millennialists, who translated their eschatological expectations into violence and revolution, to members of twentieth-century cargo cults in the Pacific, who quietly wait for their redemption from the skies.[5]

Some students of millennialist movements in modern industrialized societies, however, have become increasingly uneasy with that model. Though it does help to explain the origins of many millennialist groups, the model does not shed as much light as it should on modern British or American millennialists. Ernest Sandeen has argued that "American millenarians do not seem to have been threatened with destruction, their own world does not seem to have been collapsing, they were not dispossessed or desperate people, and they had no thought of revolution."[6] Sandeen's point is well taken, though advocates of the deprivation theory would want to point out that feelings of deprivation are always "relative"; that is, in order to be deprived, a group need only perceive that it is. A multi-millionaire who loses all but his last million in a stock-market crash is deprived in relative terms; and a group that finds its prestige slipping is also deprived, though its members may be comfortable and content in other areas of life.[7] Consequently, there is a sense in which some variation of the relative deprivation theory fits the American premillennialist experience. Many of the postmillennialists who switched over to premillennialism in the late-nineteenth and early-twentieth centuries did so because the postmillennial vision of the perfect society had not materialized. And many conservative evangelicals lost status in their denominations because of the rise of liberalism and were deprived of cultural influence due to the coming of large numbers of foreign immigrants and the resulting pluralism in American society. Certainly, it can be argued, premillennialists did suffer some kind of "psychic stress" and did believe that society was in a hopeless state of decline.[8] And yet, one should not press the deprivation theory too far. It explains some things, but not everything.

This study has argued that American premillennialism was and is primarily a *religious* movement. Although it has had some social and political consequences, premillennialism's paramount appeal is to personal and religious sentiments. For instance, the possibility of the imminent rapture has been a hedge against the fear of death. That one might enter the age to come without dying first has been a welcome thought to many people. It was widely reported, for example, that James Brookes maintained his belief in the imminent rapture because of his almost abnormal fear of death, even after he became intellectually convinced that the pretribulation rapture doctrine had no scriptural foundation.[9]

Similarly, premillennialists have cherished the prospect of momentarily meeting departed loved ones in the air at Christ's return.

For many evangelicals, the possibility of seeing a recently deceased parent, spouse, or child has been a source of immense personal comfort.[10]

More significant, however, is what Sandeen calls the "psychology of deliverance,"[11] the confidence that current toils, frustrations, disappointments, pains, or difficulties will be immediately eliminated by the appearance of Jesus Christ. Premillennialists have frequently spoken of such deliverance, so one can only guess how many people sought to escape their present circumstances by longing for the return of Christ. Many are the sufferers on beds of pain, businessmen in financial trouble, people fed up with contemporary society, or unprepared students on the eve of exams who have fervently prayed, "Even so, come, Lord Jesus!"[12]

It would be too simplistic to say, however, that people become premillennialists primarily out of some kind of psychological need for security and escape. While such factors may be significant, they can hardly be considered determinative for most people. All personal reasons aside, most premillennialists accept the doctrine because they believe that the Bible teaches it. In the long run, therefore, psychological explanations of premillennialism fail.

For the vast majority of premillennialists, the religious or doctrinal appeal is more important than the personal one. As we have already seen, the new premillennialism worked hard to keep its roots firmly planted in the conservative evangelical tradition of the nineteenth century. Premillennialists tried to relate their distinctive beliefs about the second coming to the rest of the evangelical ethos. The movement preserved evangelicalism's strong commitment to biblical authority in the face of some of the more irresponsible kinds of higher criticism. It maintained traditional evangelicalism's supernaturalism at a time when liberals were blurring the distinction between nature and supernature and denying the historicity of biblical miracles. And it preserved the historical primitivism of their evangelical predecessors. Rejecting the tendency of some liberals to think that they knew more about Christian doctrine than the apostles did, premillennialists argued that what was taught in the New Testament and believed in the early church was still binding.

This close link to conservative theology has always been an important drawing card for premillennialism. In fact, it has become so allied with conservative doctrines in general that in some groups believing one seems impossible without believing all the others. For many fundamentalists and evangelicals today, the premillennial second coming, the divinity of Jesus, the virgin birth, the resurrection, the substitutionary atonement, justification through faith, and the infallibility of the Bible come as a self-contained doctrinal package, allowing no additions or subtractions. What historian Whitney Cross said of the Millerites of the 1840s is equally true of premillennialists in the twentieth century: "Their doctrine was the logical absolute of fundamentalist orthodoxy, as perfectionism was the extreme of revivalism."[13] In other words, while premillennialists had to fight for recognition as members of the conservative alliance against liberalism at the turn of the century, they have risen to the point of dominating large segments of the current fundamentalist/ evangelical movement in the 1970s and 80s.

Premillennialism has maintained its appeal among conservative Protestants also because it seems to be empirically verified by current events. Premillennialists can point to the rise of Zionism, events surrounding World War I, and the founding of the state of Israel as proof that they read the Bible correctly. Though they tend to be rather forgetful of past mistakes and have frequently had to adjust their interpretations of particular events, they have never had to discard or substantially alter the broad outlines of their system. As dispensationalists themselves admit, not all particulars are properly in place, but things are certainly heading in the right direction. The continuing crisis between Israel and its Arab neighbors, the potential for world oil crisis, Russian expansionism, and the like fit well into the dispensational scheme of things. There may be setbacks, even occasional embarrassments, but premillennialists believe that time is on their side. As long as premillennialists continue to find ways to fit current events into their system, there seems little doubt that they will be able to appeal to significant numbers of people. In short, the atomic age and apocalypticism are made for each other. As long as the world remains a terrifying place, seemingly bent on its own destruction, the premillennialist world view will have the ring of truth for many.

Any discussion of the appeal of premillennialism would not be complete without mentioning the ironic comfort that this rather pessimistic eschatology brings to people. Despite the fact that premillennialists often sound like the world's biggest promoters of gloom and doom, they insist that their view of the future is basically optimistic. As Pat Robertson has observed, "We are not to weep as the people of the world weep when there are certain tragedies or breakups of the government or systems of the world. We are not to wring our hands and say, 'Isn't that awful?' That isn't awful at all. It's good. That is a token, an evident token of our salvation, of where God is going to take us."[14] There is something comforting about knowing that world events fit into a prophetic pattern, that God is in control, guiding everything, no matter how horrible and apparently destructive, to a redemptive end. Once premillennialists find a place for world events in their prophetic puzzle, such events cease to terrify and bewilder.

When one gets behind the prophetic charts and graphs, the speculations and erroneous predictions, one can see clearly that premillennialism is actually about religious, historical, and personal *assurance*. Premillennialists believe—they say they *know*—that everything is going to work out all right in the end. A story that has recently been circulating in some premillennialist circles can illustrate this. Some students from a theological seminary were playing basketball one night in a local gymnasium. Late in the evening the janitor arrived and prepared to lock up the building. While waiting for the game to conclude, he sat down and began reading his Bible. He was still at it when the game ended and the players began filing out. One theological student noticed that the janitor was reading from the Book of Revelation and asked him, quite smugly, if he understood what he was reading. "Sure do," the man replied. Somewhat taken aback by the janitor's confidence, the student, who had himself not quite mastered the prophetic system yet, asked a second question. "Oh, yeah? What does it all mean?" "Simple," replied the janitor, "Jesus wins."

That, in a nutshell, sums up the appeal of premillennialism for millions of people. Premillennialist eschatology provides the promise that eventually "Jesus will win," even in a world that seems to be totally out of control. It guarantees that ultimately everything will make sense and that everything will be fine. In a world like ours, that is no mean achievement.[15]

In the June 1982 issue of the *Atlantic*, William Martin, a sociologist of religion from Rice University, accurately analyzed the appeal of premillennialism in the modern world:

> Pre-millennial teaching is probably most attractive to those who feel that the world, or at least their segment of it, is out of control, and can be brought to a good end only by concerted supernatural intervention. Such feelings of marginality are likely to be especially acute when established ways of life are being threatened. To many, however, an apocalyptic outlook is simply part of the package they have inherited, and adherence is less a matter of alienation or attraction than of received tradition and perceived truth. If the Bible says these things shall come to pass, they shall come to pass, whether or not the prospect pleases. And if current events seem to offer tangible supporting evidence, then faith is strengthened and hope increased.[16]

If that is premillennialism's appeal, what are some of its effects? As we have seen, they can be substantial. In the areas of personal lifestyle, evangelism, missions, and the like, premillennialists to varying degrees have tried to live in the shadow of the second coming. The possibility of the imminent return of Christ has given a sense of urgency and significance to the daily lives of millions of people.

People who have not been reared within the movement find it hard to comprehend the power of premillennialism to shape attitudes and

behavior. As Arno Gaebelein suggested they should,[17] premillennialists by the millions never let a day go by without thinking, "Today
might be the day." If taken seriously, that possibility can put brackets
around one's life, providing boundaries for thoughts and actions. It is
a rare premillennialist indeed who has not heard the query, "Would
you really want to be doing *that* when Jesus comes?" And many who
were raised as premillennialists can tell horror stories about coming
home to empty houses or finding themselves suddenly alone in
department stores or supermarkets and instinctively concluding that
Jesus has come and left them behind. Despite the occasional terror for
the young or unrepentant, premillennialism does not seem to have a
negative effect on personal behavior. In fact, as we have seen, it
frequently can be a catalyst to holy living and personal purity.

More dubious, however, has been the effect of premillennialism
on social attitudes. Though not all premillennialists have accepted
the extreme position on the futility of reform activities, one must
finally conclude that in many cases premillennialism broke the spirit
of social concern that had played such a prominent role in historic
evangelicalism. Its hopeless view of the present order left little room
for God or for themselves to work in it. The world and the present
age belonged to Satan, and lasting reform was impossible until Jesus
returned to destroy Satan's power and set up the perfect kingdom.
As Martin Marty has said, premillennialists often give up on the
world before God does. And that refusal to get involved in social
issues has frequently kept them from fulfilling the biblical mandate
to do good and practice justice in the world. Consequently, though
there have been significant exceptions, many premillennialists have
turned their backs on social reform movements. As a result, the
social conscience of an important part of American evangelicalism
has atrophied and died. In that regard, at least, premillennialism
broke faith with the evangelical spirit that it fought so hard to
preserve.[18]

This issue invariably raises the question of premillennialist political involvement. As we have already noted, there has never been a

typical or uniform premillennialist political response. Premillennialists have taken different political and social positions and, using the same eschatology, have managed to justify them. Thus it is necessary to identify different styles of premillennialist political activity.

In his fine study of Seventh-Day Adventists and the American experience, Jonathan Butler found that Adventists interacted with their culture in three basic ways.[19] His findings are helpful in categorizing the different responses found among evangelical premillennialists.[20]

In the first category, *apolitical apocalyptic*, people choose to ignore all political questions and involvements. They curse the world and its institutions and flee from them. As James Brookes advised his fellow premillennialists in 1880: "Well would it be if the children of God were to keep aloof from the whole defiling scene." Since believers were "dead to the world," they should stay completely out of the political process, including voting in elections, because "dead men do not vote."[21] However, this form of extreme withdrawal has never been especially popular among American premillennialists. With few exceptions, they have not isolated themselves from the rest of society or built communes in the deserts or mountains to escape defilement and await the coming of Christ. While they maintain no hope for the world as it is, most premillennialists have enjoyed living in it and have been very much at home here. They share the fruits of American prosperity and, on the surface at least, are indistinguishable from their materialistic neighbors.

More premillennialists have adopted the style Butler calls *political apocalyptic*. At times believers in the second coming become interested and to some extent involved in politics because politics are useful in verifying their world view. Many premillennialists adopt the rhetoric of political discontent to substantiate their convictions that the world is getting worse, that political institutions are falling apart, and that everything is sliding toward destruction. This is understandable, given their need to show that history is going the way they think the Bible says it will. Thus they keep up with current events, become conversant in the latest political issues, and cite blatant political propaganda because it proves their position. Instead of fleeing from the world like the practitioners of apolitical apocalyptic, they keep one foot within it so that they can prove to themselves and the skeptics around them that everything really is as bad as they say it is. Their actual political involvement, however, is rather peripheral and insignificant. They are more interested in obtaining footnotes for their prophetic studies than in effectively entering the political fray. One cannot read premillennialist literature without seeing that this approach has had its share of adherents. Many premillennialists are "up on politics" but they rarely do anything about them. They need to know about political developments to be up to date; but they rarely go beyond reading about them, discussing their prophetic significance, or showing how they substantiate their predictions. Those who belong in the political apocalyptic category are interested observers, not regular participants in politics. Since the world system is passing away, there is no reason to try to do much about it.

In the last category, *political prophetic*, premillennialists actually do become politically involved. Instead of abandoning the social order or maneuvering on the fringes, some premillennialists assume political and social responsibility. Naturally, their participation in politics is highly discriminatory. Premillennialists are very selective about what they become involved in. Their approach tends to be individualistic, moralistic, and short-term. That is, they usually refuse to get involved in long-term projects for social transformation. They know that they cannot change things permanently. But they believe that there are some things that they can do. Therefore, many premillennialists decide to give the Devil "all the trouble [they] can till Jesus comes."[22]

In this way, premillennialists can combine their view of the end times with longstanding notions of America's millennial role. Throughout American history many people have viewed the nation in millennial terms. The United States is God's chosen place, the new Israel, the center of his providential activity. America is a "city set upon a hill," a beacon of freedom, prosperity, and truth for the rest of the world to follow and emulate. America's divine mission is nothing less than the transformation of the world order.[23]

In theory, at least, this millennial vision of America and premillennial eschatology are incompatible. In their more consistent moments, premillennialists have believed that there is only one kingdom of God and that no earthly nation can claim the title for itself. Despite their natural love of country, they have recognized that America is part of the world system that is passing away, that it is one of the Gentile powers that will be either destroyed at Armageddon or judged at Christ's coming.

Though it is not easy to make such diametrically opposed ideas coexist, some premillennialists have tried to find a way. As we saw in the last chapter, on the contemporary scene people like Hal Lindsey and Jerry Falwell have become enthusiastic boosters of American military might and supporters of its interests around the world. Despite his beliefs about America's ultimate prophetic fate, Lindsey believes that God is still using the United States in a special way. This is true, he has stated, because America has a large number of true believers who regularly pray for the country and its leaders, has sent out more missionaries than any other land, and has stood by the Jews through thick and thin.[24] In much the same way, Falwell has argued that America is different from other nations: "Our Founding Fathers firmly believed that America had a special destiny in the world. They were confident that God would bless their endeavors because they did not forget to acknowledge Him in all their doings."[25] Despite the country's current spiritual and moral malaise, Falwell believes that it can be saved and restored to divine favor if Americans return to the original religious vision and rediscover how to live by God's laws. As a premillennialist, Falwell knows that even if it comes, national restoration will not last forever. But he is convinced that it is a worthy cause for which to strive nonetheless. Therefore, premillennialists who fall into Butler's political prophetic category commit themselves to the political process and invariably run the risk of overaccommodating themselves to political ideologies. Their decision to help preserve the nation forces them to set aside, or at least downplay, certain parts of their eschatology. They know that the world cannot be saved by their efforts, but they do their best to postpone its demise as long as possible so that, among other things, the Lord's work might prosper until the end.

What, then, of the future of the movement? It seems certain that premillennialism is here to stay. Its dispensational version has had a loyal following within American evangelicalism for over a hundred years, and by the 1980s has established a permanent network of churches and schools. It has its own cadre of capable scholars and a remarkable literature with a large readership.[26]

The center of institutional dispensationalism is Dallas Theological Seminary. Founded in the mid-1920s by premillennialist Presbyterians, Dallas Seminary has been the academic and ideological "Vatican" of the movement ever since. The seminary's first president, Lewis Sperry Chafer, wrote dispensationalism's most influential systematic theology; and its professors have been in the forefront of premillennialist scholarship.[27] Dwight Pentecost, Norman Geisler, Charles C. Ryrie, and, most importantly, John F. Walvoord, the school's current president, are dispensationalism's most listened-to scholars.[28] Though these men are generally not read outside premillennialist circles, they are masters of their own system and provide a scholarly basis for it. Furthermore, Dallas Seminary has been the most important training ground for dispensationalist teachers and pastors. Other dispensationalist schools—colleges, Bible institutes, and seminaries—are staffed by large numbers of "Dallas men"; and many premillennialist churches prefer to hire Dallas graduates over those from their own denominational seminaries.[29]

Literature also plays an important role in the maintenance and growth of the movement. Premillennialist authors produce a steady stream of books on biblical prophecy, dispensational hermeneutics, and analyses of current events. Among others, periodicals like *Moody Monthly*, Jerry Falwell's new *Fundamentalist Journal*, and the more scholarly *Bibliotheca Sacra*, published by Dallas Seminary, keep dispensationalism before the public. The venerable Scofield Reference Bible was updated and reissued in 1967;[30] and Charles Ryrie of Dallas Seminary published his own dispensational Ryrie Study Bible in 1978.[31]

As a result, premillennialists are able to reproduce themselves theologically and ecclesiastically. Because of factors mentioned above, premillennialists have created their own well-defined subculture within American evangelicalism that needs no "outside" support to perpetuate itself. In light of the current renaissance of American fundamentalism under the leadership of men like Jerry Falwell, one must conclude that premillennialism will be able to maintain its following for some time to come. There is even evidence that it has broken out of its traditional bounds into nonevangelical circles. As was the case at the end of World War I, people outside the movement are taking notice of it and are criticizing its effects.[32] When people who are outside its normal sphere of influence acknowledge premillennialism in that way, it is safe to assume that it is having some kind of impact there.[33] One should not conclude from all this, however, that premillennialism has become established in liberal or ecumenical religious circles to any significant degree. It should be noted that the latest surge in prophetic interest began in the early 1970s, at the same time that Americans began showing interest in the occult, parapsychology, ouija boards, Eastern religions, and UFOs. Massive sales of premillennialists' books and increasing attendance at premillennialist prophetic conferences may not be an indication of authentic interest in premillennialism per se. They may simply be an example of Americans' insatiable appetite for the unusual, spectacular, and exotic. When *The Late Great Planet Earth* began showing up for sale in supermarkets, drug stores, and "secular" bookstores during the early 1970s, many shelf-stockers did not know where to put it. In many cases, they placed it alongside the latest "fad" books on extrasensory perception, out-of-body experiences, the occult, and the like. Whereas premillennialists know that there is an enormous difference between popular dispensationalism and such "pop-cultural" fads, many of the uninitiated could not tell the difference.

In short, despite some evidence to the contrary, these may not be the best of times for premillennialism after all. For one thing, American premillennialism has always been beset by internal divisions. Though we have not discussed to any great extent the hermeneutical differences among premillennialists, they have played a major role in the development of the movement in the United States. Dispensationalism was not and is not the only kind of premillennialism available to American Christians. Although it gained control of the new premillennialist movement by the turn of the century, it had to fend off a belated charge by an older, more traditional form of futurist premillennialism, which was having its own resurgence in the late nineteenth century in Europe and America among such men as Franz Delitzsch, F. L. Godet, and H. E. Meyer—all prominent European biblical commentators—and Americans Nathaniel West, John T. Duffield, and, to some extent, A. J. Gordon. That form of "historic premillennialism" did not make the absolute distinction between Israel and the church and contended that the church will live through the tribulation period and be raptured at the end of it. Though posttribulational premillennialism was evident in the early prophetic conferences, by the turn of the century its advocates had been successfully prevented from voicing their views in dispensationalist-controlled periodicals and were rarely invited to speak at prophetic conferences. Dispensationalists so effectively overcame the other view that many dispensationalists today erroneously believe that posttribulationism is new and dispensationalism is the oldest premillennial position.[34]

Those divisions still remain within American premillennialism. Even though the differences seem insignificant to outsiders, many premillennialists refuse to appear on the same platforms, serve on the same theological faculties, or be in the same churches with fellow premillennialists who hold, for example, a different view of the timing of the rapture. In such cases, the people involved believe that biblical truth, even orthodoxy, is at stake. Though they might agree on everything else, many premillennialists believe that in order for there to be Christian fellowship there must be agreement in the minute details of biblical interpretation. In more extreme cases, premillennialists have engaged in public feuds over the details of biblical prophecy, with dispensationalists asserting that nondispensationalists are on the road to liberalism and nondispensationalists claiming that their dispensational brethren are hopelessly and foolishly deluded. In some premillennialist circles, the most detested foes are fellow believers in the premillennial second coming.

Such divisions have actually intensified since World War II when posttribulationism experienced a renaissance. Premillennialist biblical scholars such as George E. Ladd, Robert Gundry, and Robert Mounce have challenged some of dispensationalism's most fundamental hermeneutical and exegetical arguments.[35] In their effort to undercut dispensational interpretation, they use some of the methods of modern, mainstream biblical scholarship. In short, many people within more moderate evangelical circles are finding in posttribulationism a way of retaining their basic premillennialist orientation while entering, at least to some degree, the world of modern biblical scholarship.[36] Such disagreements among professing premillennialists tend to divert their energies and undercut their appeal.

Furthermore, although no scientific poll or survey has ever been done to gauge the strength of premillennialism within conservative Protestantism, there is some evidence that its popularity may be on the decline in the evangelical (as opposed to fundamentalist) religious community. In early 1982, the editors of the *Evangelical Newsletter* conducted an informal poll of fifty-seven evangelical leaders, including professors, writers, and organizational heads. The editors asked them what had become of their interest in biblical prophecy over the past decade or two. Of those polled, 44 percent were less interested, 12 percent were more interested, and 44 percent experienced no change. The editors concluded that prophetic interest was waning.

> Despite Hal Lindsey, evangelical leaders are less interested in eschatology than they used to be. . . . Perhaps Israel's Six-Day War of 1967 sparked a surge in cloud-gazing that many have recovered from. Perhaps evangelicals are now reacting to the excesses of Lindsey and others. Perhaps there is just more important work to do than making charts of end events.[37]

Consequently, it seems safe to say that while militant fundamentalism retains nearly an unbroken dispensational front, that is no longer the case within American evangelical premillennialist ranks.[38]

In conclusion, American dispensational premillennialism may be entering its most perilous period. Its greatest successes tend to accentuate its greatest, and potentially most destructive, weaknesses. There was a time when the now/not-yet tension kept premillennialists from the dangers of date-setting. But that is no longer true. Since the founding of Israel in 1948 and the Six-Day War in 1967, many of premillennialism's most popular writers have become rather reckless in their predictions. When Hal Lindsey, for example, claims that the 1980s are the "terminal decade" in human history and that "all these things" must come to pass within a generation of the founding of the state of Israel, he is placing premillennialism's credibility on the line. He obviously feels confident enough in his reading of the Bible and the morning newspaper to speak in such definite terms, but if he is wrong, modern premillennialists may find themselves in the same position as the Millerites when their prophecies failed in the mid-1840s. They adjusted and survived, but their miscalculations set back American premillennialism considerably and made it a laughing stock in evangelicalism as a whole.

Dispensationalism's current problems go beyond that of date-setting. There is also the tendency to be excessively concerned with the *details* of prophetic fulfillment. This problem is not Lindsey's alone. Even the more conservative, academic spokesmen for dispensationalism are prone to look for minute fulfillments in current events. While Lindsey is obviously more sensational, there is actually little difference between his approach and that of John F. Walvoord in, for example, his *Armageddon: Oil and the Middle East Crisis* or Charles Ryrie in his *Bible and Tomorrow's News*. All three authors believe that they can identify the participants in end-time events among today's nations and have detailed scenarios of the future. The point is not that these premillennialists are doing more than they have to. According to their dispensational system, they are only doing what they must. They believe that the Bible contains a detailed and discernible plan for the end of history. Thus they would be remiss if they did not try to show how it is being worked out.

Briefly stated, dispensational premillennialism is inherently guilty of historical and theological "overassurance." In their study of different Christian approaches to history, George Marsden and Frank Roberts noted that "the tendency toward overassurance has generally been marked both by its disposition to play down the complexity and ambiguity of history and by its inclination to emphasize the clarity of the divine plan and purpose in events of the past."[39] Dispensationalists are equally overassured about events of the future. History—past, present, and future—contains no surprises. They believe they know not only where history is going, but how it is going to get there. Consequently, they are not afraid to deal with details; in fact, their hermeneutic requires them to do so. Book sales will be negligible for the premillennialist author who can only assert:

> We can be sure that history is moving toward some predetermined end and that it will culminate in the focus of evil forces and the return of Jesus Christ to set things right and inaugurate his kingdom of peace. But we cannot be sure about the details of fulfillment! The end is certain, but the means are clouded in obscurity.

The dispensational hermeneutic allows for more than that, and the dispensationalist rank and file expect more than that. Interpreters who play it too safe, premillennialists believe, are needlessly ignoring the exactness of the Bible's teachings about the future. But the truth of the matter is that those who produce too-detailed interpretations run the risk of looking foolish when history takes an unexpected turn. A study of the movement's development shows that most premillennialists believe that the risks are worth taking. While Old Testament saints regularly stoned mistaken prophets to death outside the city gates, modern premillennialist believers are willing to give their miscalculating prophets as many chances as they need. Premillennialists have made mistakes, adherents admit, but sooner or later, somebody is going to be right—about all the details. Thus, in order to be credible, premillennialists must deal with the details, but when they do, they increase the chances that they may lose their credibility if their detailed predictions do not come to pass.[40]

Historians are generally excused from making predictions about the future of historical movements—and we may be thankful for that. Though they often succumb to the temptation, prudence and common sense usually dictate silence. Only time will tell what will come of premillennialism in America. But then, that is precisely as the premillennialists would have it.

Notes

INTRODUCTION

1. Literature on the evangelical renaissance is proliferating. Some of the more significant studies include David F. Wells and John D. Woodbridge (eds.), *The Evangelicals* (New York: Abingdon, 1975); Carl F. H. Henry, *Evangelicals in Search of Identity* (Waco: Word Books, 1976); Richard Quebedeaux, *The Young Evangelicals* (New York: Harper & Row, 1974); Bernard L. Ramm, *The Evangelical Heritage* (Waco: Word Books, 1973); Donald G. Bloesch, *The Evangelical Renaissance* (Grand Rapids: Eerdmans, 1973).
2. Hal Lindsey, *The Late Great Planet Earth* (Grand Rapids: Zondervan, 1970).
3. Ernest R. Sandeen, *The Roots of Fundamentalism* (Chicago: University of Chicago Press, 1970).
4. Winthrop S. Hudson, *Religion in America* (New York: Scribner's, 1965), pp. 346–47; Martin E. Marty, *Righteous Empire* (New York: Dial Press, 1970), p. 180; William Warren Sweet, *The Story of Religion in America* (New York: Harper & Row, 1950), pp. 418–19; Sydney Ahlstrom, *A Religious History of the American People* (New Haven: Yale University Press, 1972), pp. 808–12.
5. For an overview of the historian's craft see Jacques Barzun and

Henry F. Graff, *The Modern Researcher* (3rd ed., New York: Harcourt, Brace, Jovanovich, 1977).

6. Robert F. Berkhofer, Jr., *A Behavioral Approach to Historical Analysis* (New York: Free Press, 1969).

7. Martin E. Marty, *A Nation of Behavers* (Chicago: University of Chicago Press, 1976).

8. A helpful study on millennialism is Millard J. Erickson, *Contemporary Options in Eschatology* (Grand Rapids: Baker Book House, 1977).

CHAPTER I

1. Since the King James Version was most frequently used by premillennialists during this period, it will be used for all biblical quotations.

2. Perry Miller, *Errand Into the Wilderness* (New York: Harper Torchbooks, 1956), pp. 217–39.

3. Jonathan Edwards, *Works* (4 vols., Worcester ed., Boston: Leavitt & Allen, 1843), I. For a discussion of the significance of Edwards's eschatology see C. C. Goen, "Jonathan Edwards: A New Departure in Eschatology," *Church History*, XXVII (Mar. 1959), 25–40.

4. Edwards, *Works*, I, 481.

5. Edwards, "Revival of Religion," *Works*, III, 313.

6. Quotations are from Lyman Beecher and Charles Finney. They may be found in William G. McLoughlin, Jr., *Modern Revivalism* (New York: Ronald Press, 1959), p. 105. For evangelical endeavors in this period see Charles I. Foster, *An Errand of Mercy: The Evangelical United Front, 1790–1837* (Chapel Hill: University of North Carolina Press, 1960); Donald W. Dayton, *Discovering an Evangelical Heritage* (New York: Harper & Row, 1976); Timothy L. Smith, *Revivalism and Social Reform* (New York: Harper Torchbooks, 1957).

7. See Sandeen, *Roots of Fundamentalism*, pp. 1–103, for a discussion of the rise of historicist premillennialism. The "year-day theory" was justified by reference to Numbers 14:33–34 and Ezekiel 4:4–6: "each day for a year."

8. On the Millerites see Francis D. Nichol, *The Midnight Cry* (Washington, D.C.: Review and Herald, 1944); Leroy E. Froom,

The Prophetic Faith of Our Fathers (4 vols., Washington, D.C.: Review and Herald, 1954), IV, 429–827; Edwin Scott Gaustad (ed.), *The Rise of Adventism* (New York: Harper & Row, 1974); Leon Festinger, *When Prophecy Fails* (Minneapolis: University of Minnesota Press, 1956).

9. The modern futurist movement can be traced to a Jesuit named Ribera, who proposed as early as 1590 that the prophecies concerning Antichrist would not be fulfilled until the very end of the church age, all in an attempt to undermine the Protestant claims that the papacy was in fact the Antichrist. Futurism made its way into the English-speaking world in the early nineteenth century. See George E. Ladd, *The Blessed Hope* (Grand Rapids: Eerdmans, 1956), pp. 35–40.

10. C. I. Scofield (ed.), *Scofield Reference Bible* (New York: Oxford University Press, 1909), p. 5.

11. C. I. Scofield, *Rightly Dividing the Word of Truth* (Oakland, Calif.: Western Book and Tract Company, n.d.), p. 18. Most dispensationalists counted seven dispensations, though there was some disagreement. Darby, for example, listed paradise (to the flood), Noah, Abraham, Israel, Gentiles, the Spirit, the millennium. Scofield's list included innocency (before the fall), conscience (fall to flood), human government, promise (Abraham to Moses), law (Moses to Christ), grace (the church age), kingdom (the millennium). See Arnold D. Ehlert, *A Bibliographic History of Dispensationalism* (Grand Rapids: Baker Book House, 1965). C. Norman Kraus, *Dispensationalism in America: Its Rise and Development* (Richmond: John Knox Press, 1958), pp. 23–44. Charles C. Ryrie, *Dispensationalism Today* (Chicago: Moody Press, 1965), p. 84.

12. Ehlert, *Bibliographic History*.

13. Ryrie, *Dispensationalism Today*, pp. 66–78. Daniel P. Fuller, The Hermeneutics of Dispensationalism (unpub. Th.D. diss., Northern Baptist Seminary, Chicago, 1957), pp. 24–25.

14. J. N. Darby, "The Covenants," *Collected Works,* ed. William Kelley (34 vols., London: G. Morrish, 1967), III, 75. James H. Brookes, *Israel and the Church* (St. Louis: Gospel Book and Tract Depository, n.d.), pp. 42–43. Scofield, *Reference Bible*, p. 20.

15. See Alva McClain, *Daniel's Prophecy of the Seventy Weeks* (Grand Rapids: Zondervan, 1940), pp. 12–15.

16. The numbering of the sixty-nine weeks was more difficult than might be expected. The generally accepted date of Artaxerxes' de-

cree was 444 B.C. Therefore, sixty-nine "weeks" (483 years) would have placed Messiah's rejection at A.D. 39, too late for the crucifixion of Jesus. Scofield hedged somewhat on the dating of the decree, declaring that it probably occurred sometime between 454 and 444 B.C. and assuring that "in either case we are brought to the time of Christ." Scofield, *Reference Bible*, p. 915. Brookes accepted Bishop Ussher's date (454 B.C.), argued that Christ's birth took place in 4 B.C., and thus arrived at his rejection in A.D. 29. James H. Brookes, *Maranatha* (3rd ed., New York: E. Brendell, 1874), pp. 425–26. Other dispensationalists accepted the traditional date (444 B.C.), but preferred counting years with only 360 days. With that method, they made the sixty-ninth week end on Palm Sunday. Willis Jordan, *The European War From a Bible Standpoint* (New York: Charles C. Cook, 1915), pp. 35–36. Robert Anderson, *The Coming Prince* (13th ed., London: Pickering & Inglis, n.d.), pp. 123–29. Arno C. Gaebelein, *The Prophet Daniel* (New York: "Our Hope" Publishing Office, 1936), p. 135.

17. For a complete discussion of the postponement theory see Fuller, Hermeneutics, pp. 287–337.

18. C. H. Mackintosh, *Papers on the Lord's Coming* (Chicago: Bible Institute Colportage Association, n.d.), pp. 101–2.

19. Ibid. pp. 104–5.

20. For typical presentations of this view see I. M. Haldeman, *The Coming of Christ* (Los Angeles: Bible House of Los Angeles, 1906), pp. 297–325. Leander Munhall, *The Lord's Return* (7th ed., New York: Eaton & Mains, 1898), pp. 179–80. C. H. Mackintosh, "The Double Phase of the Second Advent," *Our Hope*, XI (Nov. 1903), 322–29.

21. Samuel P. Tregelles, *The Hope of Christ's Second Coming* (London: Samuel Bagster & Sons, 1864), p. 35. Sandeen thinks the charge is pernicious and totally groundless. Sandeen, *The Roots of Fundamentalism*, p. 64.

22. David McPherson, *The Incredible Cover-Up: The True Story of the Pre-Trib Rapture* (Plainfield, N.J.: Logos International, 1975).

23. Darby, *Collected Works*, XI, 156. John Walvoord, a present-day dispensationalist, similarly states that one's doctrine of the church is more important for the doctrine of the pretribulation rapture than is any particular scriptural passage. John Walvoord, *The Rapture Question* (Findlay, O.: Dunham Publishing, 1957), p. 16.

24. Ahlstrom, *A Religious History*, pp. 133–220. Paul A. Carter, *The

Spiritual Crisis of the Gilded Age (De Kalb, Ill.: Northern Illinois University Press, 1971). Francis P. Weisenburger, *Ordeal of Faith: The Crisis of Churchgoing America, 1865–1900* (New York: Philosophical Library, 1959).

25. Henry F. May, *Protestant Churches and Industrial America* (New York: Harper Torchbooks, 1967). Aaron I. Abell, *The Urban Impact on American Protestantism, 1865–1900* (Cambridge: Harvard University Press, 1943). Robert D. Cross (ed.), *The Church and the City* (New York: Bobbs-Merrill, 1967). C. Howard Hopkins, *The Rise of the Social Gospel in American Protestantism, 1865–1915* (New Haven: Yale University Press, 1940). Robert T. Handy, *A Christian America: Protestant Hopes and Historical Realities* (New York: Oxford University Press, 1971), pp. 117–83.

26. Richard Hofstadter, *Social Darwinism in American Thought* (Boston: Beacon Press, 1944). Bert James Loewenberg, *Darwinism Comes to America, 1859–1900* (Philadelphia: Fortress Press, 1969). Stephen Neill, *The Interpretation of the New Testament, 1861–1961* (London: Oxford University Press, 1964). Ahlstrom, *A Religious History*, pp. 764–74. Hudson, *Religion in America*, pp. 263–67.

27. Henry Ward Beecher, *Yale Lectures on Preaching*, quoted in Hudson, *Religion in America*, pp. 266–67.

28. Kenneth Cauthen, *The Impact of American Religious Liberalism* (New York: Harper & Row, 1962). Lloyd J. Averill, *American Theology in the Liberal Tradition* (Philadelphia: Westminster Press, 1967). William Hutchinson, *The Modernist Impulse in American Protestantism* (Cambridge: Harvard University Press, 1976).

29. Consider the Princeton Theology, the mediating theologies of Augustus Strong and Edgar Y. Mullins, the holiness movement, the confessionalism of the Continental churches, etc.

30. James H. Brookes, *The Truth*, V (1879), 410. For more on the origins of the Bible conference movement see Kraus, *Dispensationalism in America*, pp. 71–80.

31. "Fundamentals of the Faith as Expressed in the Articles of Belief of the Niagara Bible Conference" (Chicago: Great Commission Prayer League, n.d.), reproduced in Sandeen, *The Roots of Fundamentalism*, pp. 273–77.

32. William Pettingill, "The Doctrine of the Lord's Coming as a Working Force in the Church and Community," in James M.

Gray (ed.), *The Coming and Kingdom of Christ* (Chicago: Bible Institute Colportage Association, 1914), p. 134.

33. I. M. Haldeman, *Professor Shailer Mathews' Burlesque on the Second Coming* (New York: privately printed, 1918), p. 23.

34. Sandeen, *Roots of Fundamentalism*, pp. 132–57. The addresses of the conference may be found in Nathaniel West (ed.), *Pre-Millennial Essays* (New York: Fleming H. Revell, 1879).

35. Ibid. p. 11.

36. The records of the conferences are as follows: Chicago, 1886—*Prophetic Studies of the International Prophetic Conference* (New York: Fleming H. Revell, 1886); Allegheny, Pa., 1895—*Addresses on the Second Coming of the Lord* (Pittsburgh: W. W. Waters, 1896); Boston, 1901—*Addresses of the International Prophetic Conference* (Boston: Watchword and Truth, 1901); Chicago, 1914—Gray (ed.), *The Coming and Kingdom of Christ;* Philadelphia, 1918—William L. Pettingill (ed.), *Light on Prophecy* (New York: Christian Herald, 1918); New York, 1918—Arno C. Gaebelein (ed.), *Christ and Glory* (New York: "Our Hope" Publishing Office, 1919).

37. Reuben A. Torrey, *The Return of the Lord Jesus Christ* (Los Angeles: Bible Institute of Los Angeles, 1913), p. 8.

38. William Bell Riley, *The Evolution of the Kingdom* (New York: Charles C. Cook, 1913), p. 5.

39. Quotations are from James H. Brookes, *The Truth*, XII (1886), 109–11. Ibid. XX (1894), 518.

40. J. Gresham Machen, *Christianity and Liberalism* (New York: Macmillan, 1926), pp. 49–50.

41. James H. Brookes, *The Truth*, XII (1886), 361–62, 506. Ibid. XV (1889), 203–4.

42. Mackintosh, *Papers on the Lord's Coming*, p. 56.

43. James H. Brookes, "Witnesses to the Hope," *The Truth*, XVII (1891), 310–22.

44. *Christian Workers Magazine*, XIV (Dec. 1913), 223–25. A greatly expanded list appeared at the end of the proceedings of the Chicago, 1914, conference. See Gray (ed.), *The Coming and Kingdom of Christ*.

45. *Christian Workers Magazine*, XVI (Dec. 1915), 261–64.

46. Sandeen, *Roots of Fundamentalism*, p. 231. Cornelius Woelfkin, "The Religious Appeal of Premillennialism," *Journal of Religion*, I (May 1921), 255–63.

47. List-making remained an important part of the premillennialist defense. See Thomas C. Horton, *These Premillennialists: Who Are They?* (Los Angeles: privately printed, 1921).

48. James H. Snowden, "Summary of Objections to Premillenarianism," *Biblical World*, LIII (Mar. 1919), 172–73. See also James H. Snowden, *The Coming of the Lord: Will It Be Premillennial?* (New York: Macmillan, 1919), pp. 32–34.

49. James F. Findlay, Jr., *Dwight L. Moody, American Evangelist, 1837–1899* (Chicago: University of Chicago Press, 1969), pp. 328–29.

50. *The Institute Tie*, I (Feb. 1901), 170.

51. Henry Ostrom, "My Personal Experience with the Doctrine of Our Lord's Second Coming," *Christian Workers Magazine*, XVIII (Mar. 1918), 561–64.

52. For these and other examples of the importance of premillennialist leadership see "How I Became a Premillennialist: A Symposium," *The Coming and Kingdom of Christ*, pp. 64ff. "How I Came to Believe in Our Lord's Return" (privately printed, n.d.).

53. Henry Drummond, *Dwight L. Moody: Impressions and Facts* (New York: McClure, Phillips, 1900), pp. 25–30.

54. A. T. Pierson, "Antagonism to the Bible," *Our Hope*, XV (Jan. 1909), 475.

55. Philip Mauro, *The Seventy Weeks and the Great Tribulation* (Boston: Hamilton Brothers, 1923), pp. 9–12. S. D. Gordon, *Quiet Talks on the Deeper Meaning of the War and Its Relationship to Our Lord's Return* (New York: Fleming H. Revell, 1919), pp. 149–50.

56. James H. Brookes, *The Truth*, V (1879), 314. Ibid. XXIII (1897), 80–82.

57. George Needham, "Introduction" to James H. Brookes, *Bible Reading on the Second Coming of Christ* (Springfield, Ill.: Edwin A. Wilson, 1877), p. viii. For samples of other Bible Readings see *The Truth*, II (1876), 28–32, 53–57.

58. Henry Warner Bowden, *Church History in the Age of Science* (Chapel Hill: University of North Carolina Press, 1971).

59. George P. Eckman, *When Christ Comes Again* (New York: Abingdon, 1917), pp. 48–49. See also Snowden, *The Coming of the Lord*, pp. 243–44.

60. Harris Franklin Rall, *New Testament History* (New York: Abingdon, 1914), p. 301. See also C. A. Briggs, "Millennium, Mil-

lenarianism," *The New Schaff-Herzog Encyclopedia of Religious Knowledge*, VII, 374–78. C. A. Briggs, "Origin and History of Pre-Millennialism," *Lutheran Quarterly*, IX (Apr. 1879), 244–45.

61. Albert Erdman, "Contending for the Faith," *Prophetic Studies of the International Prophetic Conference*, p. 90.

62. A critic recognized this powerful element: Francis J. McConnell, "The Causes of Premillenarianism," *Harvard Theological Review*, XII (Apr. 1919), 179–92.

63. Howard Pope in "How I Became a Premillennialist," *The Coming and Kingdom of Christ*, pp. 75–77.

64. Shirley Jackson Case, *The Millennial Hope* (Chicago: University of Chicago Press, 1918). See also Marty, *Righteous Empire*, p. 180; Findlay, *Dwight L. Moody*, p. 252.

CHAPTER 2

1. Nichol, *The Midnight Cry*, pp. 213–15, 238–40, 251. Gaustad, *Rise of Adventism*, pp. 154–72. Froom, *Prophetic Faith*, IV, 429–827.

2. Snowden, *The Coming of the Lord*, pp. 157–58. See also Snowden, "Summary of Objections to Premillenarianism," 169.

3. Dwight L. Moody, *New Sermons* (New York: Henry S. Good-speed, 1880), pp. 529–30.

4. Findlay, *Dwight L. Moody*, pp. 308–10, 317–21, 330–36.

5. William Runyan, *Dr. Gray at Moody Bible Institute* (New York: Oxford University Press, 1935), pp. 130–31.

6. Arno C. Gaebelein, *Half A Century* (New York: "Our Hope" Publishing Office, 1930), pp. 240–43.

7. *Christian Workers Magazine*, XIV (Sept. 1913), 2. Ibid. XV (June 1915), 626.

8. Torrey, *The Return of the Lord*, p. 126.

9. J. G. Princell, "Waiting, Watching, Working," *Prophetic Studies of the International Prophetic Conference*, p. 205.

10. A. C. Gaebelein, *Our Hope*, XXI (Jan. 1915), 388–89.

11. A. C. Gaebelein, *Meat in Due Season* (New York: "Our Hope" Publishing Office, 1933), p. 64.

12. A. C. Gaebelein, *Our Hope*, XIX (July 1912), 3.

13. Edmund Gosse, *Father and Son*, with Introduction and Notes by William Irvine (Boston: Houghton Mifflin, 1965), pp. 208–9.

14. J. C. Massee, "In Christ," *Christian Workers Magazine*, XIX (Mar. 1919), 461–65.

15. Gosse, *Father and Son*, pp. 209–10.

16. McLoughlin, *Modern Revivalism*, pp. 360–61.

17. Moody, *New Sermons*, p. 535.

18. J. Wilbur Chapman, *A Reason For My Hope* (New York: "Our Hope" Publishing Office, 1916), p. 4.

19. Moody, *New Sermons*, p. 535.

20. Torrey, *The Return of the Lord Jesus*, p. 131.

21. Moody, *New Sermons*, p. 532.

22. Arthur W. Pink, *The Redeemer's Return*, (Swengel, Pa.: Bible Truth Depot, 1918), p. 78.

23. R. A. Torrey, "That Blessed Hope," *Christ and Glory*, pp. 33–34.

24. William Evans, *The Coming King: The World's Next Crisis* (New York: Fleming H. Revell, 1923), pp. 103–7.

25. A. J. Gordon, quoted in A. B. Simpson, *Back to Patmos* (New York: Christian Alliance Publishing, 1914), pp. 95–96.

26. Samuel H. Kellogg, in *Bibliotheca Sacra*, VL (1888), 273.

27. James M. Gray, *Prophecy and the Lord's Return* (New York: Fleming H. Revell, 1917), p. 36.

28. Robert Speer, *The Second Coming of Christ* (New York: Gospel Publishing House, 1903), pp. 34–35.

29. R. A. Torrey, "The Second Coming A Motive for Personal Holiness," *The Coming and Kingdom of Christ*, pp. 229–31.

30. Munhall, *The Lord's Return*, pp. 76–77. For a similar story see *Our Hope*, XV (Oct. 1908), 312–13.

31. M. E. Dodd, *Jesus Is Coming to Earth Again* (Chicago: Bible Institute Colportage Association, 1917), pp. 50–51.

32. Lelia N. Morris, "What If It Were Today?" *Worship and Service Hymnal* (Chicago: Hope Publishing, 1957), #87.

33. Fanny Crosby, "Will Jesus Find Us Watching?" ibid., #85.

34. "Lewd Dressing," *Christian Workers Magazine*, XVI (Feb. 1916), 430.

35. A. R. Funderburk, "The Word of God on Women's Dress," *Moody Bible Institute Monthly*, XXII (Jan. 1922), 759. "Jail the Girls," ibid. 749. For other reactions to dress styles see A. C. Gaebelein, *Our Hope*, XXVIII (Apr. 1921), 618. "Mothers to Blame," *Moody Bible Institute Monthly*, XIII (May 1923), 407. Albert Kinzler, "What About Hair-Bobbing?" ibid. XXIV (Aug. 1924), 605.

36. *The Institute Tie,* VII (Aug. 1907), 564.

37. *Moody Bible Institute Monthly,* XXII (Oct. 1921), 599.

38. James E. Ely, *Glimpses of Bible Climaxes* (Garden City, Kans.: Businessmen's Gospel Association, 1927), pp. 110–11.

39. *The Institute Tie,* IX (July 1909), 942–43. Ibid. X (Aug. 1910), 944. *Our Hope,* XII (July 1915), 51. *Christian Workers Magazine,* XVI (Oct. 1915), 88–89. Ibid. XVI (June 1916), 738. *Moody Bible Institute Monthly,* XXV (Mar. 1925), 317–18.

CHAPTER 3

1. Case, *The Millennial Hope,* pp. 235–37.

2. Walter Rauschenbusch, *Christianity and the Social Crisis* (New York: Macmillan, 1907), pp. 202–3.

3. William B. King, quoted in Snowden, *The Coming of the Lord,* pp. 233–34.

4. Harris Franklin Rall, "Where Premillennialism Leads," *Biblical World,* LIII (Nov. 1919), 617–27. See also T. Valentine Parker, "Premillennialism: An Interpretation and Evaluation," ibid. LIII (Jan. 1919), 37–40.

5. Speer, *Second Coming of Christ,* pp. 14, 39.

6. Henry W. Frost, "The Dying Heathen," *The Institute Tie,* VIII (Nov. 1907), 181.

7. For historical overviews of the period see Kenneth Scott Latourette, *The History of the Expansion of Christianity* (7 vols., Grand Rapids: Zondervan, 1970), vols. IV–VI. Stephen Neill, *A History of Christian Missions* (London: Penguin Books, 1965), pp. 261–396.

8. John R. Mott, *The Evangelization of the World in This Generation* (New York: Student Volunteer Movement for Foreign Missions, 1900), p. 7.

9. Scofield called this verse "the most important passage in the N.T." from a dispensational perspective because it showed clearly "the distinctive work of the present, or the church age. . . . The Gospel has never anywhere converted all, but everywhere has called out *some.*" Scofield, *Reference Bible,* pp. 1169–70.

10. W. P. Mackay, "The Return of Christ and Foreign Missions," *Premillennial Essays,* pp. 456–61. Robert McW. Russell, "The Kingdom View of the Gospel as Related to the Missionary Program of Christ," *Christian Workers Magazine,* XIV (Dec. 1913), 228–34.

C. I. Scofield, *Addresses on Prophecy* (New York: "Our Hope" Publishing Office, 1910), pp. 22–23. William E. Blackstone, *Jesus Is Coming* (New York: Fleming H. Revell, 1908), pp. 131–32.

11. W. J. Erdman, "The Main Idea of the Bible," *The Institute Tie*, IX (Oct. 1908), 94.

12. Reported in C. I. Scofield, "The Doctrine of Last Things as Found in the Gospels," *The Coming and Kingdom of Christ*, p. 115.

13. Blackstone cited Acts 2:5 and 8:4, Mark 16:20, and Colossians 1:23 to prove that the world had already been evangelized. Blackstone, *Jesus Is Coming*, pp. 132–34. For the Jewish role in evangelization during the tribulation see William E. Blackstone, "Missions," *Prophetic Studies of the International Prophetic Conference*, pp. 194–202.

14. William Bell Riley, "The Significant Signs of the Times," *The Coming and Kingdom of Christ*, pp. 108–9.

15. Findlay, *Dwight L. Moody*, pp. 346–55. Sandeen, *Roots of Fundamentalism*, pp. 183–86.

16. Latourette, *Expansion of Christianity*, VI, 329, 326–31. Neill, *History of Christian Missions*, pp. 333–36. Howard Taylor, *Hudson Taylor and the China Inland Mission* (London: China Inland Mission, 1919). James H. Brookes said that all missionaries in the CIM were premillennialists—a questionable statement. *The Truth*, XV (1889), 97–99.

17. Sandeen, *Roots of Fundamentalism*, p. 187. Charles Erdman, "William Whiting Borden: An Ideal Missionary Volunteer," *Missionary Review of the World*, XXXVI (Aug. 1913), 567–77. *Christian Workers Magazine*, XIII (May 1913), 605. Ibid. XIII (Nov. 1913), 139. *Moody Bible Institute Monthly*, XXIII (June 1923), 459.

18. A. E. Thompson, *The Life of A. B. Simpson* (New York: Christian Alliance Publishing, 1920). For his premillennialism see Simpson, *Back to Patmos*. A. B. Simpson, *The Coming One* (New York: Christian Alliance Publishing, 1912). A. B. Simpson, *The Gospel of the Kingdom* (New York: Christian Alliance Publishing, 1890).

19. A. B. Simpson, quoted in J. H. Hunter, *Beside All Waters* (Harrisburg, Pa.: Christian Publications, 1964), p. 17.

20. Norris Magnuson, *Salvation in the Slums: Evangelical Social Work, 1865–1920* (Metuchen, N.J.: Scarecrow Press, 1977), pp. 14–20.

21. James H. Brookes, *The Truth*, XXII (1897), 4.

22. *Moody Bible Institute Monthly*, XXIII (May 1923), 433.

23. *The Institute Tie*, I (Oct. 1900), 37. Ibid. V (Apr. 1906), 257–58.
24. James M. Gray, *Modernism* (Chicago: Bible Institute Colportage Association, 1924), p. 87. Pettingill, *Light on Prophecy*, p. 284. G. E. Guille, *That Blessed Hope* (Chicago: Bible Institute Colportage Association, 1920), p. 36.
25. Sandeen, *Roots of Fundamentalism*, p. 186.
26. A. E. Thompson, quoted in Pettingill, *Light on Prophecy*, p. 157.

CHAPTER 4

1. Eckman, *When Christ Comes Again*, pp. 154–55. See also Case, *Millennial Hope*, pp. 240–41.
2. Robert H. Wiebe, *The Search for Order, 1877–1920* (New York: Hill & Wang, 1967). Ray Ginger, *Age of Excess: the United States from 1877 to 1914* (New York: Macmillan, 1965).
3. Josiah Strong, *Our Country* (rev. ed., New York: Baker & Taylor, 1891). The other "perils" included immigrations, Romanism, Mormonism, the changing status of religion in the schools, socialism, and accumulated wealth.
4. Otto L. Bettman, *The Good Old Days—They Were Terrible!* (New York: Random House, 1975).
5. In 1900 church membership was quite small in comparison to total population. Of 76 million in the nation, evangelical denominations could claim only 16 million, or just about 21% of the total. Edward Scott Gaustad, *Historical Atlas of Religion in America* (New York: Harper & Row, 1963), p. 52.
6. Samuel P. Hays, *The Response to Industrialism, 1885–1914* (Chicago: University of Chicago Press, 1957). Eric F. Goldman, *Rendezvous With Destiny* (New York: Vintage Books, 1952).
7. Marty, *Righteous Empire*, pp. 177–87. Jean P. Miller, Souls or the Social Order: Polemic in American Protestantism (unpub. Ph.D. diss., University of Chicago, 1969).
8. Albert Sims, *The Coming Crash* (Toronto: A. Sims, n.d.), pp. 5–16. Albert Sims, *The Near Approach of Antichrist* (Toronto: A. Sims, n.d.), pp. 12–15. *The Institute Tie*, VI (Sept. 1905), 27. *Our Hope*, XIX (Oct. 1912), 231. Ibid. XXVI (Dec. 1919), 311–12. *Christian Workers Magazine*, XV (May 1915), 55.
9. A. J. Frost, "Conditions of the Church and World at Christ's Sec-

ond Advent," *Prophetic Studies of the International Prophetic Conference*, pp. 172–77. A. C. Dixon, *Evangelism Old and New* (New York: American Tract Society, 1905), p. 178. Haldeman, *The Coming of Christ*, pp. 113–50. *The Institute Tie*, X (Aug. 1910), 944. *Christian Workers Magazine*, XV (May 1915), 55.

10. Rudolph Malek, "America's Vulnerable Spot," *Moody Bible Institute Monthly*, XXII (Nov. 1921), 655–56. *The Institute Tie*, VIII (Sept. 1907), 10–11. William G. McLoughlin, Jr., *Billy Sunday Was His Real Name* (Chicago: University of Chicago Press, 1955), pp. 146–48.

11. I. M. Haldeman, *Signs of the Times* (New York: Charles C. Cook, 1913).

12. *The Institute Tie*, VII (Apr. 1907), 337. Gray, *Modernism*. James M. Gray, *Satan and the Saint* (New York: Fleming H. Revell, 1909).

13. Blackstone, *Jesus Is Coming*, pp. 231–33.

14. Samuel J. Andrews, *Christianity and Antichristianity in Their Final Conflict* (Chicago: Bible Institute Colportage Association, 1898).

15. Lewis Sperry Chafer, *Signs of the Times* (Chicago: Bible Institute Colportage Association, 1919), pp. 12–29. Riley, *The Evolution of the Kingdom*, pp. 172–82.

16. McConnell, "The Causes of Premillenarianism," 182.

17. William Pettingill, in William B. Riley (ed.), *God Hath Spoken* (Philadelphia: Bible Conference Committee, 1919), p. 358.

18. Snowden, *The Coming of the Lord*, pp. 245–79. James Snowden, *Is the World Growing Better?* (New York: Macmillan, 1922).

19. William Newton Clarke, *An Outline of Theology* (10th ed., New York: Scribner's, 1901), pp. 429–36.

20. Case, *Millennial Hope*, p. 238.

21. Abell, *The Urban Impact on American Protestantism*, pp. 27–56, 118–223. Cross, *The Church and the City*, pp. 127–352.

22. Eckman, *When Christ Comes Again*, p. 203. See also Snowden, *Is the World Growing Better? passim*. Snowden, *The Coming of the Lord*, pp. 245–79. Case, *Millennial Hope*, pp. 278–79.

23. Blackstone, *Jesus Is Coming*, p. 148.

24. A. J. Gordon, "Latter-Day Delusions," in *Prophetic Studies of the International Prophetic Conference*, pp. 62–63. A. J. Gordon, *Ecce Venit* (New York: Fleming H. Revell, 1889), pp. 201–2. See also

Munhall, *The Lord's Return*, p. 56; E. F. Stroetter, "Christ's Coming Premillennial," *Prophetic Studies of the International Prophetic Conference*, p. 19. Blackstone, *Jesus Is Coming*, pp. 144–56.

26. James H. Brookes, "Gentile Dominion," *The Truth*, VI (1880), 536.

27. Eli Reece, *How Far Can a Premillennialist Pastor Cooperate with Social Service Programs?* (privately printed, n.d.).

28. Gaebelein, *Our Hope*, XV (Mar. 1909), 643.

29. Scofield, *Reference Bible*, p. 901. "Democracy at the Crossroads," *Christian Workers Magazine*, XIX (May 1919), 626.

30. Benjamin Parke Dewitt, *The Progressive Movement*, with Introduction by Arthur Mann (Seattle: University of Washington Press, 1968).

31. Philip Mauro, "Discontent of the Laboring Classes," *Our Hope*, XIX (Oct. 1912), 225–29.

32. A. C. Gaebelein, *Our Hope*, XIX (July 1912), 49–50. See also Sims, *The Coming Crash*, pp. 5–16.

33. Sims, *The Near Approach of Antichrist*, pp. 12–15. Sims, *The Coming Crash*, pp. 17–30.

34. *Our Hope*, XIX (Oct. 1912), 231. *The Institute Tie*, IX (Sept. 1908), 8. *The Moody Bible Institute Monthly*, XXIII (Sept. 1922), 4. Andrews, *Christianity and Antichristianity*, pp. 234–35. "The New Foe of Society," *Christian Workers Magazine*, XIV (Jan. 1914), 309–10. *Our Hope*, XV (Nov. 1908), 374–76.

35. Charles Reihl, "Solution to Prohibition," *The Truth*, XV (1889), 370–75.

36. Smith, *Revivalism and Social Reform*, pp. 148–62.

37. Parker, "Premillennialism: An Interpretation and Evaluation," 37–40. See also Rall, "Where Premillennialism Leads," 617–18.

38. Gray, *Prophecy and the Lord's Return*, p. 109.

39. Bob Jones, "The Lord's Coming as a Working Force in the Church and Community," *The Coming and Kingdom of Christ*, p. 138. *The Institute Tie*, X (July 1910), 856.

40. *The Institute Tie*, X (July 1910), 857.

41. *Christian Workers Magazine*, XIV (Aug. 1914), 800.

42. James M. Gray, "And Such Were Some of You," *Christian Workers Magazine*, XIV (Aug. 1914), 783–86.

43. Runyan, *Dr. Gray*, pp. 38–39. *The Institute Tie*, IX (Nov. 1908), 247.

44. *The Institute Tie*, IX (Sept. 1908), 18.

45. *Christian Workers Magazine*, XV (June 1920), 829. McLoughlin, *Modern Revivalism*, pp. 282–400.

46. Magnuson, *Salvation in the Slums*. George Dollar, *A History of Fundamentalism in America* (Greenville, S.C.: Bob Jones University Press, 1973), p. 367.

47. C. I. Scofield, "The World's Approaching Crisis," *Our Hope*, X (Aug. 1903), 79–80.

48. Torrey, *The Return of the Lord Jesus*, pp. 7–8.

49. Christabel Pankhurst, *The Lord Cometh!* (New York: The Book Stall, 1923), pp. 21–25.

50. David Mitchell, *The Fighting Pankhursts* (New York: Macmillan, 1967), pp. 227–28.

51. Pankhurst, *The Lord Cometh!* p. 9. See also Christabel Pankhurst, *Some Modern Problems in the Light of Biblical Prophecy* (New York: Fleming H. Revell, 1924). Christabel Pankhurst, *The World's Unrest* (Philadelphia: Sunday School Times, 1929). Christabel Pankhurst, *Seeing the Future* (New York: Harper & Row, 1929).

52. Handy, *A Christian America*, pp. 155–83.

CHAPTER 5

1. Scofield, *Reference Bible*, p. 1345.

2. Ibid. pp. 900–901. Gaebelein, *The Prophet Daniel*, pp. 73–76. See Daniel 2 and 7 for biblical references.

3. Scofield, *Reference Bible*, p. 1349. See Revelation 13:1–10, Matthew 24:15, II Thessalonians 2:3–4.

4. Daniel 9:27. When the Beast makes the covenant with Israel, Daniel's seventieth week begins, leaving seven years before the triumphant return of Christ.

5. For the rise of the false prophet, see Revelation 13:11–18. The three and a half years of terror make up the "great tribulation." Scofield, *Reference Bible*, pp. 133, 1342.

6. Ezekiel 38:1–39:25. Scofield suggested that this passage should be read along with Zechariah 12:1–4, 14:1–9; Matthew 24:14–30; Revelation 14:14–20, 19:17–21. Scofield, *Reference Bible*, p. 883. The head of the confederacy was to be Russia. Ezekiel spoke in terms of Gog, the prince of Magog, which included the territories of Rosh (Revised Version), Meshech, and Tubal. Premillennialists

identified these areas as Russia, Moscow, and Tobolsk. See Arno C. Gaebelein, *The Prophet Ezekiel* (New York: "Our Hope" Publishing Office, 1918), pp. 257–58.

7. The king of the south, Daniel 11:40, in conjunction with Ezekiel 30; the kings of the east, Revelation 16:12.

8. Revelation 19:17–21. Scofield, *Reference Bible*, pp. 1348–49.

9. In 1864, John Cumming, a British premillennialist in the historicist tradition, argued for Russian leadership of the northern confederacy: *The Destiny of Nations* (London: Hurst & Blackette, 1864). See also James Brookes, *The Truth*, II (1876), 555. Alfred Burton, *The Future of Europe* (New York: Bible Truth Press, [1890], 1915). Alfred Burton, *Russia's Destiny in the Light of Prophecy* (New York: Gospel Publishing House, 1917). *Our Hope*, XVI (July 1909), 37–38. Ibid. XVII (Jan. 1911), 464–69.

10. *Our Hope*, XXI (Sept. 1914), 146.

11. Premillennialists may have differed in details, but the general outline of events is easily discerned. See *The Institute Tie*, X (Apr. 1910), 609. Gray, *Prophecy and the Lord's Return*, pp. 26–27. Jordan, *The European War from a Bible Standpoint. Christian Workers Magazine*, XVI (May 1916), 686–87. *Our Hope*, XXI (Dec. 1914), 360–62. Ibid. XIII (Mar. 1917), 559. F. C. Jennings, *The End of the European War in the Light of Scripture* (New York: Charles C. Cook, 1915), pp. 11–24. *Christian Workers Magazine*, XV (Nov. 1914), 158–60. Philip Mauro, *The World War: How It Is Fulfilling Prophecy* (Boston: Hamilton Brothers, 1918). Charles C. Cook, *End of the Age Themes* (New York: Charles C. Cook, 1917).

12. Jennings, *The End of the European War*, pp. 35–40. Jennings, *The World Conflict in the Light of the Prophetic Word*, pp. 164–65.

13. William E. Blackstone, "The Times of the Gentiles and the War in the Light of Prophecy," *Christian Workers Magazine*, XVI (May 1916), 686–87. William J. Erdman, "An Important Query," ibid. XVII (Nov. 1916), 194.

14. S. D. Gordon, *Quiet Talks on the Deeper Meaning of the War*, p. 69.

15. *Christian Workers Magazine*, XVIII (Feb. 1918), 447.

16. Ibid. XV (Oct. 1914), 81–82. *Our Hope*, XXI (Jan. 1915), 424–27.

17. Ibid. XX (Sept. 1913), 176. Ibid. XVIII (Oct. 1911), 262. *Christian Workers Magazine*, XVI (Jan. 1916), 374.

18. Snowden, *The Coming of the Lord*, pp. 269–72.

19. *Biblical World*, XLVI (July 1915), 1.
20. Shailer Mathews, *New Faith For Old* (New York: Macmillan, 1936), pp. 196–97.
21. Eckman, *When Christ Comes Again*, pp. 9–10.
22. Shailer Mathews, *Will Christ Come Again?* (Chicago: American Institute of Sacred Literature, 1917). Quotations are from Gaebelein's review in *Our Hope*, XXIV (Jan. 1918), 407–14.
23. Shirley Jackson Case, *The Millennial Hope*. Shirley Jackson Case, *The Revelation of John* (Chicago: University of Chicago Press, 1919).
24. Snowden, *Is the World Growing Better?* Snowden, *The Coming of the Lord*.
25. George P. Mains, *Premillennialism: Non-Scriptural, Non-Historic, Non-Scientific, Non-Philosophical* (New York: Abingdon, 1920).
26. Harris Franklin Rall, *Modern Premillennialism and the Christian Hope* (New York: Abingdon, 1920).
27. See *Biblical World*, vols. LII and LIII, for A. H. Forster, "The Servant of Isaiah and the Second Coming." J. F. Vichert, "Is the Gospel Spiritual Pessimism?" James Snowden, "Summary of Objections to Premillenarianism." H. Franklin Rall, "Premillennialism: The Issue," "Premillennialism and the Bible," and "Where Premillennialism Leads."
28. Shirley Jackson Case, *Chicago Daily News*, Jan. 21, 1918.
29. Shirley Jackson Case, "The Premillennial Menace," *Biblical World*, LII (July 1918), 16–23.
30. James M. Gray, *Christian Workers Magazine*, XVIII (Mar. 1918), 548–51.
31. R. A. Torrey, XXIV (May 1918), 679–81. R. A. Torrey, *Christian Workers Magazine*, XIX (Feb. 1919), 375. As early as 1917 premillennialists were complaining about being labeled pro-German. H. A. Ironside claimed that "Men of unflinching integrity and loyalty to the Word of God have been branded as secret political agents, and their books, so far as possible, proscribed by these audacious and unprincipled leaders in the apostasy." *Our Hope*, XXXI (Apr. 1925), 628.
32. D. M. Panton, "The Present Rise and Ultimate End of Democracy," *Christian Workers Magazine*, XIX (May 1919), 637–39. Kellogg, "Premillennialism: Its Relation to Doctrine and Practice," pp. 273–74.
33. James M. Gray, "Practical and Perplexing Questions," *Christian*

Workers Magazine, XVI (Oct. 1915), 97–98. In light of the coming kingdom, Scofield declared himself a "monarchist." Scofield,
World's Approaching Crisis, pp. 22–23.

34. R. A. Torrey, *The King's Business*, V (Dec. 1914), 684.
35. Ibid. VII (Mar. 1916), 195. Ibid. VII (June 1916), 487–88. Ibid.
    VIII (Apr. 1917), 293.
36. Ibid. VIII (Oct. 1917), 867–68.
37. *Christian Workers Magazine*, XVII (July 1917), 853.
38. Ibid. XVII (Jan. 1917), 350.
39. Ibid. XVII (July 1917), 862–63.
40. Ibid. XVIII (Nov. 1917), 179–80. Ibid. XVIII (Feb. 1918), 448.
    Ibid. XVIII (Nov. 1917), 197. Ibid. XVIII (Dec. 1917), 333. Ibid.
    XVIII (Mar. 1918), 548–51. Ibid. XIX (Oct. 1918), 83.
41. Pettingill, *Light on Prophecy*, pp. 10, 111.
42. Gaebelein, *Half a Century*, p. 112.
43. R. A. Torrey, "That Blessed Hope," in Gaebelein (ed.), *Christ
    and Glory*, pp. 21–22.
44. A. C. Gaebelein, *The League of Nations in the Light of Prophecy*
    (New York: "Our Hope" Publishing Office, 1920). Haldeman,
    Why I Preach the Second Coming, pp. 121–22.
45. *Christian Workers Magazine*, XIX (Apr. 1919), 526. *Moody Bible
    Institute Monthly*, XXI (Sept. 1920), 7. Ibid. XXI (Aug. 1921),
    510–12. Ibid. XXI (Jan. 1922), 806.
46. I. R. Dean, *The Coming Kingdom* (Philadelphia: Approved Book
    Store, 1928), p. 216.
47. Torrey, "That Blessed Hope," p. 22.
48. William Bell Riley, "The Last Days, the Last War, and the Last
    King," in Gaebelein (ed.), *Christ and Glory*, pp. 161–76.
49. For another look at premillennialists and World War I see Dwight
    Wilson, *Armageddon Now!* (Grand Rapids: Baker Book House,
    1977), pp. 36–58.

CHAPTER 6

1. Wilson, *Armageddon Now!* pp. 14–35.
2. Quoted in Melvin I. Urofsky, *American Zionism from Herzl to
   the Holocaust* (Garden City, N.Y.: Anchor Books, 1976), p. 199.
3. For typical reactions to the capture of Jerusalem see *Christian*

Workers Magazine, XVIII (Jan. 1918), 396. Ibid. XVIII (Feb. 1918), 447. *Our Hope*, XXIV (Feb. 1918), 486–90. E. Newman, "Jerusalem and the Jews in View of Scripture Prophecy," in *The Jew in History and Prophecy* (Chicago: Chicago Hebrew Mission, 1918), p. 25.

4. A. E. Thompson, in Pettingill (ed.), *Light on Prophecy*, p. 144. Sandeen, *Roots of Fundamentalism*, pp. 233–35.

5. Sandeen, *Roots of Fundamentalism*, pp. 20–22, 67, 234–35.

6. Nathaniel West, *The Thousand Years in Both Testaments* (New York: Fleming H. Revell, 1889), pp. 424–26, 632. Blackstone, *Jesus Is Coming*, pp. 165, 171–72. Riley, *The Evolution of the Kingdom*, p. 48. Haldeman, *The Coming of Christ*, p. 205. J. F. Silver, *The Lord's Return* (New York: Fleming H. Revell, 1914), p. 279. Brookes, *Maranatha*, pp. 389–445.

7. Urofsky, *American Zionism*, pp. 41–230. See also Nathan Glazer, *American Judaism* (2nd ed., Chicago: University of Chicago Press, 1972).

8. E.g. *Our Hope*, X (July 1903), 3–4. Ibid. X (Nov. 1903), 339. Ibid. XIII (Aug. 1906), 119–20.

9. *The Institute Tie*, VIII (Oct. 1907), 128. *Our Hope*, X (Feb. 1904), 513–14. Blackstone, *Jesus Is Coming*, pp. 210–11. Arno C. Gaebelein, *Hath God Cast Away His People?* (New York: Gospel Publishing House, 1905).

10. *Our Hope*, V (Aug. and Sept. 1898), 101–2.

11. Gaebelein, *Hath God Cast Away His People?* pp. 200–201.

12. Gaebelein, "The Present Day Restoration Movement Among the Jews and Its Significance," *Our Hope*, XVI (Sept. 1909), 103–7. *The Institute Tie*, IX (Sept. 1908), 40.

13. Quoted in Reuben Fink (ed.), *America and Palestine* (New York: American Zionist Emergency Council, 1944), p. 21. See also Urofsky, *American Zionism*, p. 43.

14. Quoted in Anita Libman Lebeson, "Zionism Comes to Chicago," in *Early History of Zionism in America*, ed. Isidore S. Meyer (New York: American Jewish Historical Society and Theodore Herzl Foundation, 1958), pp. 168–69.

15. Daniel Fuchs, "Prophecy and the Evangelization of the Jews," in *Focus on Prophecy*, ed. Charles L. Feinberg (Westwood, N.J.: Fleming H. Revell, 1964), p. 252. Blackstone's marked Old Testament is in the public display on the history of Zionism at Herzl's grave in Israel.

16. Lebeson, "Zion Comes to Chicago," p. 169.

17. Beth M. Lindberg, *A God-Filled Life: The Story of William E. Blackstone* (Chicago: American Messianic Fellowship, n.d.), n.p.

18. J. D. Douglas (ed.), *The New International Dictionary of the Christian Church* (Grand Rapids: Zondervan, 1974), p. 135.

19. Jewish Mission of the Joint Synod of Ohio (Lutheran), 1892; Reformed Presbyterian Jewish Mission Board, 1894; Zion's Society for Israel of the Norwegian Lutherans in America, 1878; Jewish Mission of the Evangelical Synod of Missouri, Ohio, and Other States (Lutheran), 1883; New York City Extension and Missionary Society (Methodist Episcopal), 1886; Hebrew Mission of the Methodist Episcopal Church, South, 1904; plus numerous other interdenominational or nondenominational organizations.

20. James Brookes, "How To Reach the Jews," *The Truth*, XIX (1893), 135–36.

21. Arno Gaebelein, *Our Hope*, XX (Jan. 1914), 442–45.

22. *Fifty Years of Blessing: Historical Sketch of Chicago Hebrew Mission, 1887–1937* (Chicago: Chicago Hebrew Mission, 1937), published in *Jewish Era*, XLVII (Dec. 1937), 3–56.

23. J. H. Ralston, "The Conference on Behalf of Israel," *Christian Workers Magazine*, XVI (Jan. 1916), 359–60.

24. James Brookes, "Work Among the Jews," *The Truth*, XX (1894), 14–16. Sandeen, *Roots of Fundamentalism*, pp. 214–15.

25. To name a few, New York Hebrew Christian Association, 1903; Hebrew Messianic Council, Boston, 1888; Brooklyn Christian Mission to the Jews, 1892; St. Louis Jewish Christian Mission, 1898; San Francisco Hebrew Mission, 1896; New Covenant Mission to the Jews and Gentiles, Pittsburgh, 1898; Hebrew Christian Mission to the Jews, Newark, 1904.

26. Charles Meeker, "Evangelization of the American Jew," *Christian Workers Magazine*, XIX (Aug. 1919), 868.

27. F. C. Gilbert, *From Judaism to Christianity* (South Lancaster, Mass:. Good Tidings Press, 1911), p. 177.

28. Joseph Hoffman Cohn, *I Have Fought a Good Fight* (New York: American Board of Missions to the Jews, 1953), p. 42.

29. S. B. Rohold, "Missionary Work Among the Jews in the Holy Land," *Christian Workers Magazine*, XX (May 1920), 711–14. *Our Hope*, X (Aug. 1903), 104.

30. Gilbert, *From Judaism to Christianity*, pp. 251–56.

31. William W. Ketchum, "Some Interesting Things About Jews," *Christian Workers Magazine*, XX (Apr. 1920), 630–31.

32. Leopold Cohn, *A Modern Missionary to An Ancient People* (2nd ed., New York: American Board of Missions to the Jews, 1911).

33. *Down on Throop Avenue* (New York: American Board of Missions to the Jews, 1940).

34. For two accounts see J. H. Cohn, *I Have Fought a Good Fight*, pp. 96–109. Samuel Freuder, *A Missionary's Return to Judaism* (New York: Sinai Publishing, 1915).

35. Freuder, *A Missionary's Return*, pp. 164–66. J. H. Cohn, *I Have Fought a Good Fight*, pp. 204–25.

36. Ibid. p. 225.

37. "Williamsburg Mission to the Jews: Abstract of the Report of the Committee of Investigation," *Christian Workers Magazine*, XVII (Nov. 1916), 191–92.

38. Freuder, *A Missionary's Return*, pp. 36–59.

39. Ibid. pp. 7–20.

40. Lewis A. Hart, *A Jewish Reply to Christian Evangelists* (New York: Block Publishing, 1907).

41. Freuder, *A Missionary's Return*, pp. 86–94, 137–49.

42. A. C. Gaebelein, *Our Hope*, X (Aug. 1903), 104.

43. One convert tells her story in Lydia Buksbazen, *They Looked for a City* (West Collingswood, N.J.: Spearhead Press, 1955).

44. Maurice Ruben, "The Hebrew Christian Alliance Conference," *Christian Workers Magazine*, XVIII (Sept. 1917), 37.

45. A. C. Gaebelein, "Professor Heman on the Jews and the Churches," *Our Hope*, V (Aug. and Sept. 1898), 56–58.

46. A. C. Gaebelein, "The Hope of Israel Mission," *Our Hope*, V (July 1898), 40. See also E. F. Stroeter, "The Second Coming of Christ in Relation to Israel," *Addresses on the Second Coming of Christ*, pp. 150–51.

47. J. H. Cohn, *I Have Fought a Good Fight*, pp. 91–94.

48. *Protocols of the Meeting of the Learned Elders of Zion*, trans. Victor E. Marsden (London: Britons Publishing, 1922). Norman Cohn, *Warrant for Genocide: The Myth of the Jewish World Conspiracy and the "Protocols of the Elders of Zion"* (New York: Harper Torchbooks, 1969).

49. A. C. Gaebelein, *Our Hope*, XXIX (Aug. 1922), 103.

50. Charles C. Cook, "The International Jew," *The King's Business*, XII (Nov. 1921), 1087. Wilson, *Armageddon Now!* pp. 75–77.

51. James M. Gray, "The Jewish Protocols," *Moody Bible Institute Monthly*, XXII (Oct. 1921), 598.
52. W. B. Riley, *Wanted—A World Leader!* (privately printed, n.d.), pp. 41–51, 71–72.

CHAPTER 7

1. Sandeen, *Roots of Fundamentalism*, p. xv.
2. Courtland Myers, quoted in Pettingill, *Light on Prophecy*, p. 212.
3. Stewart G. Cole, *A History of Fundamentalism* (New York: Harper & Row, 1921), pp. 298–99. Sandeen, *Roots of Fundamentalism*, p. 243. Among those at the planning session were Riley, Torrey, John Campbell, William Evans, Griffith Thomas, Robert McWatty Russell, and Charles Alexander.
4. Cole, *History of Fundamentalism*, pp. 298–317. Sandeen, *Roots of Fundamentalism*, pp. 243–47. Dollar, *History of Fundamentalism in America*, pp. 159–62. Norman Furniss, *The Fundamentalist Controversy, 1918–1931* (New Haven: Yale University Press, 1954), pp. 49–56.
5. Sandeen, *Roots of Fundamentalism*, p. 246.
6. Bruce L. Shelley, *A History of Conservative Baptists* (Wheaton, Ill.: Conservative Baptist Press, 1971), pp. 7–9.
7. Curtiss Lee Laws, "Introduction," *Baptist Fundamentals* (Philadelphia: Judson Press, 1920).
8. Shelley, *History of Conservative Baptists*, p. 11.
9. Ibid. pp. 5–17. Sandeen, *Roots of Fundamentalism*, pp. 260–64. Furniss, *Fundamentalist Controversy*, pp. 103–18. Cole, *History of Fundamentalism*, pp. 65–97. Dollar, *History of Fundamentalism in America*, pp. 145–58.
10. Sandeen, *Roots of Fundamentalism*, pp. 250–60. Cole, *History of Fundamentalism*, pp. 98–131. Furniss, *Fundamentalist Controversy*, pp. 127–41. Dollar, *History of Fundamentalism in America*, pp. 173–83.
11. Sandeen, *Roots of Fundamentalism*, p. 268.
12. Darby, "The Apostasy of the Successive Dispensations," *Collected Writings*, I, 190. Darby, "God, Not the Church," ibid. IV, 366, 379.
13. Mackintosh, *Papers on the Lord's Coming*, pp. 73–74.
14. Blackstone, *Jesus Is Coming*, pp. 94–95, 154–56.

15. William G. Moorehead, "The Final Issue of the Age," *Addresses on the Second Coming*, pp. 5–27. Haldeman, *Why I Preach the Second Coming*, pp. 75–76. Haldeman, *The Coming of Christ*, pp. 108–9. A. C. Gaebelein, *Our Hope*, XII (Jan. 1907), 440–41. Ibid. XXII (Dec. 1915), 332–33.

16. A. C. Gaebelein, *Our Hope*, XXVIII (May 1922), 654. Ibid. XXX (Feb. 1924), 461–62. Ibid. XXXI (Jan. 1925), 426.

17. Sandeen, *Roots of Fundamentalism*, pp. 72–73.

18. For an interpretation of the rise of denominationalism see Sidney E. Mead, *The Lively Experiment* (New York: Harper & Row, 1963), pp. 103–33.

19. Sandeen, *Roots of Fundamentalism*, pp. 240–43.

20. Dollar, *History of Fundamentalism in America*, pp. 112–22.

21. Dollar puts Frank Norris, a Baptist from Fort Worth, Texas, and John Roach Straton, pastor at Calvary Baptist Church, New York, in this category. Ibid. pp. 122–43.

22. Dispensationalism has frequently been charged with divisiveness. Clarence Bass, *Backgrounds to Dispensationalism* (Grand Rapids: Eerdmans, 1960). Kraus, *Dispensationalism in America*, pp. 108–9. Rall, "Where Premillennialism Leads," 617–27. For a dispensationalist defense see Ryrie, *Dispensationalism Today*, pp. 78–85.

23. A. C. Gaebelein, *Our Hope*, XXVII (Dec. 1920), 332.

CHAPTER 8

1. Joel A. Carpenter, "A Shelter in the Time of Storm: Fundamentalist Institutions and the Rise of Evangelical Protestantism, 1929–1942," *Church History*, XLIX (Mar. 1980), 62–75.

2. See pp. 106–27 above.

3. *Evangel*, Feb. 7, 1925, p. 6; W. Percy Hicks, "Proposed Revival of the Old Roman Empire," ibid. Mar. 20, 1926, p. 4.

4. Ibid. (Sept. 10, 1932), p. 10. The story also appeared in *The Sunday School Times* and *Moody Bible Institute Monthly*.

5. Editorial, *Moody Bible Institute Monthly*, XXXIV (Nov. 1933), 96.

6. Ibid. XXXIV (Feb. 1934), 252.

7. See Alva J. McClain, "The Four Great Powers of the End-Time," *The King's Business*, XXXIX (Feb. 1938), 97. For an example of one who believed Mussolini was Antichrist, see Louis S. Bauman, "Socialism,

Communism, Fascism," ibid. XXVI (Aug. 1935), 293; and his *Light from Bible Prophecy* (New York: Fleming H. Revell, 1940), pp. 18–19.

8. Leonard Sale-Harrison, "The Resurrection of Imperial Rome," *Moody Bible Institute Monthly*, XXXVI (June 1936), 493–94. See also his "League of Nations and the Coming Superman," ibid. XXXVI (Aug. 1936), 605–6.

9. W. D. Herrstrom, "A Mark in Their Right Hand," ibid. XXXVIII (Mar. 1938), 375.

10. Bauman, *Light from Bible Prophecy*, pp. 20–30.

11. Scofield Reference Bible, p. 883. See also Alfred H. Burton, *Russia's Destiny in the Light of Prophecy* (New York: Gospel Publishing House, 1917). Leonard Sale-Harrison, *The Coming Great Northern Confederacy: or the Future of Russia and Germany* (London: Pickering and Inglis, 1928). For some exceptions to this interpretation of Gog and Gomer, see Wilson, *Armageddon Now!* p. 113.

12. Editorial, *Moody Bible Institute Monthly*, XXXII (Mar. 1932), 328.

13. See Thomas Chalmers, "Russia and Armageddon," *Evangel*, Apr. 14, 1934, p. 6. Dan Gilbert, "Views and Reviews of Current News," *The King's Business*, XXX (Jan. 1939), 8.

14. Louis S. Bauman, *God and Gog* (Long Beach, Calif.: Privately printed, 1934), p. 19. See also his "Gog and Gomer, Russia and Germany, and the War," *The Sunday School Times*, LXXXI (Dec. 16, 1939), 911–12.; and *Light from Bible Prophecy*, pp. 24–37.

15. Arno C. Gaebelein, "The Great Coming North-Eastern Confederacy," *Our Hope*, XLVI (1939–40), 234–35.

16. *Moody Monthly*, XXXIX (June 1939), 536. Note: in its Mar. 1938 issue, the *Moody Bible Institute Monthly* shortened its name to *Moody Monthly*.

17. Arno C. Gaebelein, "God's Hand in Prophetic Conferences," ibid. XL (Nov. 1939), 177, 129. For a description of the conference, see C. B. Nordland, "A Report of the International Prophetic Conference," ibid. XL (Jan. 1940), 249, 298.

18. Wilson, *Armageddon Now!* p. 146.

19. *Evangel*, July 12, 1941, p. 10.

20. Arno C. Gaebelein, *The Conflict of the Ages: The Mystery of Lawlessness, Its Origin, Historic Development and Coming Defeat* (New York: "Our Hope" Publishing Office, 1933), p. 72.

21. Louis S. Bauman, *Russian Events in the Light of Bible Prophecy* (New York: Fleming H. Revell, 1942), pp. 78–87.

22. See Dan Gilbert, *The Red Terror and Bible Prophecy* (Washington D.C.: The Christian Press Bureau, 1944).

23. Gaebelein, *Conflict of the Ages*, p. 99.

24. *Jewish Chronicles*, Apr. 14, 1919, quoted in ibid. p. 98.

25. Ibid. p. 99.

26. Ibid. pp. 147–48.

27. Ibid. pp. 157–58.

28. Gaebelein, *Our Hope*, XXIX (Aug. 1922), 103.

29. Gaebelein, *Conflict of the Ages*, p. 168.

30. David Rausch, "*Our Hope:* An American Fundamentalist Journal and the Holocaust, 1937–1945," *Fides et Historia*, XII (Spring, 1980), 89–103.

31. David Rausch has taken strong exception to my interpretation of Gaebelein. See his "Fundamentalism and the Jew: An Interpretive Essay," *Journal of the Evangelical Theological Society*, XXIII (June 1980), 105–12. We subsequently "debated" the issue: Timothy P. Weber, "A Reply to David Rausch's 'Fundamentalism and the Jew,'" ibid. XXIV (Mar. 1981), 67–71. David A. Rausch, "A Rejoinder to Timothy Weber's Reply," ibid. XXIV (Mar. 1981), 73–77. Timothy P. Weber, "A Surrejoinder to David Rausch's Rejoinder," ibid. XXIV (Mar. 1981), 79–82.

32. On Jewish-communist conspiracy theories, see Donald S. Strong, *Organized Anti-Semitism in America: The Rise of Group Prejudice During the Decade 1930–1940* (Westport, Conn.: Greenwood Press [1941], 1979). On Christian anti-Semitism, see Charles Y. Glock and Rodney Stark, *Christian Beliefs and Anti-Semitism* (New York: Harper Torchbooks, 1969).

33. George Marsden, *Fundamentalism and American Culture: The Shaping of Twentieth Century Evangelicalism, 1870–1925* (New York: Oxford University Press, 1980), pp. 287–88.

34. William B. Riley, "Protocols and Communism" (n.p., n.d. [1934]).

35. See p. 155 above.

36. *Moody Bible Institute Monthly*, XXVII (Sept. 1927), 3.

37. Ibid. XXXIV (Jan. 1934), 209.

38. *Time*, Nov. 12, 1934.

39. James M. Gray, "The Jewish Protocols," *Moody Bible Institute Monthly*, XXXV (Jan. 1935), 230.

40. Ibid.

41. Louis S. Bauman, *Shirts and Sheets: or Anti-Semitism, a Present-Day Sign of the First Magnitude* (Long Beach, Calif.: Privately printed, 1934), p. 18.

42. Louis S. Bauman, *The Time of Jacob's Trouble* (Long Beach, Calif.: Privately printed, 1938).

43. *Evangel*, May 18, 1935, p. 1. For another premillennialist who believed that the *Protocols* were a forgery, see Elias Newman, *The Jewish Peril and the Hidden Hand* (Minneapolis: Privately printed, 1934).

44. Bauman's work *The Time of Jacob's Trouble* is a thorough country-by-country survey of anti-Semitism.

45. Ibid. p. 17.

46. Gunther Lewy, *The Catholic Church and Nazi Germany* (New York: McGraw-Hill, 1964).

47. Peter Matheson, ed., *The Third Reich and the Churches* (Grand Rapids: Eerdmans, 1981). Ernst Christian Helmreich, *The German Churches Under Hitler* (Detroit: Wayne State University Press, 1979).

48. Editorial, *Moody Bible Institute Monthly*, XXXIV (July 1934), 506.

49. Paul Umlauf, "The New Germany and the Evangelical Church," ibid. XXXIV (Aug. 1934), 553–54.

50. Ibid.

51. Ibid. XXXV (Dec. 1934), 152.

52. Ibid XXXIV (Jan. 1934), 208.

53. Ibid. XXV (Mar. 1935), 314.

54. Ibid. XXXVI (Oct. 1935), 69.

55. Editorial, ibid. XXXIII (May 1933), 392.

56. See Bauman, *The Time of Jacob's Trouble.*

57. *Moody Monthly*, XL (Dec. 1939), 175–76. Sponsors included H. A. Ironside, Charles E. Fuller, Louis Talbot, Will Houghton, Donald Barnhouse, Charles Trumbull, L. Sale-Harrison, Max Reich, Coulson Shepherd, and George T. B. Davis.

58. Ibid. XLI (Apr. 1941).

59. Ibid. XLIII (Apr. 1943), 472.

60. Ibid. XL (July 1940), 592.

61. Rausch, "*Our Hope:* An American Fundamentalist Journal and the Holocaust, 1937–1945."

62. Joseph Taylor Britan, "An Appeal for Persecuted Israel," *Moody Monthly*, XXXIX (Feb. 1939), 316, 345.

63. Ibid. XL (Dec. 1939), inside front cover. Ibid. XL (Mar. 1940), 381.

64. Ibid. XXXIV (Feb.1934), 262–63, 294. See also "The Indestructible Jew," *The Sunday School Times*, LXXXIV (Oct. 3, 1942), 381.

65. E.g., see Henry E. Anderson, "Are God's Covenants About to Be Fulfilled?" *Moody Monthly*, XL (Nov. 1939), 128–29.

66. Harry Rimmer, *Palestine, The Coming Storm Center* (Grand Rapids: Eerdmans, 1940), quoted in ibid. (Oct. 1940), 113. See also Wilbur M.

Smith, "With the Bible in the Land of the Book," ibid. XXXIX (Oct.

67. Editorial, ibid. XLII (July 1942), 627.
68. Wilson, *Armageddon Now!* pp. 215–18.

CHAPTER 9

1. Sandeen, *Roots of Fundamentalism*, p. 202.
2. George T. B. Davis, *Rebuilding Palestine According to Prophecy* (Philadelphia: Million Testaments Campaign, 1935).
3. Thomas Chalmers, "Israel's Title to Canaan," *The King's Business*, XVII (Feb. 1926), 94.
4. See Davis, *Rebuilding Palestine According to Prophecy*, p. 112.
5. Editorial, *Moody Bible Institute Monthly*, XXXI (Jan. 1931), 346.
6. See Agnes Scott Kent, "Palestine Is for the Jew," *The King's Business*, XXII (Nov. 1931), 494. Louis Bauman, "Present Day Fulfillment of Prophecy," ibid. XXIII (July 1932), 313. *Evangel*, Feb. 4, 1933, p. 5.
7. Frederick Childe, "Christ's Answer to the Challenge of Communism and Fascism," *Evangel*, Oct. 31, 1935, p. 1. Ibid. July 4, 1936, p. 4.
8. W. F. Smalley, "Another View of the Palestine Situation," *The King's Business*, XXI (June 1930), 290–92.
9. Arno C. Gaebelein, *Our Hope*, XLVI (1939–40), 179.
10. *Evangel*, Apr. 22, 1944, p. 16.
11. T. DeCourcy Rayner, "Hidden Hands in Palestine," *Moody Monthly*, XLVIII (Dec. 1947), 264.
12. *The King's Business*, XXXIX (July 1948), 4. See also Louis T. Talbot and William W. Orr, *The New Nation of Israel and the Word of God!* (Los Angeles: The Bible Institute of Los Angeles, 1948).
13. For an excellent account of the premillennialist response to the founding of Israel, see Wilson, *Armageddon Now!* pp. 123–43.
14. Here is only a short, partial list of premillennialist studies on the prophetic significance of Israel: M. R. DeHaan, *The Jew and Palestine in Prophecy* (Grand Rapids: Zondervan, 1950). William L. Hull, *The Fall and Rise of Israel* (Grand Rapids: Zondervan, 1954). Arthur Kac, *The Rebirth of the State of Israel—Is It of God or of Men?* (Chicago: Moody Press, 1958). John Walvoord, *Israel in Prophecy* (Grand Rapids: Zondervan, 1962). William L. Hull, *Israel—Key to Prophecy* (Grand Rapids: Zondervan, 1964). Anton Darms, *The Jew Returns to Israel* (Grand

Rapids: Zondervan, 1965). Richard DeHaan, *Israel and the Nations in Prophecy* (Grand Rapids: Zondervan, 1968). Hal Lindsey, *The Promise* (Irvine, Calif.: Harvest House, 1974).

15. George T. B. Davis, "A Divine Promise That Changed History," *The Sunday School Times*, XCIX (Mar. 16, 1957) , 743–44.

16. Paul S. Allen, "Arab or Israeli?" *The Alliance Witness*, XCII (May 8, 1957), 2.

17. L. Nelson Bell, "Unfolding Destiny," *Christianity Today*, XI (July 21, 1967), 1044–45.

18. *Moody Monthly*, LXVIII (Oct. 1967).

19. Ibid. LXVII (July-Aug. 1967), 22–24. Maxwell Coder, "Jerusalem: Key to the Future," ibid. LXXIV (Oct. 1973), 32–33.

20. Hal Lindsey, *The Late Great Planet Earth* (Grand Rapids: Zondervan, 1970).

21. Lindsey's other books include *Satan Is Alive and Well on Planet Earth* (Grand Rapids: Zondervan, 1972); *There's a New World Coming* (Santa Ana, Calif.: Vision House, 1973); *The Liberation of Planet Earth* (Grand Rapids: Zondervan, 1974); *The Promise* (Irvine, Calif.: Harvest House, 1974); *The World's Final Hour: Evacuation or Extinction?* (Grand Rapids: Zondervan, 1976); *The Terminal Generation* (Old Tappan, N.J.: Fleming H. Revell, 1976); and *The 1980s: Countdown to Armageddon* (King of Prussia, Pa.: Westgate Press, 1980).

22. Lindsey, *Late Great Planet Earth*, pp. 53–58.

23. Ibid. pp. 146–79. While agreeing in general, not all dispensationalists agree with every detail of Lindsey's scenario. For example, see Tim LaHaye, *The Beginning of the End* (Wheaton: Tyndale House, 1972). Charles C. Ryrie, *The Bible and Tomorrow's News* (Wheaton: Victor Books, 1973). Thomas S. McCall and Zola Levitt, *The Coming Russian Invasion of Israel* (Chicago: Moody Press, 1974). John F. Walvoord and John E. Walvoord, *Armageddon: Oil and the Middle East Crisis* (Grand Rapids: Zondervan, 1974). John Wesley White, *WW III* (Grand Rapids: Zondervan, 1977).

24. Lindsey, *Late Great Planet Earth*, pp. 180–86.

25. Ibid. p. 168.

26. Ibid. p. 186.

27. Ibid. pp. 186–88.

28. Leading producers of these films include Mark IV Pictures, Gospel Films, and Evangelical Films.

29. See Robert Zwier, *Born-Again Politics: the New Christian Right in America* (Downers Grove, Ill.: InterVarsity Press, 1982). Robert Booth Fowler,

A *New Engagement: Evangelical Political Thought, 1966–1976* (Grand Rapids: Eerdmans, 1982).

30. Lindsey, *The 1980s: Countdown to Armageddon*, pp. 47, 61–62.

31. See *The Jupiter Effect* by John R. Gribbin and Stephen H. Plagemann. The book claimed that every 179 years the planets in the solar system become aligned in a straight line perpendicular to the sun and trigger massive earthquakes. The book caused quite a media stir; but nothing of that magnitude occurred. Ibid. pp. 30–32.

32. Ibid. p. 34.

33. Ibid. p. 146. For more on the premillennialist view of America's place in prophecy, see Thomas S. McCall, ed., *America: In History and Bible Prophecy* (Chicago: Moody Press, 1976).

34. Lindsey, *The 1980s: Countdown to Armageddon*, p. 146.

35. Ibid. p. 176.

36. Ibid. pp. 89–91, 101.

37. Ibid. p. 165.

38. Ibid. p. 171.

39. Ibid. p. 154.

40. Ibid. p. 129.

41. Ibid. p. 142.

42. Ibid. p. 157.

43. Ibid. p. 161.

44. See his footnotes, especially for chapters 9 and 10.

45. Ibid. pp. 3–7.

46. For example, see his *Listen, America!* (Garden City, N.J.: Doubleday, 1980).

47. See Timothy P. Weber, "The Second Coming Alert," *Eternity*, XXXII (Apr. 1981), 18–23.

48. Jim McKeever, *Christians Will Go Through the Tribulation: And How to Prepare for It* (Medford, Ore.: Omega Publications, 1978), p. 311.

49. Ibid., p. 209.

50. Ibid., pp. 149–51.

51. Jim McKeever, *The Almighty and the Dollar* (Medford, Ore.: Omega Publications, 1980).

52. Harry Browne, *New Profits from the Monetary Crisis* (New York: Morrow, 1978). Howard J. Ruff, *How to Prosper During the Coming Bad Years*, rev. ed. (New York: Warner Books, 1978). Howard J. Ruff, *Survive and Win in the Inflationary Eighties* (New York: Times Books, 1981).

53. Other books by McKeever include *Close Encounters of the Highest Kind* (Medford, Ore.: Omega Publications, 1978); *How You Can Be Prepared*

(Medford, Ore.: Omega Publications, 1980); and *Now You Can Understand the Book of Revelation* (Medford, Ore.: Omega Publications, 1980). He also publishes *McKeever's Individual Strategy Newsletter* and *End-Time News Digest*.

54. Mary Stewart Relfe, *When Your Money Fails* (Montgomery, Ala.: Ministries, Inc., 1981). The statistic comes from William Martin, "Waiting for the End," *The Atlantic*, CCXLIX (June 1982), 31–37.

55. Relfe, *When Your Money Fails*, pp. 113–14.

56. Ibid. pp. 231–32.

57. Mark O. Hatfield, *Between a Rock and a Hard Place* (Waco: Word Books, 1976). See also Robert Eells and Bartell Nyberg, *Lonely Walk: The Life of Senator Mark Hatfield* (Chappaqua, N.Y.: Christian Herald Books, 1979).

58. For example, William Peterson, Rufus Jones, and Frank E. Gaebelein. See Ronald J. Sider, ed., *The Chicago Declaration* (Carol Stream, Ill.: Creation House, 1974).

CONCLUSION

1. The current size of the fundamentalist/evangelical movement has been estimated at about forty million. Dwight Wilson thinks that premillennialists make up eight million of these, but there may easily be twice that number. Wilson, *Armageddon Now!* p. 12.

2. George Dollar argues that one must be a Scofield dispensationalist to qualify as a true fundamentalist. He distinguishes between fundamentalists and their more or less orthodox allies who do not adhere to dispensationalism. Dollar, *History of Fundamentalism in America*, pp. 173–83. Among the predominately premillennialist denominations are the Bible Baptist Fellowship, the General Association of Regular Baptist Churches, the Conservative Baptist Association of America, the Baptist General Conference, the Evangelical Free Church of America, the Independent Fundamental Churches of America, Plymouth Brethren, Grace Brethren, the Bible Presbyterian Church, and the Baptist Missionary Association. Hundreds of independent Baptist churches and Bible churches are premillennial, as are most Pentecostal denominations, including the largest, the Assemblies of God. In addition, there are many premillennialists in nonpremillennialist denominations such as the Southern Baptist Convention.

3. For a discussion of this "old school," see Ernest R. Sandeen, "The 'Little Tradition' and the Form of Modern Millenarianism," *The Annual Review of the Social Sciences of Religion*, IV (1980), 165–81.

4. See Sylvia L. Thrupp, ed., *Millennial Dreams in Action* (New York: Schocken Books, 1970).

5. Norman Cohn, *The Pursuit of the Millennium*, revised and expanded ed. (New York: Oxford University Press [1957], 1970). Bryan R. Wilson, *Magic and the Millennium: A Sociological Study of Religious Movements of Protest among Tribal and Third-World Peoples* (New York: Harper & Row, 1973). Peter Worsely, *The Trumpet Shall Sound: A Study of 'Cargo' Cults in Melanesia* (New York: Schocken Books, 1968).

6. Sandeen, "The 'Little Tradition' and the Form of Modern Millenarianism," 169.

7. See David Aberle, "A Note on Relative Deprivation Theory As Applied to Millenarian and Other Cult Movements," in Thrupp, ed., *Millennial Dreams in Action*, pp. 209–14.

8. See pp. 41–42 above. George Marsden uses a variation of the deprivation theory in his study of American fundamentalism. Marsden, *Fundamentalism and American Culture*.

9. Robert Cameron, *Scripture Truth About the Lord's Return* (New York: Fleming H. Revell, 1922), pp. 58–59. Robert Cameron, *Watchword and Truth*, XXIV (1902), 302. Sandeen, *Roots of Fundamentalism*, pp. 228–29.

10. Haldeman, *Why I Preach the Second Coming*, pp. 68–69. Munhall, *The Lord's Return*, pp. 66–67.

11. Sandeen, *Roots of Fundamentalism*, pp. 228–29.

12. H. P. King, *The Imperial Hope* (New York: Fleming H. Revell, 1918), p. 77. Vichert, "Is the Gospel Spiritual Pessimism?" 26–27. Woelfkin, "The Religious Appeal of Premillennialism," 255–63. Pettingill, *Light on Prophecy*, p. 261. Blackstone, *Jesus Is Coming*, p. 215.

13. Whitney R. Cross, *The Burned-over District: The Social and Intellectual History of Enthusiastic Religion in Western New York, 1800–1850* (New York: Harper Torchbooks, 1965), p. 320.

14. Quoted in Martin, "Waiting for the End," p. 34.

15. One may legitimately argue that *all* Christians, whether they are amillennialists, postmillennialists, or premillennialists, believe that "Jesus will win" at the end of history. Yet only premillennialists have created a popular movement based on their belief. In general, amillennialists do not hold prophecy conferences, have reference Bibles based

on their eschatology, translate their beliefs into various "escapist" appeals, or make their views of the end relate so explicitly to contemporary events. Because amillennialists believe that Jesus is *currently* reigning over the millennial kingdom, they are convinced that for the most part Jesus' victory has already occurred. Thus when they argue that Jesus *will* win, amillennialists mean something other than premillennialists who believe that the victory of Christ over Antichrist is still a future event. Whereas premillennialists and amillennialists concur that Christ will triumph over all his enemies, premillennialists believe that most of his victory is still to be accomplished. Premillennialists, therefore, believe that there is more to be rescued *from* in the present than do amillennialists. The present crisis is more severe, and in a sense the anticipated victory more eagerly awaited. For an excellent study of eschatology by an amillennialist, see Anthony A. Hoekema, *The Bible and the Future* (Grand Rapids: Eerdmans, 1979).

16. Quoted in Martin, "Waiting for the End," p. 34.

17. See p. 48 above.

18. Needless to say, premillennialism was not totally to blame for this phenomenon. See Moberg, *The Great Reversal*.

19. Jonathan M. Butler, "Adventism and the American Experience," in Gaustad, ed., *The Rise of Adventism*, pp. 173–206.

20. This study has concentrated exclusively on premillennialists who stayed within the evangelical "mainstream," i.e., those groups that merely added premillennialist doctrine to established evangelical orthodoxy. Thus the study ignored many other premillennial groups, including the Jehovah's Witnesses, Seventh-Day Adventists, and Pentecostals. In their own way each group deviated from the evangelical consensus. Witnesses abandoned orthodox Christology and soteriology. Adventist Sabbath and dietary practices were rejected by evangelicals at large. And evangelicals repudiated Pentecostal (and holiness) views of sanctification, the Holy Spirit, and spiritual gifts. See Robert Mapes Anderson, *Vision of the Disinherited: The Making of American Pentecostalism* (New York: Oxford University Press, 1978). Barbara Grizzuth Harrison, *Visions of Glory: A History and a Memory of Jehovah's Witnesses* (New York: Simon and Schuster, 1978). Arthur W. Spalding, *Origin and History of Seventh-Day Adventists*, 4 vols. (Washington, D.C.: Review and Herald, 1961).

21. See p. 93 above.

22. See p. 99 above.

23. H. Richard Niebuhr, *The Kingdom of God in America* (New York: Harper

& Row, 1937). Ernest L. Tuveson, *Redeemer Nation: The Idea of America's Millennial Role* (Chicago: University of Chicago Press, 1968). Conrad Cherry, ed., *God's New Israel: Religious Interpretations of American Destiny* (Englewood Cliffs, N.J.: Prentice-Hall, 1971). Peter Marshall and David Manuel, *The Light and the Glory* (Old Tappan, N.J.: Fleming H. Revell, 1977).

24. Lindsey, *The 1980s: Countdown to Armageddon*, pp. 175–76.

25. Falwell, *Listen, America!* p. 29.

26. Sandeen has argued that the development of such a "bureaucracy" is characteristic of modern millennialist movements. See his article "The 'Little Tradition' and the Form of Modern Millenarianism."

27. Lewis Sperry Chafer, *Systematic Theology*, 8 vols. (Dallas: Dallas Seminary Press, 1948).

28. Walvoord's most significant works include *The Blessed Hope and the Tribulation* (Grand Rapids: Zondervan, 1976); *Matthew: Thy Kingdom Come* (Chicago: Moody Press, 1974); *The Millennial Kingdom* (Grand Rapids: Zondervan, 1959); *The Rapture Question* (Findlay, Ohio: Dunham Publishing Co., 1957); *The Revelation of Jesus Christ* (Chicago: Moody Press, 1966); and *The Thessalonian Epistles* (Findlay, Ohio: Dunham Publishing Co., 1955).

29. Most Bible institutes remain dispensationalist in their orientation. Among dispensationalist seminaries are Talbot Theological Seminary (Calif.), Western Conservative Baptist Seminary (Ore.), Grace Theological Seminary (Ind.), Faith Theological Seminary (Pa.), Denver Baptist Seminary (Colo.), and Central Baptist Seminary (Minn.).

30. The New Scofield Reference Bible (New York: Oxford University Press, 1967). The editorial committee consisted of E. Schuyler English (chairman), Frank E. Gaebelein (former headmaster of the Stony Brook School), William Culbertson (president, Moody Bible Institute), Charles E. Feinberg (dean, Talbot Theological Seminary), Allan MacRae (president, Faith Theological Seminary), Clarence Mason, Jr. (dean, Philadelphia College of Bible), Wilbur Smith (formerly of Moody Bible Institute, Fuller Theological Seminary, and Trinty Evangelical Divinity School), and John F. Walvoord (president, Dallas Theological Seminary).

31. Charles C. Ryrie, ed., *Ryrie Study Bible* (Chicago: Moody Press, 1978).

32. Lloyd J. Averill, "Is the End Near?" *Christian Century*, C (Jan. 19, 1983), 45–48. Robert Jewett, *Jesus Against the Rapture: Seven Unexpected Prophecies* (Philadelphia: Westminster Press, 1979). C. Vanderwaal, *Hal Lindsey and Biblical Prophecy* (St. Catharines, Ont.: Paideia Press, 1978).

George C. Miladin, *Is This Really the End? A Reformed Analysis of "The Late Great Planet Earth"* (Cherry Hill, N.J.: Mack, 1972).

33. Though there is no way of knowing how extensive is the spread of premillennialist literature outside of fundamentalist and evangelical circles, my personal contacts and inquiries among liberal and "mainline" pastors reveal that a good number of laypeople in nonconservative churches have read or know about premillennialist teaching, much to the displeasure and bewilderment of their pastors.

34. Sandeen, *Roots of Fundamentalism*, pp. 208–32.

35. See, for example, George E. Ladd, *A Commentary on the Revelation of John* (Grand Rapids: Eerdmans, 1972). George E. Ladd, *A Theology of the New Testament* (Grand Rapids: Eerdmans, 1974). George E. Ladd, *The Last Things; An Eschatology for Laymen* (Grand Rapids: Eerdmans, 1978). Robert H. Gundry, *The Church and the Tribulation* (Grand Rapids: Zondervan, 1973). Robert H. Mounce, *The Book of Revelation*, The New International Commentary of the New Testament (Grand Rapids: Eerdmans, 1977). Note: Although Gundry calls himself a "modified dispensationalist," most dispensationalists believe that he has "modified" himself out of the system.

36. For example, Robert Gundry's recent commentary on Matthew used the methods of redaction criticism to an extent previously unknown among American evangelical scholars and has been severely criticized for its "accommodation" to "liberal" scholarship. Robert H. Gundry, *Matthew: A Commentary on His Literary and Theological Art* (Grand Rapids: Eerdmans, 1982).

37. "Evangelical Leaders Poll," *Evangelical Newsletter*, IX (Jan. 22, 1982), 6. It is hardly necessary to comment on the danger of making too much of such a limited and unrepresentative poll. The *Evangelical Newsletter*'s sample was rather "elitist." A more reliable poll would have to take into consideration evangelical pastors and laypeople. But, as inadequate as it is, the survey does reflect the feelings of an important segment of the evangelical community.

38. See Richard Quebedeaux, *The Young Evangelicals* (New York: Harper & Row, 1974), pp. 76–81.

39. George Marsden and Frank Roberts, eds., *A Christian View of History?* (Grand Rapids: Eerdmans, 1975), p. 10.

40. For an example of a prophetic study that tries to avoid overattention to details, see Carl E. Armerding and W. Ward Gasque, eds., *Dreams, Visions and Oracles: A Layman's Guide to Biblical Prophecy* (Grand Rapids: Baker Book House, 1977).

Selected Bibliography

BOOKS

Abell, Aaron I. *The Urban Impact on American Protestantism, 1865–1900*. Cambridge: Harvard University Press, 1943.

Addresses on the International Prophetic Conference. Boston: Watchword and Truth, 1901.

Addresses on the Second Coming of the Lord. Pittsburgh: W. W. Waters, 1896.

Ahlstrom, Sydney E. *A Religious History of the American People*. New Haven: Yale University Press, 1972.

Anderson, Robert. *The Coming Prince*. 13th ed. London: Pickering and Inglis, n.d.

Anderson, Robert Mapes. *Vision of the Disinherited: The Making of American Pentecostalism*. New York: Oxford University Press, 1978.

Andrews, Samuel J. *Christianity and Antichristianity in Their Final Conflict*. Chicago: Bible Institute Colportage Association, 1898.

Angel, Ruth, *How to Point a Jew to Christ*. New York: New York Gospel Mission to the Jews, n.d.

Armerding, Carl E., and W. Ward Gasque, eds. *Dreams, Visions and Oracles: A Layman's Guide to Biblical Prophecy*. Grand Rapids: Baker Book House, 1977.

Averill, Lloyd J. *American Theology in the Liberal Tradition*. Philadelphia: Westminster Press, 1967.

Baines, T. B. *The Lord's Coming, Israel, and the Church*. New York: Loizeaux Brothers, 1896.

Baron, David. *What Think Ye of Christ? An Appeal to the Jews*. Kansas City, Mo.: B and L, n.d.

Barton, G. A. *Does the Bible Predict the Present War?* Chicago: American Institute of Sacred Literature, 1918.

Bass, Clarence. *Backgrounds to Dispensationalism: Its Historical Genesis and Ecclesiastical Implications.* Grand Rapids: Eerdmans, 1960.

Bauman, Louis S. *God and Gog.* Long Beach, Calif.: Privately printed, 1934.

———. *Light from Bible Prophecy.* New York: Fleming H. Revell, 1940.

———. *Russian Events in the Light of Bible Prophecy.* New York: Fleming H. Revell, 1942.

———. *Shirts and Sheets: or Anti-Semitism, a Present-Day Sign of the First Magnitude.* Long Beach, Calif.: Privately printed, 1934.

———. *The Time of Jacob's Trouble.* Long Beach, Calif.: Privately printed, 1938.

Berry, George Ricker. *Premillennialism and Old Testament Prediction: A Study in Interpretation.* Chicago: University of Chicago Press, 1929.

Beiderwolf, William Edward. *The Millennium Bible.* Chicago: W. P. Blessing, 1924.

Blackstone, William E. *The Heart of the Jewish Problem.* Chicago: Chicago Hebrew Mission, n.d.

———. *Jesus Is Coming.* New York: Fleming H. Revell, 1908.

———. *The Millennium.* New York: Fleming H. Revell, 1904.

Blanchard, Charles A. *Light on the Last Days.* Chicago: Bible Institute Colportage Association, 1913.

———. *The World War and the Bible.* Chicago: Bible Institute Colportage Association, 1918.

Brookes, James H. *Bible Reading on the Second Coming.* Springfield, Ill.: Edwin A. Wilson, 1877.

———. *I Am Coming.* London: Pickering and Inglis, n.d.

———. *Israel and the Church.* St. Louis: Gospel Book and Tract Depository, n.d.

———. *Maranatha.* 3rd ed. New York: E. Brendell, 1874.

———. *Till He Come.* New York: Fleming H. Revell, 1895.

Broughton, Len G. *The Second Coming of Christ.* Philadelphia: Pepper Publishing Co., 1902.

Buksbazen, Lydia. *They Looked for a City.* West Collingswood, N.J.: Spearhead Press, 1955.

Burridge, J. H. *God's Prophetic Plan.* St. Louis: Hammond Publishing Co., 1909.

Burton, Alfred H. *The Future of Europe.* New York: Bible Truth Press, 1915.

———. *Russia's Destiny in the Light of Prophecy.* New York: Gospel Publishing House, 1917.

Caldwell, Raymond Thornton. The Social Attitudes of Modern Premillennialists. M. A. Thesis, University of Chicago, 1922.

Cameron, Robert. *The Doctrine of the Ages*. New York: Fleming H. Revell, 1896.

―――. *Scriptural Truth About the Lord's Return*, New York: Fleming H. Revell, 1922.

Carter, Paul A. *The Spiritual Crisis of the Gilded Age*. De Kalb, Ill.: Northern Illinois University Press, 1971.

Case, Shirley Jackson. *The Millennial Hope*. Chicago: University of Chicago Press, 1918.

―――. *The Revelation of John*. Chicago: University of Chicago Press, 1919.

Cauthen, Kenneth. *The Impact of American Religious Liberalism*. New York: Harper and Row, 1962.

Chafer, Lewis Sperry. *The Kingdom in History and Prophecy*. New York: Fleming H. Revell, 1915.

―――. *Signs of the Times*. Chicago: Bible Institute Colportage Association, 1919.

―――. *Systematic Theology*. 8 Vols. Dallas: Dallas Seminary Press, 1948.

Chalmers, Thomas M. *Israel and the War*. New York: Privately printed, 1916.

―――. *The Present Condition of Israel in the Light of Prophecy*. Philadelphia: American Society for Prophetic Study, 1923.

Chapman, J. Wilbur. *A Reason for My Hope*. New York: "Our Hope" Publishing Office, 1916.

Cherry, Conrad, ed. *God's New Israel: Religious Interpretations of American Destiny*. Englewood Cliffs, N.J.: Prentice-Hall, 1971.

Clarke, William Newton. *An Outline of Christian Theology*. 10th ed. New York: Charles Scribner's Sons, 1901.

Cohn, Joseph Hoffman. *I Have Fought a Good Fight*. New York: American Board of Missions to the Jews, 1953.

Cohn, Leopold. *A Modern Missionary to an Ancient People*. 2nd ed. New York: American Board of Missions to the Jews, 1911.

Cohn, Norman. *The Pursuit of the Millennium*. New York: Oxford University Press, 1957.

―――. *Warrant for Genocide: The Myth of the Jewish World Conspiracy and the "Protocols of the Elders of Zion."* New York: Harper Torchbooks, 1967.

Cole, Stewart G. *A History of Fundamentalism*. New York: Harper & Row, 1931.

Coleman, Robert H., ed. *Popular Hymnal*. Dallas: Privately printed, 1918.

Cook, Charles C. *End of the Age Themes*. New York: Charles C. Cook, 1917.

―――. *World Peace: Is It a Reasonable Hope or a Delusion?* Chicago: Bible Institute Colportage Association, 1924.

Cross, Robert D., ed. *The Church and the City*. New York: Bobbs-Merrill Co., 1967.

Cross, Whitney R. *The Burned-over District: The Social and Intellectual History of Enthusiastic Religion in Western New York, 1800–1850*. New York: Harper Torchbooks, 1965.

Cumming, John. *The Destiny of Nations*. London: Hurst and Blackette, 1864.

———. *The Great Consummation*. New York: Carleton, 1865.

Darby, John Nelson. *Collected Writings*, ed. by William Kelley. Vols. I–III. London: G. Morrish, 1967.

———. *Lectures on the Second Coming*. London: G. Morrish, 1909.

Darms, Anton. *The Jew Returns to Israel*. Grand Rapids: Zondervan, 1965.

David, George T. B. *Rebuilding Palestine According to Prophecy*. Philadelphia: Million Testaments Campaign, 1935.

Dean, I. R. *The Coming Kingdom*. Philadelphia: Approved Book Store, 1928.

DeHaan, M. R. *The Jew and Palestine in Prophecy*. Grand Rapids: Zondervan, 1950.

DeHaan, Richard. *Israel and the Nations in Prophecy*. Grand Rapids: Zondervan, 1968.

DeWitt, Benjamin Parke. *The Progressive Movement*. With an Introduction by Arthur Mann. Seattle: University of Washington Press, 1968.

Dixon, Amzi Clarence. *Evangelism Old and New*. New York: American Tract Society, 1905.

———. *Present Day Life and Religion*. Cleveland: F. M. Barton, 1925.

Dodd, M. E. *Jesus Is Coming to Earth Again*. Chicago: Bible Institute Colportage Association, 1917.

Dollar, George. *A History of Fundamentalism in America*. Greenville, S.C.: Bob Jones University Press, 1973.

Down on Throop Avenue. New York: American Board of Missions to the Jews, 1940.

Drummond, Henry. *Dwight L. Moody: Impression and Facts*. New York: McClure, Phillips and Co., 1900.

Eckman, George P. *When Christ Comes Again*. New York: Abingdon, 1917.

Eells, Robert, and Bartell Nyberg. *Lonely Walk: The Life of Senator Mark Hatfield*. Chappaqua, N.Y.: Christian Herald Books, 1979.

Ehlert, Arnold D. *A Bibliographic History of Dispensationalism*. Grand Rapids: Baker Book House, 1965.

Ely, James E. *Glimpses of Bible Climaxes*. Garden City, Kans.: Businessman's Gospel Association, 1927.

Erdman, Charles R. *The Return of Christ*. New York: George H. Doran Co., 1922.

Erdman, William J. *The Parousia of Christ a Period of Time*. Chicago: Gospel Publishing Co., n.d.

———. *The Return of Christ*. Germantown, Pa.: Privately printed, 1913.

———. *A Theory Reviewed*. Germantown, Pa.: Privately printed, n.d.

Evans, William. *The Coming King: The World's Next Great Crisis*. New York: Fleming H. Revell, 1923.

Falwell, Jerry. *Listen, America!* Garden City, N.J.: Doubleday, 1980.

Farr, F. W. *Ten Reasons for Loving His Appearing*. Chicago: Bible Institute Colportage Association, n.d.

Feinberg, Charles L., ed. *Focus on Prophecy*. Westwood, N.J.: Fleming H. Revell, 1964.

Festinger, Leon. *When Prophecy Fails*. Minneapolis: University of Minnesota Press, 1956.

Fifty Years of Blessing. Historical Sketch of the Chicago Hebrew Mission, 1887–1937. Chicago: Chicago Hebrew Mission, 1937.

Findlay, James F. *Dwight L. Moody, American Evangelist, 1837–1899*. Chicago: University of Chicago Press, 1969.

Fink, Reuben, ed. *America and Palestine*. New York: American Zionist Emergency Council, 1944.

Foster, Charles I. *An Errand of Mercy: The Evangelical United Front, 1790–1837*. Chapel Hill: University of North Carolina Press, 1960.

Fowler, Robert Booth. *A New Engagement: Evangelical Political Thought, 1966–1976*. Grand Rapids: Eerdmans, 1982.

Freuder, Samuel. *A Missionary's Return to Judaism*. New York: Sinai Publishing Co., 1915.

Froom, Leroy E. *The Prophetic Faith of Our Fathers*. Vol. IV. Washington, D.C.: Review and Herald, 1954.

Fuller, Daniel P. The Hermeneutics of Dispensationalism. Unpublished Th.D. dissertation, Northern Baptist Theological Seminary, Chicago, 1957.

Furniss, Norman F. *The Fundamentalist Controversy, 1918–1931*. New Haven: Yale University Press, 1954.

Gaebelein, Arno C. *The Conflict of the Ages: The Mystery of Lawlessness, Its Origin, Historic Development and Coming Defeat*. New York: "Our Hope" Publishing Office, 1933.

———. *Half a Century*. New York: "Our Hope" Publishing Office, 1933.

———. *The Harmony of the Prophetic Word*. New York: Fleming H. Revell, 1907.

———. *Hath God Cast Away His People?* New York: Gospel Publishing House, 1905.

————. *The League of Nations in the Light of Prophecy*. New York: "Our Hope" Publishing Office, 1920.

————. *Meat in Due Season*. New York: "Our Hope" Publishing Office, 1933.

————. *The Prophet Daniel*. New York: "Our Hope" Publishing Office, 1936.

————. *The Prophet Ezekiel*. New York: "Our Hope" Publishing Office, 1918.

————, ed. *Christ and Glory, Addresses Delivered at the New York Prophetic Conference, Carnegie Hall, November 25–28, 1918*. New York: "Our Hope" Publishing Office, 1919.

Gaebelein, Frank E. *The Story of the Scofield Reference Bible, 1909–1959*. New York: Oxford University Press, 1959.

Gaustad, Edwin Scott. *Historical Atlas of Religion in America*. New York: Harper & Row, 1963.

————, ed. *The Rise of Adventism: A Commentary on the Social and Religious Ferment of Mid-Nineteenth Century America*. New York: Harper & Row, 1974.

Gilbert, Dan. *The Red Terror and Bible Prophecy*. Washington, D.C.: The Christian Press Bureau, 1944.

Gilbert, F. C. *From Judaism to Christianity*. So. Lancaster, Mass.: Good Tidings Press, 1911.

Ginger, Ray. *Age of Excess: The United States from 1877–1914*. New York: The Macmillan Co., 1965.

Glazer, Nathan. *American Judaism*. 2nd ed. Chicago: University of Chicago Press, 1972.

Glock, Charles Y. and Rodney Stark. *Christian Beliefs and Anti-Semitism*. New York: Harper Torchbooks, 1969.

Gordon, A. J. *Ecce Venit*. New York: Fleming H. Revell, 1889.

Gordon, S. D. *Quiet Talks About Our Lord's Return*. New York: Fleming H. Revell, 1912.

————. *Quiet Talks on the Deeper Meaning of the War and Its Relation to Our Lord's Return*. New York: Fleming H. Revell, 1919.

Gosse, Edmund. *Father and Son*. With an Introduction and Notes by William Irvine. Boston: Houghton Mifflin Co., 1965.

Gray, James M. *Modernism*. Chicago: Bible Institute Colportage Association, 1924.

————. *Prophecy and the Lord's Return*. New York: Fleming H. Revell, 1917.

————. *Satan and the Saints*. New York: Fleming H. Revell, 1909.

————. *Textbook on Prophecy*. New York: Fleming H. Revell, 1919.

_____. *What the Bible Teaches About War*. Chicago: Moody Bible Institute, n.d.

_____, ed. *The Coming and Kingdom of Christ*. Chicago: Bible Institute Colportage Association, 1914.

Guille, G. E. *That Blessed Hope*. Chicago: Bible Institute Colportage Association, 1920.

Grounds, Vernon C. *Evangelism and Social Responsibility*. Scottsdale, Pa.: Herald Press, 1969.

_____. *Revolution and the Christian Faith*. A Holman Book. Philadelphia: Lippincott, 1971.

Gundry, Robert H. *The Church and the Tribulation*. Grand Rapids: Zondervan, 1973.

_____. *Matthew: A Commentary on His Literary and Theological Art*. Grand Rapids: Eerdmans, 1982.

Haldeman, I. M. *The Coming of Christ*. Los Angeles: Bible House, 1906.

_____. *How to Study the Bible*. New York: Charles C. Cook, 1913.

_____. *Professor Shailer Mathews's Burlesque on the Second Coming*. New York: Privately printed, 1918.

_____. *The Signs of the Times*. 4th ed. New York: Charles C. Cook, 1913.

_____. *This Hour Not the Hour of Peace*. New York: Charles C. Cook, 1915.

_____. *Why I Preach the Second Coming*. New York: Fleming H. Revell, 1919.

Handy, Robert T. *A Christian America: Protestant Hopes and Historical Realities*. New York: Oxford University Press, 1971.

_____, ed. *The Social Gospel, 1870–1920: Gladden, Ely, and Rauschenbusch*. A Library of Protestant Thought. New York: Oxford University Press, 1966.

Harkness, Robert. *Reuben Archer Torrey: The Man, His Message*. Chicago: Bible Institute Colportage Association, 1929.

Harrison, Barbara Grizzuth. *Vision of Glory: A History and a Memory of Jehovah's Witnesses*. New York: Simon and Schuster, 1978.

Harrison, Norman B. *His Sure Return*. Chicago: Bible Institute Colportage Association, 1926.

Hart, Lewis A. *A Jewish Reply to Christian Evangelists*. New York: Block Publishing Co., 1906.

Hatfield, Mark O. *Between a Rock and a Hard Place*. Waco: Word Books, 1976.

Hays, Samuel P. *The Response to Industrialism, 1885–1914*. Chicago: University of Chicago Press, 1957.

Helmreich, Ernst Christian. *The German Churches Under Hitler.* Detroit: Wayne State University Press, 1979.

Hoekema, Anthony A. *The Bible and the Future.* Grand Rapids: Eerdmans, 1979.

Holden, John. *Will the Christ Return?* New York: Fleming H. Revell, 1918.

Hopkins, C. Howard. *The Rise of the Social Gospel in American Protestantism, 1865–1915.* New Haven: Yale University Press, 1940.

Horton, Thomas C. *These Pre-Millennialists: Who Are They?* Los Angeles: Privately printed, 1921.

How Can We Haste His Coming? New York: Christian Alliance Publishing Co., n.d.

Hudson, Winthrop S. *Religion in America.* New York: Charles Scribner's Sons, 1965.

Hull, William L. *The Fall and Rise of Israel.* Grand Rapids: Zondervan, 1954.
————. *Israel—Key to Prophecy.* Grand Rapids: Zondervan, 1964.

Hunter, J. H. *Beside All Waters.* Harrisburg, Pa.: Christian Publications, 1964.

Ironside, Henry A. *The Midnight Cry.* New York: Loizeaux Brothers, n.d.

Israel—Past, Present, and Future. Chicago: Chicago Hebrew Mission, 1915.

Jennings, F. C. *The End of the European War in the Light of Scripture.* New York: Charles C. Cook, 1915.

————. *The World Conflict in the Light of the Prophetic Word.* New York: "Our Hope" Publishing Office, 1917.

The Jew in History and Prophecy. Chicago: Chicago Hebrew Mission, 1918.

Johnson, Howard A., ed. *Winning Jews to Christ.* Chicago: The Christian Mission to Israel, 1919.

Jordon, Willis F. *The European War From a Bible Standpoint.* New York: Charles C. Cook, 1915.

Kac, Arthur. *The Rebirth of the State of Israel—Is It of God or of Men?* Chicago: Moody Press, 1964.

Kellogg, Samuel H. *Are Premillennialists Right?* New York: Fleming H. Revell, 1923.

King, H. P. *The Imperial Hope.* New York: Fleming H. Revell, 1918.

Kraus, C. Norman. *Dispensationalism in America: Its Rise and Development.* Richmond: John Knox Press, 1958.

Kromminga, D. H. *The Millennium in the Church: Studies in the History of Christian Chiliasm.* Grand Rapids: Eerdmans, 1945.

Ladd, George E. *The Blessed Hope.* Grand Rapids: Eerdmans, 1956.

————. *A Commentary on the Revelation of John.* Grand Rapids: Eerdmans, 1972.

———. *Crucial Questions About the Kingdom of God*. Grand Rapids: Eerdmans, 1952.

———. *Jesus and the Kingdom*. New York: Harper & Row, 1964.

———. *The Last Things: An Eschatology for Laymen*. Grand Rapids: Eerdmans, 1978.

———. *A Theology of the New Testament*. Grand Rapids: Eerdmans, 1974.

LaHaye, Tim. *The Beginning of the End*. Wheaton, Ill.: Tyndale House, 1972.

Larkin, Clarence. *The Second Coming of Christ*. Philadelphia: Privately printed, 1922.

Latourette, Kenneth Scott. *The History of the Expansion of Christianity*. Vols. IV-VI. Grand Rapids: Zondervan, 1970.

Lewy, Gunther. *The Catholic Church and Nazi Germany*. New York: McGraw-Hill, 1964.

Lindberg, Beth M. *A God-Filled Life: The Story of William E. Blackstone*. Chicago: American Messianic Fellowship, n.d.

Lindsey, Hal. *The Late Great Planet Earth*. Grand Rapids: Zondervan, 1970.

———. *The Liberation of Planet Earth*. Grand Rapids: Zondervan, 1974.

———. *The 1980s: Countdown to Armageddon*. King of Prussia, Pa.: Westgate Press, 1980.

———. *The Promise*. Irvine, Calif.: Harvest House, 1974.

———. *Satan Is Alive and Well on Planet Earth*. Grand Rapids: Zondervan, 1972.

———. *The Terminal Generation*. Old Tappan, N.J.: Fleming H. Revell, 1976.

———. *There's a New World Coming*. Santa Ana, Calif.: Vision House, 1973.

———. *The World's Final Hour: Evacuation or Extinction?* Grand Rapids: Zondervan, 1976.

Look Out! He Is Coming! Framingham, Mass.: Christian Workers Union, n.d.

McCall, Thomas, and Zola Levitt. *The Coming Russian Invasion of Israel*. Chicago: Moody Press, 1974.

———, ed. *America: In History and Bible Prophecy*. Chicago: Moody Press, 1976.

McCartney, Richard Hayes. *The Secret Rapture, Delusion and Snare*. Chicago: James Watson and Co., 1926.

McClain, Alva. *Daniel's Prophecy of the Seventy Weeks*. Grand Rapids: Zondervan, 1940.

McConkey, James H. *The End of the Age*. Pittsburgh: Silver Publishing Co., 1919.

McCown, C. C. *The Promise of His Coming*. New York: The Macmillan Co., 1921.

McEwen, Robert Ward. "Factors in the Modern Survival of Millennialism." Ph.D. dissertation, University of Chicago, 1933.

Machen, J. Gresham. *Christianity and Liberalism*. New York: The Macmillan Co., 1926.

McKeever, Jim. *The Almighty and the Dollar*. Medford, Ore.: Omega Publications, 1980.

―――. *Christians Will Go Through the Tribulation: And How to Prepare for It*. Medford, Ore.: Omega Publications, 1978.

―――. *Close Encounters of the Highest Kind*. Medford, Ore.: Omega Publications, 1978.

―――. *How You Can Be Prepared*. Medford, Ore.: Omega Publications, 1980.

―――. *Now You Can Understand the Book of Revelation*. Medford, Ore.: Omega Publications, 1980.

Mackintosh, C. H. *Papers on the Lord's Coming*. Chicago: Bible Institute Colportage Association, n.d.

McLoughlin, William G., Jr. *Modern Revivalism: Charles Grandison Finney to Billy Graham*. New York: Ronald Press, 1959.

McPherson, Dave. *The Incredible Cover-up: The True Story of the Pre-Trib Rapture*. Plainsfield, N.J.: Logos International, 1975.

Magnuson, Norris A. *Salvation in the Slums: Evangelical Social Work, 1865–1920*. Metuchen, N.J.: Scarecrow Press, 1977.

Mains, George P. *Premillennialism: Non-Scriptural, Non-Historic, Non-Scientific, Non-Philosophical*. New York: Abingdon, 1920.

Marsden, George. *Fundamentalism and American Culture: The Shaping of Twentieth Century Evangelicalism, 1870–1925*. New York: Oxford University Press, 1980.

Marsden, George, and Frank Roberts, eds. *A Christian View of History?* Grand Rapids: Eerdmans, 1975.

Marty, Martin E. *A Nation of Behavers*. Chicago: University of Chicago Press, 1976.

―――. *Righteous Empire*. New York: Dial Press, 1970.

Marvin, E. P. *Maranatha*. Louisville: Pickett Publishing Co., 1902.

Mason, John. *Why We Expect Jesus Now*. New York: Fleming H. Revell, 1893.

Matheson, Peter, ed. *The Third Reich and the Churches*. Grand Rapids: Eerdmans, 1981.

Mathews, Shailer. *The Faith of Modernism*. New York: The Macmillan Co., 1924.

_____. *New Faith for Old*. New York: The Macmillan Co., 1936.

_____. *Will Christ Come Again?* Chicago: American Institute of Sacred Literature, 1917.

Matthew Twenty-Four, or the Second Coming of Christ. Mountain View, Calif.: Pacific Press Publishing Association, 1890.

Matthews, Mark. *The Second Coming of Christ*. New York: The Book Stall, n.d.

Mauro, Philip. *After This*. New York: Fleming H. Revell, 1918.

_____. *Bringing Back the King*. New York: Fleming H. Revell, 1920.

_____. *Dr. Shailer Mathews on the Christ's Return*. Swengel, Pa.: Bible Truth Depot, 1918.

_____. *God's Present Kingdom, With an Examination of Modern Dispensationalism*. Boston: Hamilton Brothers, 1928.

_____. *The Hope of Israel—What Is It?* Boston: Hamilton Brothers, 1929.

_____. *The Seventy Weeks and the Great Tribulation*. Boston: Hamilton Brothers, 1923.

_____. *The World War: How It Is Fulfilling Prophecy*. Boston: Hamilton Brothers, 1918.

May, Henry F. *Protestant Churches and Industrial America*. New York: Harper Torchbooks, 1967.

Mead, Sideny E. *The Lively Experiment*. New York: Harper & Row, 1963.

Meyer, Isidore S., ed. *Early History of Zionism in America*. New York: American Jewish Historical Society and Theodore Herzl Foundation, 1958.

Miller, Jean P. "Souls or the Social Order: Polemic in American Protestantism." Ph.D. dissertation, University of Chicago, 1969.

Miller, Perry. *Errand Into the Wilderness*. New York: Harper Torchbooks, 1956.

Miller, Robert Moats. *American Protestantism and Social Issues, 1919–1939*. Chapel Hill: University of North Carolina Press, 1958.

Mitchell, David. *The Fighting Pankhursts*. New York: The Macmillan Co., 1967.

Moberg, David O. *The Great Reversal: Evangelism versus Social Concern*. A Holman Book. Philadelphia: Lippincott, 1972.

Moody, Dwight L. *New Sermons*. New York: Henry S. Goodspeed, 1880.

_____ et al. *The Second Coming of Christ*. Chicago: Bible Institute Colportage Association, 1896.

Morgan, G. Campbell. *God's Method With Man*. New York: Fleming H. Revell, 1898.

Morrison, H. C. *The World War in Prophecy*. Louisville: Pentecostal Publishing Co., 1917.

Mott, John R. *The Evangelization of the World in This Generation*. New York: Student Volunteer Movement for Foreign Missions, 1900.

Mounce, Robert H. *The Book of Revelation*. The International Commentary on the New Testament. Grand Rapids: Eerdmans, 1977.

Munhall, Leander. *The Lord's Return*. 7th ed. New York: Eaton and Mains, 1898.

————, ed. *Anti-Higher Criticism*. New York: Fleming H. Revell, 1894.

Needham, George C., ed. *Primitive Paths to Prophecy*. Chicago: Gospel Publishing Co., 1891.

Neill, Stephen. *A History of Christian Missions*. London: Penguin Books, 1965.

Newman, Elias. *The Jewish Peril and the Hidden Hand*. Minneapolis: Privately Printed, 1934.

Nichol, Francis D. *The Midnight Cry*. Washington, D.C.: Review and Herald, 1944.

Niebuhr, H. Richard. *The Kingdom of God in America*. New York: Harper & Row, 1937.

Ottman, F. C. *The Coming Day*. Philadelphia: Sunday School Times, 1921.

————. *God's Oath. A Study of an Unfulfilled Promise of God*. New York: George H. Doran, 1911.

————. *Imperialism and Christ*. New York: Charles C. Cook, 1912.

Pankhurst, Christabel. *The Lord Cometh!* New York: The Book Stall, 1923.

————. *Seeing the Future*. New York: Harper & Row, 1929.

————. *Some Modern Problems in the Light of Bible Prophecy*. New York: Fleming H. Revell, 1924.

————. *The World's Unrest*. Philadelphia: Sunday School Times, 1929.

Parlane, W. A. *Elements of Dispensational Truth*. New York: Charles C. Cook, 1905.

Pentecost, Dwight. *Things to Come*. Grand Rapids: Dunham, 1958.

Pettingill, William L., ed. *Light on Prophecy: Proceedings and Addresses at the Philadelphia Prophetic Conference, May 28–30, 1918*. New York: The Christian Herald, 1918.

Pink, Arthur W. *The Antichrist*. Swengel, Pa.: Bible Truth Depot, 1923.

————. *The Millennium*. Swengel, Pa.; Bible Truth Depot, n.d.

————. *The Redeemer's Return*. Swengel, Pa.: Bible Truth Depot, 1918.

Pollock, A. J. *Why Does God Allow This War?* New York: Loizeaux Brothers, n.d.

Prophetic Studies of the International Prophetic Conference. New York: Fleming H. Revell, 1886.

Protocols of the Meeting of the Learned Elders of Zion. Translated by Victor E. Marsden. London: The Britons Publishing Society, 1922.

Putnam, C. E. *Jesus' Coming and the Kingdom.* Chicago: Bible Institute Colportage Association, 1920.

_____. *Non-Millennialism vs. Premillennialism, Which Harmonizes the Word?* Chicago: Bible Institute Colportage Association, 1921.

Quebedeaux, Richard. *The Young Evangelicals.* New York: Harper & Row, 1974.

Rall, Harris Franklin. *Modern Premillennialism and the Christian Hope.* New York: Abingdon, 1920.

_____. *New Testament History.* New York: Abingdon, 1914.

Rauschenbusch, Walter. *Christianity and the Social Crisis.* New York: The Macmillan Co., 1907.

_____. *Christianizing the Social Order.* New York: The Macmillan Co., 1912.

Reece, Eli. *How Far Can a Premillennial Pastor Co-operate with Social Service Programs?* Privately printed, n.d.

Relfe, Mary Stewart. *When Your Money Fails.* Montgomery, Ala.: Ministries, Inc., 1981.

Riley, William Bell. *The Evolution of the Kingdom.* New York: Charles C. Cook, 1913.

_____. *Is Christ Coming Again?* Grand Rapids: Zondervan, n.d.

_____. "Protocols and Communism." Privately printed [1934].

_____. *Wanted—A World Leader!* Privately printed, n.d.

_____, ed. *God Hath Spoken.* Philadelphia: Bible Conference Committee, 1919.

Rimmer, Harry. *Palestine, The Coming Storm Center.* Grand Rapids: Eerdmans, 1940.

Rodd, John E. *The Last Days: Text Book on the Second Coming of Christ.* Chicago: Evangelical Publishing Co., n.d.

_____. *Our Lord's Second Coming: A Comprehensive, Consecutive and Emphasized New Testament Reading on This Momentous Subject.* New York: Charles C. Cook, n.d.

Rohold, S. B. *The War and the Jew.* Toronto: The Macmillan Co. of Canada, 1915.

Ross, John Jacob. *The Sign of His Coming, or the Near Approach of the End.* New York: Charles C. Cook, 1918.

Runyan, William M. *Dr. Gray at Moody Bible Institute.* New York: Oxford University Press, 1935.

Rutgers, William H. *Premillennialism in America*. Goes, Holland: Osterbaan and Le Gointre, 1930.

Ryrie, Charles C. *The Bible and Tomorrow's News*. Wheaton, Ill.: Victor Books, 1973.

———. *Dispensationalism Today*. Chicago: Moody Press, 1965.

———, ed. *Ryrie Study Bible*. Chicago: Moody Press, 1978.

Sale-Harrison, Leonard. *The Coming Great Northern Confederacy: or the Future of Russia and Germany*. London: Pickering and Inglis, 1928.

———. *The League of Nations*. Harrisburg, Pa.: Evangelical Press, 1930.

———. *The Wonders of the Great Unveiling*. Philadelphia: Evangelical Press, 1930.

Sandeen, Ernest R. *The Roots of Fundamentalism: British and American Millenarianism, 1800–1930*. Chicago: University of Chicago Press, 1970.

Scofield, C. I. *Addresses on Prophecy*. New York: "Our Hope" Publishing Office, 1910.

———. *Rightly Dividing the Word of Truth*. Oakland, Calif.: Western Book and Tract Company, n.d.

———. *Will the Church Pass Through the Great Tribulation?* Philadelphia: Philadelphia School of Bible, 1917.

———, ed. The Scofield Reference Bible. New York: Oxford University Press [1909], 1917.

———, ed. The New Scofield Reference Bible. New York: Oxford University Press, 1967.

Shelley, Bruce. *A History of Conservative Baptists*. Wheaton, Ill.: Conservative Baptist Press, 1971.

Sider, Ronald J., ed. *The Chicago Declaration*. Carol Stream, Ill.: Creation House, 1974.

Silver, J. F. *The Lord's Return*. New York: Fleming H. Revell, 1914.

Simpson, A. B. *Back to Patmos*. New York: Christian Alliance Publishing Co., 1914.

———. *The Coming One*. New York: Christian Alliance Publishing Co., 1912.

———. *The Gospel of the Kingdom*. New York: Christian Alliance Publishing Co., 1890.

Sims, Albert. *The Coming Crash*. Toronto: Privately printed, n.d.

———. *Deepening Shadows and Coming Glories*. Toronto: Privately printed, n.d.

———. *The Near Approach to Antichrist*. Toronto: Privately printed, n.d.

Smith, Oswald J. *Is the Antichrist at Hand?* 5th ed. Toronto: Tabernacle Publishers, 1926.

Smith, Timothy L. *Revivalism and Social Reform*. New York: Harper Torchbooks, 1957.

Smock, C. M. *God's Dispensations Compared and Contrasted*. Chicago: Bible Institute Colportage Association, 1918.

Snowden, James H. *The Coming of the Lord: Will It Be Premillennial?* New York: The Macmillan Co., 1919.

_____. *Is the World Growing Better?* New York: The Macmillan Co., 1919.

Spalding, Arthur W. *Origin and History of Seventh-Day Adventists*. 4 vols. Washington, D.C.: Review and Herald, 1965.

Speer, Robert E. *The Second Coming of Christ*. New York: Gospel Publishing Co., 1903.

Stowe, Harriet Beecher, et al. *He's Coming To-morrow*. New York: Fleming H. Revell, 1896.

Stroh, Grant. *The Next World Crisis*. Chicago: Bible Institute Colportage Association, 1914.

_____. *When God Comes Down to Earth*. Chicago: Bible Institute Colportage Association, 1914.

Strong, Donald S. *Organized Anti-Semitism in America: The Rise of Group Prejudice During the Decade 1930–1940*. Westport, Conn.: Greenwood Press, [1941], 1979.

Strong, Josiah. *Our Country*. Rev. ed. New York: Baker & Taylor, 1891.

Sutcliffe, B. B. *The Responsibility of the Church in Relation to Israel*. Chicago: Chicago Hebrew Mission, n.d.

Talbot, Louis T., and William W. Orr. *The New Nation of Israel and the Word of God!* Los Angeles: The Bible Institute of Los Angeles, 1948.

Taylor, Howard. *Hudson Taylor and the China Inland Mission*. London: China Inland Mission, 1919.

Taylor, J. M. *The Second Coming of Christ and Some Reasons Why I Think It Is Near*. Bismark, N.D.: Privately printed, 1917.

Thompson, A. E. *The Life of A. B. Simpson*. New York: Christian Alliance Publishing Co., 1920.

Thrupp, Sylvia L., ed. *Millennial Dreams in Action*. New York: Schocken Books, 1970.

Torrey, Reuben A. *How to Study the Bible for Greater Profit*. New York: Fleming H. Revell, 1896.

_____. *The Return of the Lord Jesus*. Los Angeles: Bible Institute of Los Angeles, 1913.

_____, ed. *The Higher Criticism and the New Theology*. New York: Gospel Publishing House, 1911.

Tregelles, Samuel P. *The Hope of Christ's Second Coming*. London: Samuel Bagster and Sons, 1864.

Trumbell, Charles G., ed. *How I Came to Believe in Our Lord's Return and Why I Believe the Lord's Return Is Near*. Chicago: Bible Institute Colportage Association, 1934.

Tuveson, Ernest L. *Millennium and Utopia: A Study in the Background of the Idea of Progress*. Berkeley: University of California Press, 1949.

_____. *Redeemer Nation: The Idea of America's Millennial Role*. Chicago: University of Chicago Press, 1968.

Twenty Reasons for Believing That the Second Coming of the Lord Is Near. New York: Fleming H. Revell, 1878.

Tyng, Stephen H., Jr. *He Will Come*. New York: Muchlow and Simon, 1877.

Urofsky, Melvin I. *American Zionism from Herzl to the Holocaust*. Garden City, N.Y.: Anchor Books, 1976.

Van Burkalow, J. T. *The Lost Prophecy*. New York: Fleming H. Revell, 1924.

Walvoord, John F. *The Blessed Hope and the Tribulation*. Grand Rapids: Zondervan, 1976.

_____. *Israel in Prophecy*. Grand Rapids: Zondervan, 1968.

_____. *Matthew: Thy Kingdom Come*. Chicago: Moody Press, 1974.

_____. *The Millennial Kingdom*. Grand Rapids: Zondervan, 1976.

_____. *The Rapture Question*. Findlay, Ohio: Dunham Publishing Co., 1957.

_____. *The Revelation of Jesus Christ*. Chicago: Moody Press, 1966.

_____. *The Thessalonian Epistles*. Findlay, Ohio: Dunham Publishing Co., 1955.

Walvoord, John F., and John E. Walvoord. *Armageddon: Oil and the Middle East Crisis*. Grand Rapids: Zondervan, 1974.

Weber, Timothy P. *The Future Explored*. Wheaton, Ill.: Victor Books, 1978.

Weisberger, Bernard A. *They Gathered at the River*. Chicago: Quadrangle Books, 1958.

Weisenburger, Francis P. *Ordeal of Faith: The Crisis of Churchgoing America, 1865–1900*. New York: Philosophical Library, 1959.

West, Nathaniel. *The Present Condition and Future Glory of Believers and the Earth*. St. Louis: Gospel Book and Tract Depository, n.d.

_____. *The Thousand Years in Both Testaments*. New York: Fleming H. Revell, 1889.

_____, ed. *Premillennial Essays*. New York: Fleming H. Revell, 1879.

When and How Ought I to Expect My Lord? New York: Loizeaux Brothers, 1890.

White, John Wesley, *WW III*. Grand Rapids: Zondervan, 1977.

Wiebe, Robert H. *The Search for Order, 1877–1920*. New York: Hill & Wang, 1967.

Wight, Francis Asa. *Babylon the Harlot*. Scottdale, Pa.: YMCA, 1925.

_____. *The Beast, Modernism and the Evangelical Faith*. Boston: The Stratford Co., 1926.

_____. *The Kingdom of God, or the Reign of Heaven Among Men*. New York: Fleming H. Revell, 1923.

Wilson, Bryan R. *Magic and the Millennium: A Sociological Study of Religious Movements of Protest among Tribal and Third-World Peoples*. New York: Harper & Row, 1973.

Wilson, Dwight. *Armageddon Now!* Grand Rapids: Baker Book House, 1977.

Wilson, W. H. *The Destiny of Russia and the Signs of the Times*. Chicago: Privately printed, 1914.

Wimberly, C. F. *Behold the Morning!* New York: Fleming H. Revell, 1916.

Wood, Ross. *The Present in the Light of Prophecy*. Cincinnati: Privately printed, 1933.

Worsely, Peter. *The Trumpet Shall Sound: A Study of "Cargo" Cults in Melanesia*. New York: Schocken Books, 1968.

Zwier, Robert. *Born-Again Politics: The New Christian Right in America*. Downers Grove, Ill.: InterVarsity Press, 1982.

PERIODICALS

Anderson, Henry E. "Are God's Covenants About to be Fulfilled?" *Moody Monthly*, XL (November 1939), 128–29.

Bear, James E. "Historic Premillennialism." *Union Seminary Review*, LV (1944), 193–211.

_____. "The People of God According to the Fathers of the Early Church." *Union Seminary Review*, LII (July 1941), 371–72.

Bell, L. Nelson. "Unfolding Destiny." *Christianity Today*, XI (July 21, 1967), 1044–45.

Blackstone, William E. "He May Come Today." *Our Hope*, XXVIII (December 1921), 370.

_____. "The Times of the Gentiles and the War in the Light of Prophecy." *Christian Workers Magazine*, XVI (May 1916), 686–87.

Briggs, Charles A. "Origin and History of Pre-Millennialism." *Lutheran Quarterly*, IX (April 1879), 207–45.

Britan, Joseph Taylor. "An Appeal for Persecuted Israel." *Moody Monthly*, XXXIX (February 1939), 316, 345.

———. "Why Our Nation Should Not Disarm." *Moody Bible Institute Monthly*, XXI (August 1921), 510–12.

Brookes, James H. "Cutting the Nerves." *The Truth*, XVI (1890), 37–38.

———. "Gentile Dominion." *The Truth*, VI (1880), 536.

———. "How I Became a Premillennialist." *The Truth*, XXII (1896), 331–33.

———. "How to Reach the Jews." *The Truth*, XIX (1893), 135–36.

———. "Work Among the Jews." *The Truth*, XX (1894), 14–16.

Brown, Ira V. "Watchers for the Second Coming: The Millenarian Tradition in America." *Mississippi Valley Historical Review*, XXXIX (December, 1952), 441–58.

Cameron, Robert. "Discrediting the Second Advent." *The Truth*, XXI (March 1895), 166–71.

———. "To the Friends of Prophetic Truth." *Watchword and Truth*, XXIV (1902), 134–36.

Carpenter, Joel. "A Shelter in the Time of Storm: Fundamentalist Institutions and the Rise of Evangelical Protestantism, 1929–1942." *Church History*, XLIX (March 1980), 62–75.

Case, Shirley Jackson. "Gentile Forms of Millennial Hope." *Biblical World*, XLVI (April 1915), 67.

———. "The Premillennial Menace." *Biblical World*, LII (July 1918), 16–23.

Chafer, Lewis Sperry. "Dispensationalism." *Bibliotheca Sacra*, XIIIC (October 1936), 390–449.

Chalmers, Thomas. "Israel's Title to Canaan." *The King's Business*, XVII (February 1926), 94.

Cleland, T. H. "The Celestial and the Terrestrial." *The Truth*, VII (1881), 464–65.

Coder, Maxwell. "Jerusalem: Key to the Future." *Moody Monthly*, LXXIV (October 1973), 32–33.

"Converting the Jews." *Moody Bible Institute Monthly*, XXIV (February 1924), 282.

"Counting Our Assets." *Biblical World*, XLVI (July 1915), 1.

Cross, George. "Millenarianism in Christian History." *Biblical World*, XLVI (July 1915), 3.

Davis, George T. B. "A Divine Promise That Changed History." *The Sunday School Times*, XCIX (March 16, 1957), 743–44.

"Democracy at the Crossroads." *Christian Workers Magazine*, XIX (May 1919), 626.

"Eminent Exponents of Premillennialism." *Christian Workers Magazine*, XIV (December 1913), 223–25.

Erdman, Charles R. "William Whiting Borden: An Ideal Missionary Volunteer." *Missionary Review of the World*, XXXVI (August 1913), 567–77.

Erdman, William J. "An Important Query." *Christian Workers Magazine*, XVII (November 1916), 194.

_____. "The Main Idea of the Bible." *The Institute Tie*, IX (October, 1908), 94.

"Evangelical Leaders Poll." *Evangelical Newsletter*, IX (January 22, 1982), 6.

Evans, William. "The War in Europe in Relation to Christianity and the Church." *Christian Workers Magazine*, XV (November 1914), 158–60.

Fereday, W. W. "The Present Crisis." *Our Hope*, XXI (December 1914), 360–62.

Forster, A. H. "The Servant of Isaiah and the Second Coming." *The Biblical World*, LII (September 1918), 194–95.

Frost, Henry W. "The Dying Heathen." *The Institute Tie*, VII (November 1907), 181.

Funderburk, A. R. "The Word of God on Women's Dress." *Moody Bible Institute Monthly*, XXII (January 1922), 759.

Gaebelein, Arno C. "The Awful European Conflagration: The War Has Come." *Our Hope*, XXI (September 1914), 146.

_____. "Current Events." *Our Hope*, XXXIX (May 1933), 687.

_____. "God's Hand in Prophetic Conferences." *Moody Monthly*, XL (November 1939), 117, 129.

_____. "The Great Coming North-Eastern Confederacy." *Our Hope*, XLVI (1939–40), 234–35.

Goen, C. C. "Jonathan Edwards: A New Departure in Eschatology." *Church History*, XXVII (March 1959), 25–40.

Gosnell, L. W. "The Capture of Jerusalem." *Christian Workers Magazine*, XVIII (January 1918), 396.

Gray, James M. "And Such Were Some of You." *Christian Workers Magazine*, XIV (August 1914), 783–86.

_____. "The Battle of Armageddon." *Christian Workers Magazine*, XV (October 1914), 81–82.

_____. "The Bible, Prophecy, and the War." *Christian Workers Magazine*, XIX (October 1918), 45–55.

_____. "The Capture of Jerusalem." *Christian Workers Magazine*, XVIII (February 1918), 447.

―――. "Current Criticism of Premillennial Truth." *Christian Workers Magazine*, XVIII (March 1918), 548–51.

―――. "The Jewish Peril and How to Meet It." *Moody Bible Institute Monthly*, XXI (July 1921), 469–71.

―――. "The Jewish Protocols." *Moody Bible Institute Monthly*, XXXV (January 1935), 230.

―――. "The League of Nations and the Danger of Federation." *Moody Bible Institute Monthly*, XXI (September 1920), 7.

Gretter, D. "Disarmament and the Signs of the Times." *Moody Bible Institute Monthly*, XXII (January 1922), 806.

Herrstrom, W. D. "A Mark in Their Right Hand." *Moody Bible Institute Monthly*, XXXVIII (March 1938), 375.

"Jail the Girls." *Moody Bible Institute Monthly*, XXII (January 1922), 749.

Jennings, F. C. "Retrograde Doctrine Tested." *Our Hope*, XXXIX (November 1932), 288.

"The Jewish Protocols." *Moody Bible Institute Monthly*, XXII (October 1921), 598.

Kellogg, Samuel H. "Is the Advent Pre-Millennial?" *Presbyterian Review*, III (1882), 475–502.

―――. "Premillennialism: Its Relation to Doctrine and Practice." *Bibliotheca Sacra*, VL (1888), 234–74.

Ketchum, William W. "Some Interesting Things About Jews." *Christian Workers Magazine*, XX (April 1920), 630–31.

Kinzler, Albert. "What About Hair-Bobbing?" *Moody Bible Institute Monthly*, XXIV (August 1924), 605.

Klein, P. A. "Compulsory Military Service." *Christian Workers Magazine*, XVI (July 1916), 835–36.

"The League of Nations." *Christian Workers Magazine*, XIX (April 1919), 526.

"Lewd Dressing." *Christian Workers Magazine*, XVI (February 1916), 430.

McConnel, Francis P. "The Causes of Pre-Millennialism." *Harvard Theological Review*, XII (April 1919), 179–92.

Mackintosh, C. H. "The Double Phase of the Second Advent." *Our Hope*, X (November 1903), 322–29.

Malek, Rudolph. "America's Vulnerable Spot." *Moody Bible Institute Monthly*, XXII (November 1921), 655–56.

Martin, William. "Waiting for the End." *The Atlantic*, CCXLIX (June 1982), 31–37.

Marvin, E. P. "The Jews—God's Witnesses." *Christian Workers Magazine*, XI (December 1910), 274–315.

Massee, J. C. "In Christ." *Christian Workers Magazine*, XIX (March 1919), 461–65.

Mauro, Philip. "Discontent of the Laboring Classes." *Our Hope*, XIX (October 1912), 225–29.

Meeker, Charles P. "The Evangelization of the American Jew." *Christian Workers Magazine*, XIX (August 1919), 868.

"The Menace of the Movies." *Christian Workers Magazine*, XVI (June 1916), 758.

Miller, L. Ray. "May Christians Attend Picture Shows?" *Moody Bible Institute Monthly*, XXV (March 1925), 317–18.

"Mothers to Blame." *Moody Bible Institute Monthly*, XXIII (May 1923), 407.

Needham, Mrs. George C. "Armageddon." *Our Hope*, XXI (January 1915), 424–27.

Ostrom, Henry. "My Personal Experience with the Doctrine of Our Lord's Second Coming." *Christian Workers Magazine*, XVII (March 1918), 561–64.

Panton, D. M. "The Present Rise and Ultimate End of Democracy." *Christian Workers Magazine*, XIX (May 1919), 637–39.

Parker, T. Valentine. "Premillennialism: An Interpretation and an Evaluation." *Biblical World*, LIII (January 1919), 37–40.

———. "The Second Advent and Modern Thought." *Bibliotheca Sacra*, LXVIII (October 1911), 600.

Patterson, R. M. "Pre-Millenarianism," *Princeton Review*, IV (1879), 415–34.

Pierson, A. T. "Antagonism to the Bible." *Our Hope*, XV (January 1909), 475.

Rall, Harris Franklin. "Premillennialism and the Bible." *Biblical World*, LIII (September 1919), 459–69.

———. "Premillennialism: The Issue." *Biblical World*, LIII (July 1919), 339–47.

———. "Where Premillennialism Leads." *Biblical World*, LIII (November 1919), 617–27.

Ralston, J. H. "The Conference on Behalf of Israel." *Christian Workers Magazine*, XVI (January 1916), 359–60.

Rausch, David A. "Fundamentalism and the Jew: An Interpretive Essay." *Journal of the Evangelical Theological Society*, XXIII (June 1980), 105–12.

———. "Our Hope: An American Fundamentalist Journal and the Holocaust, 1937–1945." *Fides et Historia*, XII (Spring 1980), 89–103.

———. "A Rejoinder to Timothy Weber's Reply." *Journal of the Evangelical Theological Society*, XXIV (March 1981), 73–77.

Rayner, T. DeCourcy. "Hidden Hands in Palestine." *Moody Monthly*, XLVIII (December 1947), 264.

Reihl, Charles. "Solution to Prohibition." *The Truth*, XV (1889), 370–79.

Robinson, J. J. "Is Social Service a Part of the Apostasy?" *Christian Workers Magazine*, XIV (July 1914), 729–32.

Ruben, Maurice. "The Hebrew Christian Alliance Conference." *Christian Workers Magazine*, XVIII (September 1917), 37.

Russell, Robert McWatty. "The Kingdom View of the Gospel As Related to the Missionary Program of Christ." *Christian Workers Magazine*, XIV (December 1913), 228–34.

"Safe for Democracy." *Christian Workers Magazine*, XVII (July 1917), 853.

Sale-Harrison, Leonard. "The League of Nations and the Coming Superman." *Moody Bible Institute Monthly*, XXXVI (August 1936) 605–6.

———. "The Resurrection of Imperial Rome." *Moody Bible Institute Monthly*, XXXVI (June 1936), 493–94.

Sandeen, Ernest R. "The "Little Tradition" and the Form of Modern Millenarianism." *The Annual Review of the Social Sciences of Religion*, IV (1980), 165–81.

Schor, Samuel. "Notable Developments of Zionism." *Christian Workers Magazine*, XVII (September 1917), 44.

Scofield, C. I. "The World's Approaching Crisis." *Our Hope*, X (August 1903), 79–80.

Scott, Walter. "Europe in a Blaze." *Our Hope*, XXI (November 1914), 279–83.

———. "The Near Prophetic Crisis." *Our Hope*, XVII (January 1911), 464–69.

Sheldon, Charles F. "Modernism and Ecclesiastical Tragedy." *Moody Bible Institute Monthly*, XXIII (June 1923), 472.

Smalley, W. F. "Another View of the Palestine Situation." *The King's Business*, XXI (June 1930), 290–92.

Smith, David E. "Millenarian Scholarship in America." *America Quarterly*, XVII (1965), 535–49.

Snowden, James H. "Summary of Objections to Premillenarianism." *Biblical World*, LIII (March 1919), 165–73.

Stanfield, J. M. "Morals of the Picture Show." *Christian Workers Magazine*, XVI (October 1915), 88–89.

Toews, H. F. "The Doctrine of Non-Resistance." *Christian Workers Magazine*, XVII (July 1917), 862–63.

Torrey, R. A. "Unprincipled Methods of Post-Millennialists." *Our Hope*, XXIV (May 1918), 679–81.

Umlauf, Paul. "The New Germany and the Evangelical Church." *Moody Bible Institute Monthly*, XXXIV (August 1934), 553–54.

Vaus, James A. "Work Among the Jews." *The King's Business*, VIII (May 1917), 425.

Vichert, J. F. "Is the Gospel Spiritual Pessimism?" *Biblical World*, LIII (January 1919), 26–36.

Weber, Timothy P. "A Reply to David Rausch's 'Fundamentalism and the Jew.'" *Journal of the Evangelical Theological Society*, XXIV (March 1981), 67–71.

_____. "The Second Coming Alert." *Eternity*, XXXII (April 1981), 18–23.

_____. "A Surrejoinder to David Rausch's Rejoinder." *Journal of the Evangelical Theological Society*, XXIV (March 1981), 79–82.

"Williamsburg Mission to the Jews: Abstract of the Report of the Committee of Investigation." *Christian Workers Magazine*, XVII (November 1916), 191–92.

Woelfkin, Cornelius. "The Religious Appeal of Premillennialism." *Journal of Religion*, I (May 1921), 255–63.

Index